IN THE LAND OF
GIANTS

IN THE LAND OF
GIANTS

My Life in Basketball

Tyrone "Muggsy" Bogues
and David Levine

Little, Brown and Company
Boston   New York   Toronto   London

First Edition

Library of Congress Cataloging-in-Publication Data

Bogues, Tyrone.
    In the land of giants : my life in basketball / Tyrone "Muggsy" Bogues and David Levine.
        p. cm.
    ISBN 0-316-10173-7
    1. Bogues, Tyrone.   2. Basketball players — United States — Biography.   3. Stature, Short.   I. Levine, David. II. Title.
    GV884.B64A3   1994
    796.323'092 — dc20
    [B]   94-26479

10 9 8 7 6 5 4 3 2 1

Designed by Barbara Werden

MV-NY

Published simultaneously in Canada by
Little, Brown & Company (Canada) Limited

Printed in the United States of America

Little man whip a big man every time if
the little man's in the right and keeps a-comin'.
— motto of the old west Texas Rangers

CONTENTS

ACKNOWLEDGMENTS

T HE AUTHORS wish to thank the following for their help in preparing this book: Rob Urbach and Falk Associates Management Enterprises; David Black and Black Inc. Literary Agency; Lev Fruchter and Susan Raihofer of Black Inc.; Bill Phillips and Little, Brown; Steve Schneider of Little, Brown; the Charlotte Hornets front office, especially media relations director Harold Kaufman and associates Jason Brannon and Keith Kroehler; John Justus, sports information director at Wake Forest University; Tim Wilkin and John Rolfe for research assistance; Rick Bonnell and his book, "Charlotte Hornets: Sharpening the Stinger"; Tucker Mitchell and his book, "Hornets Never Lie"; Ken Davis for a great title idea; Minor Hinson in Charlotte, and Lauren Frank and Lea Swaim in Washington, D.C., for their hospitality; the Levine family for all their love and support; Sue Malone for everything; and the entire Bogues family, but especially Elaine Bogues for her scrapbooks and her charm, and Kim Bogues for her good humor and her home cooking.

Special thanks to everyone, too numerous to list here, who took the time to give their thoughts and memories of Muggsy.

Finally, to the memory of Reggie Lewis, with love.

People always say we'll never see another Larry Bird. But I've always felt we have a better chance of seeing another Larry Bird than we do another Muggsy Bogues. Nobody has ever done what Muggsy is doing.
— Allan Bristow, Charlotte Hornets head coach

W E'RE LIVE AT THE HIVE! The Bugs Are Back!

Is this Intro to Entomology 101? No, this is the intro to the NBA, 1993–94. The Hive is what the locals affectionately call their home gym, the Charlotte Coliseum, located on, yes, Hive Drive, in Charlotte, North Carolina. The Bugs, of course, are the home team Charlotte Hornets. And they are indeed back tonight, November 5, 1993, for the first game of their sixth season of professional basketball.

Both "Live at the Hive" and "The Bugs Are Back" are reminders that this is the NBA of the '90s, where marketing slogans, flashy graphics, musical themes, and advertising campaigns are at least equal in importance to the talent of the players hired to run the floor. Marketing will be crucial to keep interest high during the long, cold winter months that stretch seemingly forever between training camp in October and the finals of the playoffs in June. But opening night is its own reward. On this night, marketing is redundant.

Tonight the Hive is buzzing on its own. The Hornets have just come off their most successful season: in the spring of 1993, they made the playoffs for the first time in franchise history. They surprised many by beating the lofty Boston Celtics in the first round of that postseason, and then gave a commendable showing against the New York Knicks before losing four games to one. The Hornets, something of an NBA doormat for their first four years of existence, broke through that spring to national prominence. Playing before large audiences in two of the most important NBA cities got the

Hornets noticed by the national media as never before. Charlotte's two biggest stars, burly power forward Larry Johnson and glowering center Alonzo Mourning, were already well known through their college exploits, at the University of Nevada–Las Vegas and Georgetown, respectively, and through some national advertising campaigns (most notably, Johnson in drag as "Grandmama," the high-flying, slam-dunking old lady with the gray hair, pearls, clutch bag, and gold tooth in the hilarious Converse campaign). But the team as a whole was better known for its league-leading home attendance, its attractive Alexander Julian–designed teal uniforms, and the popular Hugo the Hornet logo and mascot, than it was for its basketball prowess.

Indeed, most casual fans would be hard pressed to name a third Hornet, after Larry and 'Zo. At best, they might think a minute, dislodge a memory, and wonder, "Oh, the little guy, Muggsy, he's on the Hornets, right?"

Right. In fact, the little guy, five-foot-three-inch Tyrone "Muggsy" Bogues, is as popular around Charlotte as his two more famous teammates. An original Hornet, taken in the expansion draft that helped stock Charlotte's first season with players discarded from other teams, Muggsy Bogues instantly became a focal point for a bad team, an identity for a new franchise desperately looking for one.

But tonight that seems like generations ago. Tonight the Hornets enter the 1993–94 season as legitimate contenders for the NBA's Eastern Conference championship. One writer, from the estimable *New York Times*, has gone so far as to predict that the Hornets will win the conference crown, and others have them going deep into the playoffs. (Injuries to several key players, however, will prevent those predictions from coming true.) And that's just one of the story angles that has the Hive inundated with an orgy of media attention that includes not one, not two, but *four* live television broadcast crews, including Japan's NHK Network — Charlotte's first quadruple-cast — plus taped TV and radio broadcasts for French and Spanish audiences, writers from national and international publications, corporate sponsors, league officials, and local muckety-mucks.

The main reason is that the Chicago Bulls are Charlotte's opponent, and this is the Bulls' first regular season game of the post–Michael Jordan era. Jordan's stunning retirement just weeks earlier had shocked the sports world, and there is much interest in how the three-time defending champions will react. Other story angles include the debut of Chicago's newest star, the European Toni Kukoc; the emergence of Johnson and Mourning as possible successors to Jordan's status as king of the court; how the Hornets and Bulls now match up as conference rivals; and a few lesser subplots.

In the center of all this commotion is Charlotte's littlest big man, the starting point guard who is smaller than many of the teenage ball boys who shag rebounds during warmups. As is his custom during the pregame ritual, he laughs, he jokes, he challenges his teammates to shooting contests, he flits about like, well, like a bug, energizing his team and the crowd. He talks, and talks again, and talks some more, gabbing with friends and foes who tower above him, a smile seemingly engraved onto his face. He is a happy Lilliputian in a nation of intense Gullivers, an unlikely intruder in the land of giants.

He is Muggsy Bogues, the smallest man ever to play in the National Basketball Association.

Context is everything, of course. If normal-size people stand next to Muggsy Bogues in normal situations — that is, away from the basketball court — Muggsy appears well within the normal rules of human dimensions. Sure, he is shorter than the average man, who is five-eight or so, but not by so much as to be noticed. In fact, because he is, at 145 solid pounds, far stronger and more muscular than most five-three men, and because he swaggers with the puffed-up air of confidence that all athletes possess, he seems to take up more space than his volume would suggest. He appears, if anything, a bit taller than his actual height. Walking down the street or shopping in the mall, Muggsy Bogues is likely to run into other men his size or shorter, and most will be close enough in height to look him squarely in the eye. In other words, in the context of real life, Muggsy Bogues is no different than the guy who occupies the office down the hall or the guy who delivers your mail, no different than your accountant or dentist or mechanic, no different than you or me.

It is in the context of basketball that Muggsy Bogues is noticeably special. "You don't really get the full effect of Muggsy," says his coach, Allan Bristow, "until you go up and stand next to him." Bristow speaks from his own perspective. He is himself a giant, standing six-seven (he played ten solid seasons in the ABA and NBA, from 1973 through 1983, for four different teams), and when he stands next to Muggsy, you do indeed begin to get the full effect. Put Muggsy next to a seven-footer like Alonzo Mourning, and the effect is stunning.

But then, placing Muggsy Bogues on an NBA court at all is stunning in its own right, so stunning, in fact, that many casual basketball followers are finally taking notice. Bogues, in fact, is on a roll, constantly juggling a busy schedule of off-court endeavors. At this particular point in time, just before the start of the 1993–94 season, he is scheduled to film commercials for CNN's weekly NBA highlights show. (He is paired with Philadelphia's towering rookie Shawn Bradley, who stands a lofty seven-six — talk about context!) He is also being followed around for two days by another film crew, this one from CBS's prime-time show "How'd They Do That?" A Japanese film crew has for some reason decided that the Hornets are to be "Japan's Team" — although "they know *nothing* about basketball," their American producer/translator tells me sadly — and the crew is in town for several weeks filming Muggsy and other Hornets. He is also entertaining family from out of town; meeting with his agent, David Falk; screening a newly produced video on his life story, entitled "Don't Tell Me No!"; negotiating endorsement deals with Reebok, Sprite, AT&T, and a couple of other companies; trying to find time for his collaborator; racing to practice once or twice a day in preparation for the season; and spending time with his wife, Kim, and his three children whenever possible — all the while living with his family in a tiny hotel suite for far too long, as the renovations on his beautiful suburban house drag on and on and on. . . .

Just another week in the life of an NBA star.

That Muggsy Bogues should inhabit this life is remarkable for so many reasons. He grew up in the slums of Baltimore, the youngest of four children. His father, arrested when Muggsy was twelve, was sentenced to twenty years in prison for armed robbery. His mother, forced onto welfare, went back to school, and then to work to support her family. Her kids all grew up among the drugs and violence that pervade America's inner cities, and struggled to stay clean and safe. As with so many children of the streets, sports was both safe haven and salvation; more than just a place to go, the gyms and courts and rec centers of the inner city are a source of self-confidence, peopled with teachers, coaches, and role models who help steer aimless, hopeless kids toward at least a chance of a better life.

The Bogues children had that going for them. What they didn't have, and what most people would consider essential to success in sports — especially basketball — was height.

The NBA has not always been the land of giants. The very man who invented the game, Dr. James Naismith, was considered big for his time — he played center on his college football team — yet he stood just five-ten. The game he invented in 1891 was for the average-size athlete, and the early pro game remained that way. Robert W. Peterson, in his history of pro basketball, *Cages to Jump Shots*, writes that "a modern NBA player who stepped onto a 1915 basketball court would be at sea. He would find himself a giant among pygmies. Most early pros were barely above the average height for adult males, and several pioneer stars stood only a few inches above five feet."

That is, Muggsy height.

For nearly half a century, basketball was earthbound. Gravity held players prisoner. There was no jump shot. There were no alley-oops, no glass-cleaning rebounds, no monster dunks. It was a two-dimensional game played by short white men taking two-handed set shots. Speed and agility ruled over strength and height and vertical leap. "Joe Lapchick," Peterson writes, "center for the Original Celtics, the most famous team in basketball's first half-century, was considered a giant at 6-5. Although no statistics are available on average heights of early players, it is likely that the average during basketball's first fifty years was under six feet."

In those dark days, to be tall was to be a freak. In society at large, excessive height was considered almost shameful, and certainly unathletic. But things changed over the next few decades. In the 1930s and '40s more and more six- and six-and-a-half-footers appeared, but they were usually confined to playing the center position, and they were stereotypically gangly and poorly coordinated.

In 1946, though, a six-ten giant named George Mikan turned pro, and by 1950 he was voted the greatest player of basketball's first fifty years — after just four years of playing time. Mikan has been called the first *good* big man, and he opened the floodgates. Not only was he the most effective player of his time, he was the most popular, and he helped push attendance to new heights as well. Team owners may not have understood pick-and-rolls, but they sure understood gate receipts, and soon, tall was all. From Wilt and Bill Russell in the late 1950s and '60s, to Kareem and Bill Walton in the '70s, to a six-nine guard — a six-nine guard!!— named Magic in the '80s, all these men and more like them transformed basketball from what it was to what it is.

In so doing, they effectively put people like Muggsy Bogues out of business. While the average height of American men has risen only slightly since the turn of the century, the average height of an NBA player has skyrocketed to over six and a half feet. Over the past two decades, there have been only a handful of players under six feet; players like Calvin Murphy, Spud Webb, Charlie Criss, and Michael Adams were all between five-seven and five-ten. These days, in fact, you have to be quite tall just to be called small: Boston's Nate Archibald was known as "Tiny," and he was six-one.

And yet Muggsy Bogues, nearly a foot shy of Tiny, is one of just twenty-seven men in the entire world: a starting point guard in the NBA. What's more, he is among the league leaders in assists and steals every year. He's one of only three players — the others being John Stockton of the Utah Jazz and Kevin Johnson of the Phoenix Suns — to record six hundred or more assists six years in a row. He has led the league in assist-to-turnover ratio five times in six years. His scoring average hit double figures in 1992–93, and he was one of only a few players throughout the league who averaged a "double-double" — double figures in two categories; in Muggsy's case, assists and scoring — for the entire 1993–94 season. He plays well over thirty minutes per game. Even his rebounding improves every year. He's not a gimmick. He's not a freak. He's one of the premier point guards in the league, and at the top of his game.

Muggsy Bogues is still not as well known as his more famous teammates and opponents, but within the "industry" of basketball, he is perhaps the most respected player around. As Allan Bristow says, there will be other Larry Birds in basketball's future. There will be other Magic Johnsons, other Michael Jordans, other Shaquille O'Neals. But ask anyone involved in the NBA if there will ever be another five-three starting point guard, and you will not find a single person who says yes. Muggsy Bogues is, in every sense imaginable, unique.

DAVID LEVINE

IN THE LAND OF
GIANTS

Playing My Game

*It all starts with Muggsy. He sets the tone for everything. He is
the spark plug. How many times I gotta tell y'all this?*
— Larry Johnson, Charlotte Hornets forward

PATRICK EWING WAS SHOCKED. I could see it in his eyes.
The big, seven-foot center of the New York Knicks had
come off a pick and received a pass near the top of the key.
He positioned the ball in his right hand — his shooting hand.
He pump-faked once to get Alonzo Mourning off his feet, squared
his shoulders to the basket, eyed the target, brought the ball to his
eyes, took a little jump, and prepared to fire.

He never saw me coming.

Whapppp!

In the small amount of time between Ewing catching the ball
and shooting, less than a second, I came racing over from his right,
timed my jump just right, got a good, clean takeoff, and swatted the
ball away just before it left his shooting hand.

Patrick couldn't believe it. His shot had been blocked by someone
whose head barely came up to the letters on his basketball jersey.
Man, was he pissed!

I pounced on the loose ball and raced past him up court. I could
see his expression — surprise, confusion, a little anger — but then
I left him behind to start a fast break and score two points for us.
On the way back down court, I ran up to him, smiled my biggest

smile, and said, "Thanks, big fella. Now you're on my highlight film."

All he could do was laugh. And keep an eye on me for the rest of the game.

The fans, of course, went crazy, but that's nothing new. Fans have always taken to me. It's been that way as long as I've been playing the game. I've always been a favorite of both home and away crowds. I'd like to think it's because I play so hard all the time I'm on the floor, that I play with intensity and passion, that I have fun on the court and I like to entertain the crowd. And I know in my heart that is all part of it.

Mostly, though, it is because I am five feet, three inches tall.

In my mind, my size is no big deal. I've been playing against bigger guys my whole life. I've always been the smallest guy around, as a baby, as a little kid, in high school. I think I stopped growing altogether by the time I was ten years old. To be honest, it seems like I've been five-three my whole life. I don't ever remember growing. In elementary school I was five-three. In high school I was five-three. It's strange, isn't it? I think my mom was the first woman ever to give birth to a five-three baby.

But other people make a big deal of my size, especially in comparison to the guys I play against. See, to me, those other guys are just "footers": six-footers, seven-footers, and probably eight-footers someday. But I never believed only "footers" could play the game of basketball. People have always tried to tell me that, of course. From the first day I picked up a basketball, they told me to give it up. I was too small. I'd never make it. It was hopeless, no matter how good I was. I had to be big to play.

I never listened to any of them. To me, basketball is about talent, and heart, and desire. It's not about size. It's not a game for people who are big. It's a game for people who can play.

A lot of people still say it's unbelievable that a guy my size can play in the NBA — even though I have been doing it since I was drafted in the first round by the Washington Bullets in 1987, even though I have been a starting point guard for six years now, even though I am among the league leaders in assists, steals, and some other categories every year. Well, they just don't understand. Even if they can't believe it, I always did. And if there is one key to any success I have had in the game of basketball, and in anything else I have achieved in my life, it is that. I always believed in myself.

I have to admit, though, that playing in the NBA is amazing. Especially my first couple of years in the league. Going up against guys I had watched on television, guys who were supposed to be the best in the world, gave me a thrill that's hard to describe. Isiah, Magic, Larry Bird — you watch these guys your whole life, and then, man, there you are on the court with them. Internally I was very nervous, very excited. But I never showed any of those feelings. I kept it all in. I still do. I like to have fun on the court, and I am always hugging and joking and yelling at my teammates to keep them focused and in the game. But those are positive emotions. You can't show any negative emotions on the court. At the NBA level, guys will eat you up if they think you are scared or nervous. We are all like dogs — we can smell fear.

One of the biggest ways guys hide their fear is by trash talking. A lot of people have the wrong idea about trash talking. For most players, guys from the streets who grew up playing ball, trash talk is just a part of the game. It's a part of our life, really. Usually it doesn't mean anything. It sounds a lot worse than it is, especially if you don't understand the culture it comes from. Sure, sometimes it gets out of control, and guys get genuinely upset and fight. But usually it's harmless, just a way to get the opponent off his game by making him mad — or making him laugh. I'm not a talker on the court much, unless I go up against someone I know. For instance, in 1988–89, my second NBA season, we were in New York and I was up against Mark Jackson. Mark and I had been talking at the 1987 NBA draft, when we were both first round choices — me with the Bullets, him with the New York Knicks. That day, when my name was called as the twelfth pick overall, I told him excitedly that I'd see him at the Garden and we'd go one-on-one in front of all New York. I reminded him of that.

"Hey, honey," I said. (I like to call guys "honey" when I'm working on them. It's just one of my things.) "Here I am. I'm gonna teach you some new things."

He'd say, "Well, here I am, little man. Now I'm gonna take you down to the post."

"C'mon, big fella, you know it ain't that easy," I said. "I'm gonna take you out on the wing."

"You know I'll eat you up."

He was coming off his phenomenal rookie season, so I tried to ride him about that: "You know, honey, that rookie of the year thing was a fluke."

We went at it all night. But that's unusual. Sometimes I'll do it to try to take someone out of their game. One night Michael Jordan tried a crossover dribble on me, but I stopped him. He pulled back, so I started talking: "Oh, you won't get away with that. Come on, honey, show me what you really got."

He tried another fancy move to shake loose from me, but I was right with him: "I ain't goin' nowhere, big fella. You can't lose me."

He smiled. Then he passed off.

Another time I tried it on Charles Barkley. Now, as most people know, Charles talks much trash. On this one occasion he fouled me hard as I drove to the hoop. We were beating them big, by twenty or thirty, and it seemed like he was trying to take me out of the game. As I got off the floor I looked up at him, acting really angry and aggressive, and said, "Hey, big fella, you trying to hurt me? You don't know where I come from. I'll hurt *you.* I'll take *you* out!"

The big fella looked at me and started laughing. "I wouldn't try to hurt you, Muggs," he said. "You know that."

People often want to know what the game looks like from my level, standing waist-high among all those giants. Well, it's hard for me to say. Since I've always been the shortest guy on the court, I only know the game from my level. I can't compare it to how a seven-footer sees the game.

I do know this, though. People say that basketball is played above the rim. That's true only about 20 percent of the game. The rest of the time the ball is in someone's hands, and he's on the floor. The ball's on the floor more than it's in the air.

And when it's down there, I have the edge. You don't start your shot over your head. You've got to bring the ball up. I'm right there where the ball starts. Same thing with rebounds. A guy gets a board, his first thought is to gather it in to his chest or waist. I'm right there, too. I'm waiting. I just reach in and *pop!* it's out.

When I'm playing my game, I am the happiest man alive. Once I step on the court I feel free. You can have so many problems in your life, but when you're on the basketball court it just eliminates everything. It totally blocks the world out of your mind. I have so much love for the game, it is totally indescribable. You can say I'm in heaven. You can put the most far-fetched, exaggerated words you know in my mouth, because that's how much it means to me and a lot of people who play this game. When I'm out on the fast break, when there is a three-on-one and the ball is in my hands and I'm in the middle of the court and I have an opportunity to trick my opponent and get the ball into the hands of one of my big fellas, I get this great feeling coming over me, like something spectacular is about to happen. Something magical.

In a lot of ways, my whole life has been magical. The odds against anyone making the NBA are huge. In my case, they were probably twice as huge, because I am half the size of the average NBA player. Not only did I have to avoid the harsh temptations of my early life growing up in the projects of Baltimore, I had to overcome the endless doubts that someone my height could play any form of organized ball. As a little kid I was picked on or passed over when choosing sides for a game. In recreation leagues I was looked at as the cute little one. No one ever thought I'd play high school ball. When I did play in high school I was taunted and laughed at by opposing players and fans. No one thought I had a chance at *any* college ball, and certainly not Division I, major college ball. And when I did make it, at Wake Forest University, I was a national curiosity for a long time before I was considered a talented player. The pros? C'mon. A lot of big coaches, scouts, and so-called experts doubted that I could play even minor league pro ball, and as long as I've been in the NBA I've been called a gimmick, a novelty act, a promotional stunt to fill seats while management waits until someone better comes along to take my place. (By the way, it's been seven years now, and everyone is still waiting.)

I'm not angry or bitter about this anymore. I'm just stating it as fact. That's the way it has been my whole life. As a kid, though, I was sometimes very angry about it. There were times I'd run crying to my mom when kids teased me. Other times, I'd just burn up inside if some kid said something about my height or passed me over when picking sides for a game. I'd be furious when a coach doubted my ability or took me out of a game. But over time I learned to use that anger constructively. I turned it against my opponents and those who doubted me. I learned early on not to show that it upset me, to pull it inside and use it as a powerful motivation. People tell me they still see this in me to this day. Even in practice, if someone on my own team beats me somehow — steals the ball from me, or tricks me into a turnover — they say I get this fire in my eye, a look that says, "No one is gonna make me look bad and get away with it." I can feel it bubbling inside me, a feeling that I have to get back at the guy, to steal the ball back from him, or drive past him, anything to let him know he can't take advantage of me. And I almost always do. I just cannot stand to be beaten at anything, anytime.

I've been that way for a long time now. I learned that it was the only way I could succeed, because no one has ever taken me seriously. Except me.

And that's how I became the smallest player in the history of the NBA.

I don't want you to think I go around with a chip on my shoulder. I'm not looking to show people up. Most of the time, this little fella is an easy-going, fun-loving guy. I think I am known for my big smile as much as for my size, because I am almost always smiling. I'm a joker. I love being with my friends and family, I even love hanging with my opponents. It's only when I am challenged that the fire starts to burn.

And being my size never stops presenting a challenge. Every day I walk out the door I have to prove myself all over again. That's what makes my story so interesting. I think my story inspires a lot of people, especially kids, and I am really proud of that. Everyone encounters a lot of negativity through life, but my life proves that anyone can overcome that negativity. You can do anything you want to do in life, if you have a fierce belief in yourself, a strong will, a big heart, and some role models to inspire you.

These aren't just ideas or pipe dreams. They are true. I'm a real-life example.

Remember, size isn't only measured from ground level up. Size is about more than just feet and inches. A lot of people will tell you, even though they are six or twelve or twenty inches taller than me, that they still look up to the little fella.

Little Ty

I missed the day everyone started calling him "Muggsy." A couple days later we were playing ball, and everyone's going, "Muggsy! Muggsy! Muggsy!" I'm wondering, Who's Muggsy? When we were real young kids I had always called him "Little Ty." Or "Shorty."
— Reggie Williams, Denver Nuggets forward

THE LAFAYETTE COURT HOUSING PROJECT in East Baltimore had been home for both my mom's and pop's families for quite some time, a couple of generations I think, when I was born into the neighborhood on January 9, 1965.

Both sides of the family were on the short side. My mom, Elaine Bogues, is only four-eleven. My pops, the late Richard Bogues, was five-six. My older brothers, Richard and Anthony, are five-seven and five-five, and my older sister, Sherron, is five-one. My aunts and uncles and grandparents and cousins all check in with around the same numbers. You can call us Bogueses the "Fives Family." I knew I had no chance of ever getting out of the five-foot range, no matter how hard I wished and dreamed about growing taller.

After two boys and a girl, my mom wanted another girl to even things out, but she was plenty happy when I showed up healthy. After having her first three kids, she lost two other babies before they were born. I'm sure glad they kept trying.

In fact, I think that maybe because my folks kept trying so hard, went through so much trouble and pain to have me, I was born with more determination than most people. Their determination to have me somehow got into me. I was not to be denied. And from that moment on it has been a part of my personality. I mean, everyone in my family is strong-willed, even my grandparents. They all played sports, for instance, and I've been told they all played as hard-nosed as me and my brothers and sister do. But I think everyone in my family will tell you I have more of it than anyone. As long as I can remember I have always been determined. There is no time in my life that I can remember letting someone else tell me what to do or deciding how I should live my life.

Whatever I'd set my mind on, I'd do. When I tried to learn to ride a regular bicycle, I was so small I could hardly get on it. It took me a good week to learn. I tore that bike up, and myself, too. But I did it.

For my first couple of years we lived on the tenth floor of an apartment building, and one of my mom's favorite stories is about when I was just one or two years old and I said I was going to go down all the stairs by myself. She told me if I did she'd break my legs. Well, one day she was looking for me, and I was nowhere around. She got nervous and started hollering, until my brother Anthony yelled up from the ground floor, "He's down here!" Sure enough, I had thrown my bottle down and went after it. (I needed an excuse to go down, and that seemed a good one!) She gave me a good beating for doing that, but she was sure surprised I could do it.

I don't quite remember doing that; it's not a clear picture in my mind, more like a blur of memory. But it sure is my style and always has been. I can remember being told, "Don't swing on the monkey bars!" Well, tell me not to do something, and I have to do it. Of course, I slipped and fell on my head, and was knocked cold for a few minutes. But I did it. I don't like to say I do things on a dare, but to me challenges are like dares. I can't say no to a challenge.

Like I said, maybe this stubbornness, this determination, was born into me. All I know is that, as time has passed, it has become an asset. I have always had to accomplish things no one thought I could. Especially on the basketball court. I was never satisfied with just being competitive. I always wanted more. I always had to take it to the fullest extent possible, to make whatever I dreamed of happen.

Anyway, that's how I came into the neighborhood, and I am glad for it. No, my parents didn't name me Muggsy. They called me Tyrone Curtis Bogues, Ty for short. These days, everyone calls me Muggsy, or Muggs, or some other nickname, even my wife and kids. I've been Muggsy for so long (since I was around ten years old — I'll tell you later how that name came about), I even have to catch myself sometimes when I am signing checks or other important papers; I start to write "Muggsy," and have to remind myself to sign "Tyrone."

To this day, though, my mom still calls me Ty. And I have to admit, I really like that. My mom and I have a very special relationship, and it's even more special that she calls me by the name she gave me.

Lafayette Court is on Orleans Street, not far from downtown Baltimore. It's not much to look at. The main apartment complex is that ten-story building with several apartments on each floor. There's an outside hallway that's screened in, and from it you can look down on the main courtyard. There's not much grass or trees, and the fences that surround the playing areas and basketball courts are kind of ratty. The outdoor courts are overgrown — the asphalt is cracked, and weeds grow in the cracks. The rims are usually bent, and there are never any nets. But we had an indoor court at the recreation center, which was about a hundred yards from my house and was where my brothers and sister and I spent most of our time anyway.

Across the main courtyard is a row of two-story apartments. My family moved from the ten-story high-rise into one of those when I was young, and that's where I remember growing up — 1115 Orleans Street.

It is tough talking about life in the projects. I can only describe my feelings about it as mixed, or conflicted. I go back and forth on it myself. I guess it is because the ghetto is a complicated place. People from outside the ghetto think it's all drugs and killings and gangs, that people are always afraid and always hungry and life is just always terrible. But that's not the case. As with all things, there is good and bad everywhere. Nothing is just black or white. And one of the ways I have learned to cope with bad things is to downplay them, or to focus on the good things.

The result is that if you ask me today if I think growing up in the ghetto was a horrible experience, I will tell you No. In fact, speaking as an adult, I can tell you honestly that I am as proud as I can be about where I grew up. I am not one of those guys who will forget where he came from, or is embarrassed because he came from a place that some people look down on. Not me. Whenever I am in Baltimore, I make sure to head back to the old neighborhood. A lot of my friends still live there — I am also not the kind of guy who forgets his old friends. Maybe life hasn't worked out for them the way it has for me. I know I've been extremely fortunate, and some of my friends have not been so lucky. But they will always be my friends, and I will always be a Lafayette kid at heart. I love that I come from where I do. Growing up in the projects made me and my family strong. It made me who I am today.

But having said that, I also have to be honest and say that growing up in the ghetto was often terrible. Inner-city life is harsh. I can't lie about that. Life for us was never easy.

People were crowded into small apartments, sometimes five and six to a room. My two brothers and I were all in one room so my sister could have her own. We had no control over our apartment's temperature settings, and the radiators would make it so hot in the winter we had to open windows just to keep from suffocating. Things like lights and elevators never worked; I'd have to walk up those ten flights of stairs in the dark, not knowing who might be hanging around. But I was also scared of using the elevator sometimes, and being trapped in this small space with somebody I did not know.

I'd hate to turn on the light switch in the kitchen every morning, because the roaches would be everywhere. There were mice, and rats, too. For a long time I was afraid to walk past any row of bushes because a rat might jump out of it.

The area was infested with drugs back then, of course. As a kid I'd see people with swollen, puffy hands, feet, and legs; I thought they were from lifting weights, until I learned they were the signs of heroin use. Dealings drugs was the only way a lot of guys could put money in their pockets and food on their tables. There were loan sharks, who loaned money; I don't know what their interest rates were, but you can bet they beat the bank's. These guys had a nasty reputation, nastier even than the dealers'. They'd beat up people to within an inch of their life — but never kill them, because a dead man can't repay a loan. There was also a lot of drinking, and gambling, and pimping, and stealing, and a lot of gangster activity.

And there was violence. Gunfire was as common as dogs barking. The drug dealers fought over their territories, and the gangs fought over turf, same as they do today. My friends and I had to dive under cars or over fences pretty often. We'd be walking home from school, or walking to the rec center, when suddenly, out of nowhere — *Pop! Pop! Pop!* I scraped a lot of elbows and knees that way, tore a lot of clothing. I like to joke about it now, and say that's how I learned to run so fast. But it was terrifying for a little kid just trying to get home. I often say that city people are "hard" and suburban or country folks are "soft." Well, we are hard because we had to become hard at too early an age. It is tough to be a little kid in the projects.

I witnessed some truly horrible things, things no one should see, especially not a child. I was walking out of the rec center one day, minding my own business, when I saw two guys arguing very heatedly. I figured out that one of them was a loan shark, so I knew it might get ugly. I had no idea how ugly. One of the guys pulled out an ice pick and started jabbing it into the other fellow. I was so shocked I couldn't move. The victim fought and fought, and finally got away. I don't know how he had the strength. He must have been stabbed a dozen times and was bleeding all over the place as he staggered down the street.

I saw another guy beaten to death with a baseball bat — a sickening thing to see, let me tell you, maybe the worst thing I ever saw in my life. I don't remember how it started or who was involved, but I'll never forget that scene. I can still see that guy swinging the bat with both hands. I can still hear the sound of the bat crushing the other guy's skull. It makes me feel sick inside, to this very day.

We weren't even safe on the basketball courts. I can remember an argument during a game, just the usual argument that always comes up in the course of a game. Well, this one got more and more nasty, until one of the kids walked off the court, came back a few minutes later, pulled out a gun, and blew the other kid away — just shot him in the back as he was going in for a layup.

So you can see how a person gets hard in the city.

Some of these victims weren't just guys in the neighborhood — they were my friends. I've lost too many good friends to the streets. Some who survived ended up in jail. That's life in the ghetto. It's the same in every city in America. Some good ball players — some good people — never got the chance to show their talents.

It very easily could have been me. The difference between Muggsy Bogues, NBA player, and Muggsy Bogues, dead body, is so small it scares me just to think about it. You see, I was a victim of the streets, too. When I was just five years old, I was shot.

I was unlucky enough to be in the wrong place at the wrong time. Across Orleans Street from our apartment was a small store. Now, my mom and pop always told us kids never to cross the street, because the traffic was dangerous and they wanted us to stay close to home. Well, we went over there anyway. I was with my sister, Sherron, and some other kids when we saw an older boy fighting with his girlfriend. The boy got so angry or frustrated that he picked up a rock and threw it through the store window. The guy who owned that store was a mean old guy, and he came running out of the store, yelling, "Who did this?" The boy who did it pointed over to us and said, "Those kids did it."

The owner ducked into a little shed and came out with a shotgun. We all scattered. Sherron, who was holding my hand, let go of me. I tried to climb a chain-link fence, but I started to slip on loose gravel or dirt. That's when the old man started firing.

I heard the shots before I felt anything, but I knew he had hit me. Shotgun pellets hit me in the right arm, on the inside of the bicep, and all up and down my right leg. I went down in a heap by the fence. An older kid named Rickey saw me, picked me up, and carried me away, across the street. Pellets just missed him. My sister and brother were just missed, too. I think Rickey saved my life, because the guy kept shooting until he was out of ammunition.

Everyone was hysterical. At that point no one knew if he had been shooting pellets or bullets, and of course bullets would have done a lot more damage. My mom was crying, my brothers and sister were crying, I was crying. My pops was furious, and he went after the old guy. He was going to do something harsh, I'm sure, but I don't know what happened — my mom may have talked him out of it — and I don't know if the guy was arrested or what. I only remember lying in the ambulance, five years old and bleeding all over, and being scared to death.

Luckily, the wounds were not serious. They removed as many of the pellets as they could, patched me up, and sent me home. They didn't get all the pellets, though, and I still have a few in my arm to this day. They don't hurt or anything, but I can feel them there. They always remind me of how precious life is and how quickly it can be taken away. I usually don't take the good things in life for granted, but when I begin to, I only need to feel those metal slugs in my arm. They remind me of all the friends I've lost. And I know it could as easily have been me as them. You don't have to be a bad guy to die in the streets. Plenty of good people die, too.

The hardest part about growing up in the projects is simply surviving, but staying out of trouble is almost as difficult. Trouble can find you, of course, and you can be an innocent victim, like I was when I got shot. But you can also find trouble. It is everywhere you look. And I'm not saying we were perfect. We weren't the Brady Bunch. Far from it. I got into some trouble now and then, like any other kid.

Sometimes it was pretty harmless. I remember getting caught skipping school. I was very young, and this was a prekindergarten school. Kids in the neighborhood alternated days; some of my friends went to school one day, and I went another day. This one time I saw my friends hanging out and just figured there wasn't any school that day. I didn't skip intentionally, I just got confused. My brother saw me hanging out, and told my mom. She didn't believe him: "That couldn't have been Ty, he's at school."

My brother said no, he was sure it was me. My mom stuck her head out the door and yelled, "Ty, you down there?"

"Yes, ma'am," I said innocently.

Well, she gave me one good beating for that. It was a dreadful moment for young Ty. She taped two rulers together and tore up my butt so bad I couldn't wait to get to school the next day. I never made that mistake again.

(I would try to trick her, though. I'd complain of an upset stomach to get out of school. But she'd outsmart me. She'd give me that awful Pepto Bismol. "You feel better now, Ty?" "Yes, ma'am." "Good. Then get off to school.")

Sometimes, though, the trouble wasn't so innocent. One of the worst things I ever did was when I was ten. It's a story I've never told anyone, not even my family, that's how much it affected me. Looking back now, it's not such a big thing — just a stupid thing that a lot of kids do. But it shook me up so much that even now it's hard to talk about it.

What happened was, myself and four of my buddies were in the Kmart to buy some gym socks, because we had a game going. Well, before we got to the socks we stopped off at the candy counter. Before we knew it, we had spent all our money on candy. As we were leaving the store, one of us remembered we had come in for socks, and we knew we couldn't play without them. So we headed back to the clothes department and we stuffed some socks into our pants. It was the first time I had ever tried to steal something.

We got caught, of course. A security guard saw what we did, and he dragged us back into his office, where he scared us all near to death.

"Number one," he said, "I have already called the police. Number two, I have already called your parents. Number three, I don't know if you know it, but what you did is against the law, and you are going to pay the price for breaking the law."

After about a ten-minute interrogation and lecture, he left the room and locked the door behind him. He left us alone for about twenty-five minutes, which we spent crying and bawling and being scared beyond belief. He had us thinking we were going to be thrown in jail for a hundred years — that is, if we survived the beating our parents were going to give us. We were five terrified little kids.

When he finally came back, we figured we were goners. But he said only that he was keeping our names and pictures on file for six months, and if we ever did anything like this again, he was going to make sure we did double hard time in the state pen. He hadn't called the cops, or our parents. He just let us go.

That was one smart security guard. Talk about scared straight — I never came close to stealing anything again.

The biggest source of trouble, of course, was drugs. I'm not going to lie to you, I saw drugs around me. You couldn't avoid it. Some of my friends got into selling and using it. I always tried to keep away from it, to keep it at arm's length, and my friends respected me for that. There were temptations, but no one tried to pressure me into it, and I could make my own decisions.

I think it was easier to avoid drugs if you chose to when I was a kid. In a lot of ways things were very different then from what they are now. Back then, people looked out for each other more than they do now. The projects were almost like a small town, where everyone knew everyone else. And everyone looked out for the kids. The older generation respected kids then. I mean, there was always a bad element around, but back then, they didn't force drugs on the kids. They did their thing, but they left the kids alone. It's not like today, where it's all about making a lot of money by getting kids hooked early. We knew it was there, but we could stay away from it.

Our mom wouldn't allow us to use drugs. She would have killed us if she thought we were. But more important, she always taught us we didn't have to use drugs, that we had other choices. She worked for a living, and she taught us the value of work, that you have to be strong to survive, that you have to look the other way.

See, it's not just about the drugs. There have always been drugs, and you can't get rid of them. It's about the people. People make their own choices. If you have choices, you don't need drugs. Drugs are only for people who think they don't have any other choice.

My folks always worked, so we were never really poor. At least I never thought we were poor. I mean, we obviously weren't rolling in money, and things were always tight, but we never went without anything. There was always enough food on the table. We always had decent clothes. I always had new sneakers when I needed them, and a ball to play with. Every week, my mom would bring us some kind of present. Even if it was just a new pair of socks, or a candy bar, it was a special treat. She did it automatically. And by doing that, we never felt deprived.

So you see, we weren't perfect kids and the neighborhood wasn't a perfect place. And still, despite all this, I look back on my childhood only fondly. And I do that for a reason. I'm not naive, and I won't sugarcoat things. I will acknowledge that there were horrible things to ghetto life. But I will not dwell on them. I refuse to. In fact, I will use them to motivate me, to make me a better person.

I look at it like this: it wasn't an easy life, but it was the best for me. I lived through some rough things. I was tested early, and I came through. It helped give me the confidence that I could do anything I wanted, if I set my mind to it.

I'll repeat something I said earlier: I think that one of the main keys to my success is that I use negative emotions as internal motivation. Whether it's the violence I saw, or the things people said about my height, or whatever else might be used against me, I turn it around and say, "Oh yeah? Well, I'll show you!" I keep it inside, but I never forget it. To the outside world, I'll focus on the good things. I have learned that there are always plenty of positive things if you pay attention to them.

That's why, even with all the hardship, I can also honestly say that I had great times in the projects. If people outside the ghetto want to think it was all gloom and doom, I can't help that. I am here to tell you, I had a lot of fun.

Our families had all been living at Lafayette for so long it was quite comfortable. In those days, people had respect for their homes. They took care of their yards. The yards were small, for sure, but families kept the grass cut, the weeds pulled, the stoops swept. There were rose bushes everywhere. People can't believe that we had roses in the projects, but we did. Red roses, yellow roses, white roses. The neighbor ladies would surely let us know if we were playing too close to their gardens.

Back then, we could stay outside all night and not worry at all. As long as we were within sight of our parents, we could sleep out on our little front porch or on the courtyard lawn in front of the apartments. And we felt totally safe.

These days, kids can't really do any of those things. Today it's all in the open, the drugs, the friends killing each other. Even the little things like taking care of the lawns and stoops has mostly disappeared. It's very sad to see what has happened. I think that also accounts for some of my conflicted feelings. There is no question that the city is worse now than when I was coming up, and that it is harder to see it in any kind of positive light.

Still, the city is my home — I wouldn't trade it for anything. You can get an education on the streets. It's an environment that can bring out the worst in an individual, or the best. I think for me and my family it brought out the best. And it keeps us grounded. No matter how much success I might have or money I might make, or how much fame I get from being on television, I can never get a big head, because my family will kick my butt if I do. We all know where we came from, and we will never change. My mom still works in the city of Baltimore, and a lot of people at her office don't even know that her son is a professional basketball player. When they find out, they say, "Well, why didn't you tell us?" That's not her style. That's not us. As she says, "We just go about our natural ways."

How did Tyrone become "Muggsy?" To understand that, you have to understand the neighborhood, and now that you do, I can explain.

In those parts, everyone had a nickname. Everyone. It is a tradition, I guess you could call it, and it goes back a long way. Even my father had a nickname. His name was Richard, but everyone always called him "Billy Bogues" — both names. Not just Billy, but Billy Bogues, and said with a little attitude, a little respect. I'm not sure how he got the name, but it doesn't matter. A lot of nicknames just take over, and people forget why they got them. My brother Anthony, for instance, is called "Stroh," and my brother Richard is called "Chuckie." I don't have any idea why. But it's always Stroh and Chuckie, and it always will be.

In my group, we had "Jimmy Golf," and "O.J.," and "Doctor Crip." My best friend was a kid we called "Russ"; you probably know him as Reggie Williams, who was a star in high school and at Georgetown University and now plays for the Denver Nuggets.

Russ is still my very best friend to this day, and it's amazing that the two of us, who have known each other forever, grew up together, and love each other so much, are both in the NBA. Reg and I were inseparable as kids. My mom called us Mutt and Jeff, because he was so tall and I was so small, because he was always shy and quiet and I was always outgoing and talkative. We were a perfect match. They used to say back home that if you were looking for Reg, you found Ty, and if you were looking for Ty, you found Reg. We were that close.

As for me, when I was a very young kid I was known as "Apple," because I had a bald, shiny little head, and I guess I looked like a shiny brown apple.

But that changed forever one day when I was around ten. People always ask me who my heroes and role models were when I was a kid, expecting me to name some pro player from the NBA or ABA. The fact is, my own personal hero at the time was a kid in the neighborhood named Dwayne Wood. Dwayne was a little older than me — I hung out with his younger nephew Darryl, who was the guy we called O.J. — and was playing for Dunbar High School, which is located just across the street from Lafayette Court. Dwayne is only about five-five, but he could really play. (He went on to play at Virginia Tech.) I bugged him to play me one-on-one all the time. We played ball a lot together on the streets, and he was the guy who made me realize I could play with anyone, no matter my size. That's why he was always my idol.

We were playing ball one day, and I was being my usual pesky self, stealing the ball from everyone, running the break, making the passes to my big men — basically playing the same game I play today. After one play where I created all sorts of havoc, Dwayne just yelled out, "Hey, Ty, you're out there muggin' everybody!"

Now at the time, my friends and I were big fans of the Bowery Boys movies, which ran on TV all the time. We loved to watch them because those kids reminded us of ourselves, tough, street smart, wise-guy kids, and all of them had nicknames like us. In fact, the leader of the Bowery Boys was called Muggsy. And since I was already the leader of my group, it all just came together. "Muggin' " became "Muggsy." It happened almost instantly.

I have to admit the name Muggsy kind of bothered me at first, because it sounded like I was really a mugger. But when a name sticks to you, there's nothing you can do about it. And "Muggsy" stuck with me because it was perfect. Soon enough I knew it was a name of respect, a name for a leader.

Even then, I was leading my troops. In the projects, you have to make your own fun, and I kept my boys busy. It wasn't all basketball, either. I was always getting football or baseball games together. We rode our bikes all over Baltimore — that's probably how I developed such strong leg muscles. We had those old-style roller skates that you attached to your sneakers with a skate key. We'd skate all over the neighborhood with our keys around our necks, or go to Dead Man Hill and nearly kill ourselves. Every Christmas, all the kids would gather and skate all day, grabbing car bumpers and hitching rides. There would be around two hundred kids, just skating all over the place.

I was almost always the instigator. I might have been the smallest kid around, but I was always in charge. I was always fearless, leading the break, getting things moving, heading up court.

I was always the point guard.

3

Life in the Projects

*He was more spoiled than the others, because he's the youngest.
I always carried him around everywhere. People gave him
whatever he wanted. He had that smile. . . .*
— Elaine Bogues

EVEN THOUGH THINGS WERE ALWAYS TIGHT at home financially, my folks kept us kids busy. My dad had an old, beat-up car, and we'd go to drive-in movies. All of us would pile into that car, then sit outside eating popcorn and watching movies. We all loved amusement parks, and we'd go at least once a year. My mom even scraped together enough money for a bus trip to Coney Island one summer. To this day I still love amusement parks. I take my own kids, and I spend more time on the rides than they do. You can't get me off the roller coaster!

Now that I am a parent of three kids, I really appreciate my own parents. My folks did a great job of raising us. I have complete respect for them. Especially my mom. She really kept the family together. She worked hard at that while I was young, when my dad was off working, and even harder when he was sent to prison.

My dad — well, talking about him is a bit more complicated. In the same way I have conflicted feelings about the ghetto, I have conflicted feelings about Pops. For a lot of the same reasons, too. In a lot of ways, he was like the ghetto itself. He had a lot of good qualities to him. But he also had a lot of problems.

Pops always had a regular job. He worked down at the docks as a stevedore, unloading ship's cargo. He had some irregular hours: he'd be off work a few days, then work a couple days straight, then work some nights. Sometimes he'd travel to New York or other ports to work. He was out a lot. Whenever we asked where he was, my mom always said he was working, and we had no reason to doubt that.

I am being truthful when I say that we kids didn't know much about what in the projects is called his "street life." It's not that we were naive, or stupid. Like I said earlier, in those days the older generation kept their business away from kids for the most part. We respected our dad. We were afraid of him, too. We didn't get into his business.

But he didn't get into ours, either. He wasn't very affectionate with us. He would play with us whenever we were all around the house, or if we were at the beach together, but he wasn't the kind of dad to say, "Let's go play catch" or "Let's go work on your game."

I have to say, he was there for all the important things. He made sure he was around at Christmas, and he always had something for us kids. He was there for birthdays, for Easter, days like that. And unfortunately, that is more than you can say for a lot of the men in the ghetto. Some of my friends never saw their fathers.

But he was no Brady Bunch dad. As a youngster, I didn't understand why he wasn't around, why he wouldn't be interested in me or my basketball abilities. He never asked how I was doing, even though by the age of eleven or twelve I was well known around the neighborhood, and even around the city's other rec leagues as a star player. All kids want the respect of their father, and I knew he respected me, but he was just not very concerned with my sports.

I understand now that when he wasn't at home, he was out hustling for whatever money he could make, doing whatever it took to make sure his family had enough to eat. He got into some things he shouldn't have. He was selling drugs. He committed stickups and robberies. I don't think he was a hard-core gangster, but from time to time he was involved in crime. There is no denying that. He was living a life of the streets. And eventually he paid the price for it.

The first time I can remember him getting into trouble occurred one winter when we were pretty young. We had this huge snow-storm, twenty inches or something, and the city shut down. My dad began looting with some other men and came home with a new carpet and a big color television set. My mom wouldn't allow it. She made him take it back, and he did. I guess he didn't want to hear her mouth. (Elaine Bogues can speak her mind — she may be only four-eleven, but Little 'Lainey *will* be heard!)

I thought that was just an isolated incident, something he just got caught up in. I wasn't proud of him for doing it, but I didn't pay much mind, either. I'm sure my mom had a sense of what my dad was into, but probably didn't want to know. I know that I never saw anything other than that one time. I never heard stories about him being involved with drugs or crime.

That's why I was so shocked when he was arrested. He got caught in a stickup and was arrested for armed robbery. I was twelve years old, and my mom came to us one night and told us Pops was going away for a long time — he was sentenced to twenty years at the federal prison in Jessup, Maryland.

We couldn't understand it. We asked my mom all kinds of ques-tions: Why was he doing this? Didn't he have a job? What was he doing with a gun? Why did he have to go away? I was really upset. I was at an age where a kid needs both his parents around. My dad might not have been the most supportive father in the world, but I knew I could count on him being there if I really needed him. A kid that age needs a male around the house. I had seen families with just the mom at home, and I really didn't want that. I was scared.

Those were some tough times, boy. My mom stood by Pops, and visited him every week. But I had a hard time visiting at first. I hated going to see him in prison. It made me uncomfortable, and

I didn't go as often as I should have. I regret that now. But I was still angry and hurt by what he had done. I didn't handle it as well as I could have. I was young, and I guess I was mad that he wasn't around for us.

But over time, things changed between us. While he was in prison, my mom would bring him all the newspaper stories about me that ran while I was in high school, and he started to understand that I was becoming a good ballplayer. He really became interested and grew to be very proud of me. He even kept scrapbooks of all the clippings my mom brought him, and he showed me off to his friends in prison whenever I came by. At first that made me uncomfortable, all these guys in prison calling, "Hey, Muggsy! Muggsy!" at me, like they were my fans. But I grew to be proud of it, because it made my dad proud. I am sure he was the proudest dad in prison. Eventually I figured, hey, prison was something I had to get used to, and I couldn't let it bother me.

As the years passed, I think his being in prison actually helped bring us closer together. He had time to think about us kids, and our relationship, and he really tried to correct his mistakes. He wrote me many letters, usually once or twice a week. He tried to communicate to me who he was, why he had done some of the things he did. And he did a good job. He never came right out and said what he had done, or why, but I could read between the lines. I came to understand him more, to know that he was doing those things for us, to try to make our lives a little better. He wasn't a bad man; he was a good man who had done some bad things.

As we got older, we were both sad that he wasn't around for my glory days in high school. I am sure he really missed being a part of that aspect of my life, and he would have loved to have the opportunity to watch me develop through high school and college.

But through all those years I know that in my heart and in his heart we were together. It's one of the strongest feelings I have. When I got to high school, he was like my second coach. He really got involved in the game — he even started coaching a prison team — and his getting more involved in basketball because of me and who I was, truly brought us closer together. I would drop him a line every so often, encouraging him and his team, or I'd send him some plays to run. We learned to communicate our feelings through basketball.

In the end I refused to let his being in prison affect my relationship with him in a negative way. Whatever problems we had became smaller and smaller. We still had our conflicts, like most fathers and sons, but he was my dad first, last, and always.

A lot of kids in the projects were badly hurt by not having a father around for a role model. But I was lucky enough to have some uncles and my older brothers to act as role models. Other kids were not so lucky, and that's one of the reasons many young boys join gangs — gang leaders are older boys who sometimes take the place of missing dads. I was very fortunate to have my uncles to keep me straight.

My mom had the biggest impact of all, though. She was both a mom and a dad to me. She gave me all the confidence I needed.

When other kids would taunt me about my height, or tell me to give up basketball, I'd run crying to her. She didn't know the first thing about sports, but she'd tell me, "Ty, don't worry about it. No one can run your life. They can't judge your heart. Whatever you want to do, whatever you believe in, do it."

When I cried to her that I wanted to be taller, she said, "You'll do fine, Ty. God doesn't make mistakes."

When my dad went to prison, my mom was on public assistance for a while. But she knew that wasn't the way to make life better, so she went to school at night, and got a job as a secretary. We all stuck together and supported her and each other. And we all worked during the summers to help out. My mom and sister and brothers think I got away with a lot. It bugs them that I had the job of sitting in the rec center all afternoon handing out lunches to other kids. They say I didn't do any chores around the house, either. I think I pitched in plenty, but maybe I did scam a little. When the little fella smiles that smile . . .

I was close to all my siblings. I'd tag along after my older brothers like every younger brother does, until they'd get annoyed and tell me to get lost. I'd pretend to leave, then follow them some more. We hung around together all the time, playing sports and goofing around. The Bogues boys were always tight, and we still are. They help out at my summer basketball camps — they are both good players, too — and I hang with them whenever we get the chance to be together.

My sister was close to me, since I was the youngest and she was closest to my age. She really looked out for me during those years, and we spent a lot of time together. I learned a lot about basketball from her. She was a good player, an all-star in high school, and got inducted into the Dunbar High School Hall of Fame after she graduated.

She had the same game I do. She was quick, pushed the ball up the floor, and concentrated on steals and assists. Scoring wasn't important as long as your big men (or women) were getting the ball. Let them score, and get the assist, the "dime" as we call it.

Sherron is my biggest fan. And my biggest critic. She went to all my games as a kid, and even though you couldn't see her — at five-one, she was hard to find in a crowd — you could always hear her. Ask anyone who went to my games as a kid and they can all do an impersonation of Sherron yelling at me: "Go get 'em, shorty! Yeah!" "Get that apple, little man!" "Shoot the rock, Muggs!" (Even my own sister wants me to shoot more!)

She's still the first to get on my case after a game. I call her "Coach," or sometimes I call her "Helen," because that sounds like an old lady's name, the kind of old lady who is always bugging you or lecturing you about something. And that's her — she calls me up after watching me play on TV:

"What's the problem, Helen?"

"You gotta take that open shot, short man."

"All right, Helen."

"How many dimes you get tonight, shorty?"

"I got ten dimes, Helen."

"Well, give up a few dimes and take that shot!"

"Okay, Coach Helen."

My family is so close, I call them after every game. I did all through college, and still do in the pros. Sometimes it gets comical. My mom will tell my brothers or sister, "I just talked to Ty," and they will say, "But I just talked to him, too."

My family has meant everything to my being where I am today. Because of the love and support I got from my mom and the rest of my family, and because I was able to focus on the positive things, I never thought our life was so bad. I knew I wanted to make it better, but it wasn't desperation. It was gradual, a step-by-step process. And I knew basketball was the way to do it. As a youngster I knew basketball would help get me into a good high school like Dunbar, so I worked toward that. Later on, when I realized my parents couldn't afford to send me to college, I knew ball would help me get a scholarship. I knew it would let me travel, meet new people, see some things I might not see otherwise, and then, if things worked out, it would let me earn a living and feed my family.

I learned early on that basketball was best used as a tool to help you get other things. In the ghetto, basketball — all sports, really — is more than just a game. It's a way of life. For many kids, it's the only thing around to keep you out of trouble. But this way of life attracted some undesirable things to it, because successful people always draw a bad element that wants to be a part of that success. As a result, no matter how successful you might become, you always have to keep focused on making the next step. If you get caught up into the lifestyle of the moment, you are in danger. There are a ton of examples of people who lost sight of where they wanted to go, and suffered for it.

All the kids at Lafayette at that time, and really all of Baltimore, knew the story of Skip Wise. He was our inspiration, and our warning. Our best example and worst example. He personified the choices we had and the dangers of making the wrong choices.

Skip "Honeydip" Wise, a Lafayette boy, was the greatest schoolyard player of the time in Baltimore. Everyone said he was going to be the next Oscar Robertson. He was *the man* — the sweetest-shooting, sweetest-ballhandling, sweetest-moving guy I ever saw. He had lost one of his toes in an accident, and still he always had that ol' Honeydip strut. We watched him at the rec center, then at Dunbar, and then in the Atlantic Coast Conference at Clemson, and he set the tone for every kid who played back then. We all looked up to him. The crowds would chant "Honeydip! Honeydip!" and all the kids around would dream they were Skip Wise. He was a true role model. Until he ran into problems.

After making all-conference as a freshman, he had academic problems. He also had a big contract offer from the ABA Baltimore Claws, so he left school and turned pro. But when the ABA and NBA merged, the Claws folded, and he didn't hook up with any other team. He began hanging around the old neighborhood and getting into some bad habits. He had lived the lifestyle of a famous person as a kid, and now his friends took care of him and made sure he had nice clothes and fancy boots, and women wanted a part of him, and the drug dealers wanted to associate with him. It all caught up with him. He got arrested for selling drugs and served some time in prison.

Like I said earlier, it comes to individual decisions. He made his decisions, he was living his life, and he didn't see what he could lose. He knows that now. I still see Skip back home — he's out of prison and doing pretty well — and we play ball together sometimes. He constantly tells me, "Shorty, I am sure glad you didn't follow in my footsteps."

I use Skip as an example. He was on top of the world, and as high as he got, he still fell off, because he lost focus. It can happen to anyone. I know it could have happened to me. The same type of guys that hung around Honeydip hung around me. But I learned the things I shouldn't do. These guys were my friends, and they still are, but they always respected me for not getting involved with their lifestyle. They knew I was trying to make it through basketball, and they didn't try to get me off my path. They didn't pressure me, and I don't judge them. You will never, ever get me to say that these are bad guys.

But they are doing what I consider bad things, and I don't associate with the negative side of their lives. I don't approve or condone using drugs at all. Believe me, no one knows more about the damage drugs do. You always have choices, and drugs should never be your choice. A lot of these guys who are my friends had the talent to go somewhere with basketball. They at least could have played college ball, gotten an education, and moved on to a better life. But some people get impatient, they don't look further down the road than what they see right in front of them. They see what they can have right now — the quick score — and they take it. They don't see how it hurts them later on. I don't think any kid should make that choice.

I know it's not easy. It's hard to "just say no" when you can see that saying yes can get you a lot of nice things in the short run. I certainly had my temptations. I had moments where I lost focus. But basketball was always my savior. You know how a VCR always has to be on channel three to get a clear picture? Well, I was like a VCR — I had to be on the basketball channel to stay focused. If I slipped to another channel, things got blurry.

I was able to stay on the basketball channel because of help from my friends and family. Especially friends like Reggie Williams, who always had the same focus. As I've told you, Reg is my best friend, and I don't ever remember a time not knowing him. I will always consider Reg my single best friend, and he'll say the same about me. A lot of it comes from that time in our lives when we kept each other on track. We talked about staying focused all the time. We never let each other get caught up in the outside activities that could hurt us. I think we clicked so well because we have such different personalities. I was outgoing, he was quiet, but we had so much in common.

I know I couldn't have made it without friends like Reg. Just like I know I couldn't have made it without my family. My parents, my brothers and sister, and people like Reggie Williams helped make me a strong person. I always knew who I was. I never felt like I wasn't somebody special. I believe that even if I wasn't successful at basketball, I still would have been successful at something else. But basketball opened doors for me, broadened my horizons, took me places I wanted to go, earned me respect. That's what I looked to basketball for.

That, and the love of playing the game.

4

Ball Was All

We grew up with the attitude that if you didn't play ball, you weren't considered a person. There wasn't anything else to do except get in trouble.
— David Wingate, Charlotte Hornets forward/guard

DAVID WINGATE IS RIGHT. 'Gate is another old friend from Baltimore. He didn't live in Lafayette, but in another project nearby called Cecil. We played against each other as kids before we teamed up in high school, and now we're teammates again on the Hornets.

And he was right — all we ever did was play ball. We'd play in the heaviest snow, clearing a spot just big enough to shoot. We'd play in pouring rain and in the heat of summer. All day, every day, in the rec center if it was open, on the streets if it wasn't.

My mom always knew where I was — which is why she let me do it. She never had to worry about me, because she knew I was either at the rec center or on the outdoor courts. I used to set my watch back a couple of hours, so that whenever I had to be home by a certain time I could always play longer and have an excuse. I'd be due home for dinner at six, and I'd show up at seven-thirty. She'd start to holler, and I'd say, "But my watch says it's six. This dang watch must be slow." I did that more than a few times. I knew she was on to me, but she didn't mind as long as I was playing ball.

I think that all my earliest memories are about basketball. Sher-ron and I would bend coat hangers into circles, tie them to a wall or a dresser with clothesline, and set up goals in her room. We'd have one-on-one games with a nerf ball or a rolled-up sock. The whole neighborhood would be in there playing, all the kids. We'd clear her bed and all her stuff out of the way, and have some *serious* games. We'd be slam dunking over each other, banging off the walls, making a big mess of things, until my mom or pops would yell at us for making too much noise. We'd stop for a minute, then start up again.

I still remember getting my first real basketball. My godmother gave it to me when I was eight years old. I woke up Christmas morning, and there was this box. I opened it, put air in the ball, and went down to the court and played, even though it was early in the morning and freezing cold.

As a kid, I always had a ball with me. Always. I slept with the ball, I dribbled up and down the stairs, I set up a slalom course of cardboard boxes and dribbled through it as fast as I could.

The funniest thing was me dribbling when I took out the trash. I made it a challenge to take the trash bag in one hand all the way down the stairs to the dumpster while dribbling with the other hand. At first I wasn't very good, and people in other apartments would be hanging out their windows and doors, watching me and laughing. I had trash spilling all over the place, and they'd be giving me all kinds of heck. But I had the last laugh. It wasn't long before I could make it all the way down to the dumpster without spilling a thing.

I would follow my brothers or sister to the pickup games and watch the older kids play. They'd never pick me because I was so small, and it burned me up. I'd be furious, and I would go off and try to prove them wrong. I knew even then I couldn't be passive, or compassionate. I couldn't let people push me around or talk trash to me. If I let that happen I wouldn't get anywhere. Some-times, trash talk can be more damaging than pushing and shoving. I just used it all as motivation.

What bugged me was that no one ever said to me, "Muggsy, you shouldn't play because you aren't good enough." It was always, "You can't play because you are too short." That really made me mad. To this day, people say the same thing. After so many years in the NBA they still say I'm too short, not that I can't play. If I'm not doing the job, criticize that. Criticize my basketball. I can accept that. But don't criticize me for something that I don't have that you think I should have, like height.

So, when the older kids wouldn't let us play, we'd get a couple of empty milk crates, and tie them to the chain-link fence. My friends Reg, O.J., and I would have our own games. I think that's the last time I dunked — into a milk crate. We had some serious milk crate games. We would be dunking into these milk crates and wondering how tall we'd get, thinking we'd be tall enough to dunk into the real goals, pretending we were throwing it down like Doctor J. But it was just dreaming. Sometimes Sherron would play with us, and deep down, we both knew we weren't going to get much taller.

When kids would make fun of my height — saying things like, "You're so short, when you sit on the curb your legs dangle in the air" — it hurt me. Little kids are sensitive. You want to be liked, to be included in things, but when other kids say things like that you feel like you are not part of the crowd, like you are somehow deformed. I'd get depressed and wonder why I couldn't be as tall as the other kids. But I never let it take over my life. I knew that if I could prove myself to them, they would have to overlook my height.

My friends and I made sure we showed off, and that the older kids saw what we could do. And it worked. Eventually, the older kids could see I had some ability, and they would pick me. And then everyone in the neighborhood saw me differently. The little fella could *play*. From then on I was always chosen for teams.

People ask why I didn't get discouraged about being left out or being called too short, why I just didn't give up and walk away from all that abuse. I didn't give up, because I knew I was good at it. From playing with Dwayne Wood and my sister and brothers, I knew I had enough talent to compete with the other kids. If I wasn't good at it, I might have given it up, but I knew I had promise. All I needed was a chance to show my stuff, and once I got it, I got respect. Once I drove past a big kid, or shot over him, or stole the ball a few times from him, he stopped looking at me as this little short kid, and started looking at me as a good player. That's why I've always been so passionate about basketball. I love the game itself, but I also love that it earned me the respect of people who doubted me. Other kids still made jokes about my size, but now it was with admiration, and that made all the difference.

We had great times playing on the streets, but the best times of all were at the rec center. That place was the center of my world for as long as I was growing up. A man named Leon Howard was the rec center director then, and he loves to tell about the first time he saw me. The center had a summer camp for the little kids. They'd get about a hundred kids every summer. I was in the five-and-six-year-old group, and Mr. Howard would see this tiny kid trying to climb onto the folding chairs. He says that I could hardly get up on them, I was so small, but I wouldn't let anyone help me. I was so aggressive, my size was no big deal to me.

Every morning the kids had to say the Pledge of Allegiance before the programs started. And every morning, I wanted to hold the flag. Mr. Howard says I would run into the place first thing in the morning and get the flag before anyone else had a chance. He finally had to tell me, "Now, Tyrone, you can't hold it every morning. Let someone else have a chance."

Mr. Howard says he could tell I was a leader, even then: "You watch the way a person walks, like a peacock, with his head held up, walking with a little strut. That's what Tyrone had back then. Head up, with a little strut. Even then, he was the smallest kid around, but he wasn't afraid of anybody."

Every apartment or housing complex had a rec center back then. There were something like a hundred or more rec leagues throughout Baltimore. The center was open late, after school, and all day on weekends. It was open all summer long.

They ran all kinds of programs besides basketball. There was Ping-Pong, pool, wrestling, football, even dancing. I did it all. In fact, I won a city-wide Ping-Pong tournament when I was around twelve, and I was the state junior wrestling champion in the sixty-five-pound division one year. A lot of people were telling me that wrestling should be my sport, that I could get a college scholarship if I gave up basketball and stuck to wrestling. My own wrestling coach, Dwight Warren, did everything in his power to persuade me to stick to wrestling. Now, I liked wrestling a lot, but I *loved* basketball. And that love carried me further than wrestling ever could have. Mr. Warren says that I taught him a lesson — he never says what a kid *should* do anymore.

When I was very young, I wasn't allowed to go to the rec center by myself. I used to beg my brothers and sister to take me, or I'd sneak away to get there myself. As I got older I just went there on my own. We spent all our time there. We'd race home from school, throw our books down, and race over to the center. Often we'd get there even before it had opened, and we'd wait around in front until Mr. Howard or someone else came by to unlock the doors.

I started playing in a house league at age nine for a coach named Larry Holley. We had some wild house games back then — myself on one team, Reggie Williams on another, just taking it to each other. Mr. Holley was the first coach to give me a real chance, the first to not look at my size but just at my playing. At this point I could see a pattern developing. Every time I took a step up in basketball, I had to prove myself all over again. First it was on the playground, where the older kids refused to let me play until I proved I could hold my own. Then in the rec leagues, where each new coach wondered if I was too small. Then in high school, and college, and the pros. Every time it happened, I learned the lesson of internal motivation. It didn't come easily — it still doesn't. There were times I would get upset and angry, times I would lose control, but I was still just a kid, and I had to learn the lesson over and over.

For example, my next coach was a very special man, Edger Bell Lee. We all called him "Tweetie Bird." I'll never forget him. I remember one time when he took me out of a game and I was furious. After the game, he dropped me off at my house, and as he was pulling away I grabbed a rock. I lost my head. I wasn't trying to do any damage, but I smashed his car's rear window. I couldn't believe I had done that: "Oh, man, I just busted Tweetie Bird's window!" I ran up to him. "Mr. Lee, Mr. Lee, I'm sorry, I'm real sorry." He didn't say a word. He just drove off. When he showed up for the next game the window was all taped up. Oh, my, I felt so bad. But he never said a word. He knew it was my natural competitiveness and I think he didn't want to take that away from me.

Like I said, Mr. Lee was a wonderful guy. He had a little car, a two-door Nova, and he'd pile twelve kids into it to take us to the other rec centers to play games. One time we were late, and Tweetie Bird said we had just ten minutes to warm up once we got there. One of my teammates started moaning, "Oh, Tweetie Bird, it takes ten minutes to get dressed, we won't have time to warm up." Tweetie Bird just said, "Son, you can set the whole world on fire in ten minutes." We all busted up. He was a real jokester.

Another time, we were driving to a game and came to a stoplight, and he sees a young lady waiting at a bus stop. He stops the car, leans out the window, and says, "Hey, pretty girl, you look like a squirrel. Are you crackin' any nuts today?" Oh, man, we just fell out. I remember it to this day, almost twenty years later. Mr. Lee kept us all together. He treated us well, and we loved playing for him. He would always spring for cookies and soda after every game. He'd buy those three-for-a-dollar boxes of cookies and we'd go crazy.

Those early days were great. I started playing in the rec leagues, first the Baltimore Neighborhood League for ten-to-twelve-year-old kids, and then the Urban Coalition League for thirteen-and-fourteen-year-olds. We had me and Reg, Darryl Wood, all my friends together playing ball. We were *good*. And we played some serious competition from the other rec centers. Our biggest competitor, though, was the Cecil projects. They had two kids as good as Reg and me. One was David Wingate, who could really run the floor and shoot the ball. The other was a quiet little skinny kid they called "Truck." His real name was Reggie Lewis, the future captain of the Boston Celtics. For the next couple of years, I competed against Reggie Lewis every weekend and all summer long. We were rivals then, but soon enough we played together on the same team, in high school, and we became friends. Then, through our college days, and into the pros, we just grew closer and closer. We had a lot of history together, from the time we were ten years old until he met his tragic end in 1993. Now that he's gone, I cherish the time we had together more than ever.

For years, the whole city watched those rec league games that had Reg Williams and myself against David Wingate and Reggie Lewis. There were other good players throughout the rec league, but those games were special. Of course, back then we didn't know how special it was, that we would all soon be playing together in high school, and then against each other in college, and that we would all someday get to the pros. We dreamed about it, but all kids have those dreams. We were just out there to have fun and play hard and beat each other's butts. Russ and Muggs against 'Gate and Truck. We were the talk of the city.

My mom didn't come to many of the rec league games. She didn't know or care much about sports. And she thought her being there would put extra pressure on me. But that never bothered me. People were already coming to watch the little fella play, even when I was young.

The crowds at those rec league games were always standing room only. We had hundreds of people in the gym, especially at the big games like Lafayette-Madison, or Lafayette-Cecil. People would come out to see me, because they couldn't believe that this little boy could play at that level. And I was always prepared. I'd go out there and please the crowd. Even then, as a ten- or twelve-year-old, I loved to put on a show.

After Tweetie Bird, my coach was Mr. Howard, the rec center

director. We called him "Fat Man." He had played college ball —
one of his college teammates was Curly Neal, the Harlem Globe-
trotters star. Mr. Howard is the one who really began to teach me
the fundamentals of basketball. He took me aside and set up special
drills. He had me dribbling around chairs he set up on the floor,
working on my crossover dribble, working on changing direction,
dribbling with just my fingertips to get the feel of the ball, dribbling
with my head up so I wouldn't have to look at the ball. He taught
me so much.

I practiced all the time. When I was taking out the trash, I'd be
thinking about Mr. Howard, trying fancy moves and spilling gar-
bage everywhere, until I could switch the ball and the trash bag
from hand to hand without spilling a drop or missing a dribble.

He worked on everything in my game to make it better. He
worked on my passing, he worked on my shooting, by holding a
broomstick over his head to get me used to shooting over taller
players, to get me putting more arch on my shot.

Mr. Howard was one of the few people who never doubted my
ability. Most people in the area had big families, and if the older
brothers and sisters played and were pretty good, then he figured
the younger kids would be good too. He knew that my older brothers and sister were good players. He also knew my uncle, who was
an aggressive player.

Under Mr. Howard's coaching, I got better and better. When I
was thirteen I was named the MVP at our rec league tournament.
He couldn't believe this little guy running around the way I did. I
surprised even him.

When we won that league tournament, we were all supposed to
get a trophy, but we had more kids on our team than they had
trophies. So when I got the MVP trophy I gave my team trophy to
one of the kids who didn't get one. I just considered it another
assist, and I know it made him happy.

The rec center was supposed to close at five-thirty every day, but
Mr. Howard, Reg, and I would usually stay later, just playing ball.
We were like his kids, and he liked hanging around with us. He

used to say we were model kids. "If you were to talk to them, you wouldn't believe they were from public housing," he says. It was because we were athletes, and athletes always hang together instead of hanging out on the streets at night. We were always at the gym. We were gym rats. Mr. Howard would show up on Saturdays and we would have already pulled the doors open and started playing. He'd pretend to get mad and say, "I'm gonna call the police on you."

"You ain't gonna call no police," we'd say, and we'd all laugh.

Plus, we were pretty good players, so he was willing to take the time to teach us. He really knew the game. Reg, being kind of shy and preferring to be at home, would usually leave before I did. Mr. Howard and I would talk about all kinds of things. He became almost a second father to me, giving me advice and helping me stay out of trouble. And we'd play one-on-one.

During lunch hours all of us kids would sit around arguing that we could beat him at all sorts of competitions — shooting baskets, Ping-Pong, cards, whatever. One time, O.J. and I lined up to race him the length of the court. We both beat him the first time, but he said it didn't count and we had to do it again, this time just to the far foul line. We ran again, and we beat him again. Again he says it doesn't count. This time it's to half-court. Now he beats us, and we are furious. Plus, he cheated. He'd get a running start before he would say, "Go." Oh, we were angry.

He still kids us about it. He knew he couldn't beat us at a long race, but at a short distance he could, because his legs were longer. And he knew he could cheat, because we were too young to say anything. Besides, we liked him, so we let him get away with it. We'd argue like crazy — "You cheated!" "No I didn't. It just *looks* like I did" — but it was all in fun.

The rec center saved my life. I can't say strongly enough how important it was for me and my family and friends. Every night, every day during the summer, it wasn't anything to see a hundred and fifty, two hundred kids in there, playing pool and Ping-Pong, checkers and cards, doing arts and crafts. It was so crowded you couldn't move. It saved a lot of kids from the street, and it gave the community something to be proud of.

Sports was important for the neighborhood. People looked forward to those games, and we were guaranteed something like a hundred people at them. They were so proud of their kids doing well, which helped keep the community balanced during that time. It made them proud to say they were from Lafayette. Mr. Howard and other adults always told the kids to be proud of where they came from. Mr. Howard constantly told us we could make it in society just like anybody else. He'd say, "Realize that these circumstances are beyond your control. You can't help it if your parents aren't financially able to move you out to some nicer area. Be proud of where you come from."

During that time, sports helped a lot with that pride. Nowadays, though, they don't have rec centers anymore. The city doesn't have the money to keep them open. It breaks my heart to go back to Lafayette and see a sign on the door that the rec center is closed. I am sure that many of the problems in the area now could be solved if the kids had someplace to go, something to do other than get in trouble. They don't have the choices I had.

I am convinced that none of the good things that happened to me would have happened without the people I met through the rec center and the basketball leagues. People like Tweetie Bird and Mr. Howard were role models for us. They kept us straight and focused. And friends like Reggie and Darryl and all my other pals also kept one another in line. Competing against people like Reggie Lewis and David Wingate made us tough and prepared us for life. Competition is a big motivator; it gets you to try things you might not try, and accomplish things that no one thinks you can accomplish.

People outside the projects might take things like their kids' basketball games for granted. They have other things to keep their kids busy and to develop their self-esteem. In the inner-city, sports were sometimes the only source of pride and accomplishment for a lot of struggling families. People who say that sports aren't important are wrong. Sports are *everything* in the ghetto. Sometimes it's the only positive thing in a world full of negative things.

Through sports, we stayed out of trouble, we kept our lives moving forward. And as a result, we got to go to a great high school, and play on the greatest high school basketball team ever.

It's So Hard to Be a Poet

I know why the caged bird sings, ah me,
When his wing is bruised and his bosom sore —
When he beats his bars and he would be free;
It is not a carol of joy or glee,
But a prayer that he sends from his heart's deep core,
But a plea, that upward to Heaven he flings —
I know why the caged bird sings!
        — Paul Lawrence Dunbar, "Sympathy"

P AUL LAWRENCE DUNBAR was a famous African American poet who lived from 1872 to 1906, and there are several inner-city schools around the country named after him. The one at 1400 Orleans Street in Baltimore was almost like a holy place to the kids of the projects. Like a lot of things in the ghetto, you wouldn't know by looking at it. "Regrettably," wrote Franz Lidz in a 1981 issue of *Sports Illustrated,* "the school lacks the beauty of its namesake's best verse. Cramped amid drab housing projects, Dunbar has all the charm of a government warehouse."

But we knew better. Dunbar High is no prep school, but it does offer its students a solid education if they are willing to work — it is not only the athletes who move on to college from there. Still, athletics, and especially basketball, is one of the prime tickets out.

The teams at Dunbar are called the Poets. The Poets weren't really considered a basketball power until Skip Wise and his team-mates upset Washington, D.C.'s powerful DeMatha High, which then had future NBA all-star Adrian Dantley, in 1973. That team was coached by the legendary William "Sugar" Cain, a former Harlem Globetrotter who coached the team for thirty-two years, but that DeMatha game was his last before he retired.

Two years later, a former pro football player named Bob Wade took over as basketball coach and athletic director at Dunbar. He had played for the Washington Redskins in the late '60s, and his coach was Vince Lombardi. Discipline, naturally, was a big part of Coach Wade's outlook. The Poets were always successful during the late '70s, winning several consecutive Baltimore Public Schools championships. He coached Dwayne Wood and my brother Anthony, and he had a lot of talented players at the school.

But Coach Wade already had his eyes on us younger kids, barely in our teens, playing in the rec centers and on the outdoor courts of the nearby housing projects. There were a number of truly talented players, all of us the same age — give or take a year — and we might find our way onto the same high school team sometime around 1981–82.

Coach Wade hoped it would be his team.

I caught his eye pretty early on. In the mid '70s, the Dunbar gym was opened to community groups once the school's own sports and recreation programs had been completed. It was a big deal for the local kids to play on the Dunbar court, and I really enjoyed it as much as anyone. I didn't know it then, but Coach Wade's office overlooked the gym, and on occasion he would look through his window and watch the kids play. He'd see little me, just eleven or twelve years old and the size of an eight-year-old, playing with kids older than I was. He noticed how I was usually one of the first kids chosen in pickup games, how I would often control the offensive flow of the game with ball handling and passing, and how my defensive pressure gave opposing players a terrible time when they tried dribbling the ball up against me.

He was intrigued. I could more than hold my own against thirteen- and fourteen-year-olds. But high school athletes are seventeen, eighteen years old. They aren't boys anymore. They are stronger, and faster, and can jump higher. Coach Wade had played small point guards before. But I was *small*. Still, over the years, he kept an eye on me.

Of course, he didn't have to convince me to come to play for him. Dunbar High was the only place any city kid who played ball wanted to go. It had the tradition, the crowds, the great gym. It was where Honeydip had played, and Dwayne Wood. All the best players from Lafayette Court went there, and so did the kids from Cecil and some of the other projects. All the time we were coming up, my friends and I talked about the day we would put on that Poets uniform and show our stuff.

So you can imagine how devastated I was when I found out that I had to attend another school as a freshman.

Even though Dunbar was located right across the street from Lafayette, kids from our project were actually zoned to go to another school, Southern High. But like a lot of cities with big public school systems, Baltimore let kids transfer from one school to another to take courses that weren't offered at every school. That allowed students and athletes to transfer to Dunbar, which offered courses that Southern didn't.

I hadn't even considered Southern High. Southern was a bad school with a bad basketball team. Dunbar was a good school with a good team. If you had a choice, which would *you* choose?

To transfer, we had to declare that we wanted to study dental technology, which Dunbar offered but Southern didn't. Now, none of us really dreamed of being dental technicians; I'm not going to lie about that. We weren't attending Dunbar to learn to clean teeth. Everyone else knew it, too. That was just the way the system worked.

David Wingate, who is a year older than Reg and me, got into Dunbar first. Reg, Darryl Wood, and I, along with Reggie Lewis, all would come over the next year. That was the plan, anyway. But somehow, my academic records from junior high got lost, and I missed the transfer deadline. I still think someone at Southern hid them so I would have to stay there. I was furious. All my boys were running for the Poets and I was stuck at Southern.

I planned to just work on my grades so that I could transfer the next year, and play a little for Southern. The coach there, whose name is Meredith Smith, had this preconditioning program, but I dropped out of it. I was in shape, I knew I could make that team easily, and I wanted to concentrate on schoolwork, so I didn't do some of the running. Well, Coach Smith decided he was going to be a hard guy about it. When he held tryouts, he called out about twenty names of kids who could try out for the varsity. Sure enough, my name wasn't among them. I just started laughing. All the other kids asked, "What about Muggs?"

I still felt like playing some ball that particular day, so I went over to the junior varsity tryout and just tore those poor kids up. I had a field day. But that was it. I wasn't going to play JV ball for a lousy team. I figured I'd just do my schoolwork, and play some more rec league ball to stay in shape. Mr. Howard got me into the fourteen-to-sixteen-year-old leagues to keep my skills sharp and be ready for Dunbar the next season.

Going to Southern was awful. I could have walked to Dunbar, but Southern was miles away. I had to take two different city buses, because school buses didn't run in our neighborhood. I had to get up in the middle of the night, stand in the dark, in the rain and snow and cold, wait for the bus, then transfer to another bus. It took almost an hour each way to get there and back every day. It was dreadful.

Meanwhile, Southern's team was struggling. They got off to a 1–5 or 1–6 start. Just before the deadline when they could add more players, Coach Smith came to me and asked me to come and play for him. I was still mad, and had some attitude, so I gave him a hard time. I wasn't too mature about it, I guess. I was still learning how to control my anger, and sometimes I didn't control it very well. But I talked to Mr. Howard about it, and he thought I should play. He thought I should get some high school experience, which was a lot different than rec league ball, and by getting a feel for the high school game I'd make a smoother transition to Dunbar. I followed his advice, and told the coach I would play.

I didn't start the first game. The team fell behind, so Coach Smith finally put me in. I never came back out. I took over, and we became a totally different team. We won many of the rest of our games. I put up some strong numbers, including scoring in double figures pretty often — I was shooting a lot — and getting my share of dimes.

We were still a weak team, though. This was no Dunbar. I remember one game we played against Lake Clifton High, which had a great team, maybe even better than Dunbar at the time. We were down by five points late in the game. Coach Smith puts me in, and I steal the ball on the first possession, feed a guy for a layup, and we're down by three. They bring the ball back up and come at me again, and I steal it again. My big man gets another perfect layup. Now we are down by one and there are about twenty seconds left in the game. The ball comes back in, they bring it up against me once more, and I steal the ball again. I throw it down to my teammate under the basket, and the guy misses the layup! We lose by one.

Of course, at the end of the year Coach Smith tried to get me to stay at Southern. I just laughed. I couldn't wait to get to Dunbar. While I was at Southern I would go to all the Dunbar games. In the big games, my boys would look up at me in the stands, and we all knew I should be down there with them. In the last game of the season they played one of their big rivals, a private Catholic school called Calvert Hall, for the city championship. It was a great game, a legendary game, that Calvert Hall won in triple overtime after trailing by nine with only 1:52 left in regulation. When it was over, Coach Wade looked up at me in the stands and shrugged. We both knew I could have been the difference. That was a hurtful feeling, seeing my boys lose that one. I felt for Reg, for O.J., for 'Gate, for all the guys. All they were missing was a true point guard, a playmaker who could make the team go. That was my role.

And once I got there for my junior year, boy, did we go.

*   *   *

When I transferred from Southern to Dunbar for my junior year —
high school lasted three years for us; we went from freshmen directly to juniors and then seniors — Coach Smith knew there was
no way he could stop me. I could have stayed at Southern, been
comfortable, been a star. But I knew that if I had stayed I would
have been just another little kid in the city league, and probably
would have been overlooked. At Dunbar, I knew I could get noticed, maybe get some national exposure, and that would help me
get a college scholarship.

(I should mention that, these days, Southern has a very good
basketball team, one of the best in the city, and Mr. Smith is still the
coach.)

I was so excited to get to Dunbar. I was also a little nervous. I
knew all the guys on the team, and had been playing with them for
as long as I could remember, but I still had some butterflies that
first day of practice. There were Reg and 'Gate as the starting
forwards and O.J. as the returning point guard. They also had Gary
Graham, a great shooter, at the big guard, and another transfer,
Tim Dawson, at center. The second team had guys like Keith James
and Derrick Lewis, and Reggie Lewis was really coming into his
own and could have started anywhere else in the city. Our bench
was better than most other first teams in the city. These guys had
been winning for a long time. They had only lost three games the
year before. The Poets had a winning tradition going back to before
I was born. All of a sudden I'm coming in to take a spot on the
team. I admit, my gut was bubbling.

Plus, there were a lot of expectations because I was the missing
piece. And I had to get accustomed to Coach Wade, his tempera-
ment, what he would accept and wouldn't accept. We had to feel
each other out, because I think he still wondered if I could really
play at the high school level. I think he had some doubts. But after
our first practice, he knew I would hold my own. He knew I was his
starting point guard.

At that first practice, he killed us. He left us gasping for air. We practiced long, from three-thirty to seven-thirty or eight o'clock every night after school. We'd go into the gym when it was daylight, and come out into pitch dark. When it came to working us, there was no one like Coach Wade. I think we were the only high school team in the country that practiced that way. In fact, I know it. I've talked with other players about their high schools, and no one has been able to match my Bob Wade stories.

And it was beneficial. Those practices were so hard, but we loved them. We loved working. We never complained about it.

Coach Wade had all kinds of tricks. He'd bring out sandbags and bricks and make us run suicide drills, dragging the bags or carrying the bricks in our hands. We'd run with bricks in our hands, and if anyone dropped a brick, we'd start the whole darn thing over again.

All the hard work paid off, though. Coach Wade was a discipline coach, which we needed. We all could have gone off on our own, because we all thought we were good enough to be stars. We all could have been egotistical, playing for ourselves and our own stats. But Coach kept us together. He made us a team. He got us wanting to win a league title.

We were sharp, boy. Precise. In pregame warmups we had the best layup lines in the world. Dunks, alley-oops, we really put on a show. We were as tight as any team I've ever been on, college or pro. I mean, with Williams, Wingate, Lewis, me, Dawson, Graham, and all the others, we had a team that could have beaten some college teams right then.

And even though we all were stars, we had no ego problems at all. We were so tight. We loved each other like brothers, and I think the rest of the school respected us for that. Around school there was a togetherness about the players on that team. We looked out for each other.

I was pretty popular throughout the school. I always tried to be friendly and to make other students feel good about themselves. I knew that athletes were put up on a pedestal, but I wanted to make the other kids feel special too. I enjoyed a lot of my school activities.

I got along well with my classmates and most of my teachers. But the fact is, I spent most of my time with the other players on the team.

We were close, and it was all because of Coach Wade. He honestly cared for each of us, on and off the court. He taught us the value of self-discipline and prepared us all for life. Coach is very well spoken, and easily heard. If he sees something he doesn't like, he is going to put his foot down. He'll step up and say so.

He talked to us all the time about staying away from the wrong element. People in the community respected him and what he was doing, so if they saw any of us kids doing anything wrong or hanging out with the wrong guys, they would call him up and tell him. It was like he had a whole network of spies working for him. And he would challenge the kids with it. He'd say, "I understand you weren't in class today" or "You were seen hanging out with so-and-so." And if it was true, he would punish the whole team. He'd make us run with bricks and sandbags. If we ever asked why we were being punished, he'd just say, "Ask your teammate so-and-so. He'll tell you why." And then the other kids would get on him, too. It was effective, boy. He kept our noses clean.

With me, coming in new, he let me work my kinks out and let me be me. That helped me relax. Once I understood what he wanted, I knew my role. I kept everyone going. I hollered at guys, kept everyone focused, not letting their minds wander. That's what he wanted from me, to be the floor leader.

I can still remember getting my first Poets uniform. Maroon, with gold and white trim, and the word POETS on the front and a little zigzag design on the side. Putting on those little cookie-cutter shorts — boy, were they short in those days! But I liked them; they showed off my leg muscles. I felt like one stocky little fella out there. I had my number 14 on the back, which I wore all through high school and into college. I loved putting on that uniform.

And I can still remember our cheers. We'd bust out of the locker room for our layup line, and the crowd would go wild. Cheerleaders dancing all over the floor, leading the cheers:

Poets!
It's so hard, it's so hard to be a Poet!
It's so hard!
Go Fight Win!
Shake that thing!
Gimme a G, Gimme an O, Gimme an F, Gimme an I, Gimme a G,
Gimme an H, Gimme a T, Gimme a W, Gimme an I, Gimme an N!
What's it spell? Go Fight Win!
Shake that thing!

Ooh, that was *it!* We'd get the opening tip, and the ball would come to me.

Dribble Dribble
Shoot Shoot
Take that ball to the hoop hoop hoop!
Dribble Dribble
Shoot Shoot
Take that ball to the hoop hoop hoop!

I'd bring the ball up, so geeked up that my heart would be pounding. The crowds were always standing room, the gym so crowded that the floor would actually sweat. I'd hear my sister yelling from behind the bench: "Go shorty! Yeah!"

I'm telling you, there was nothing like a Dunbar game. To this day, even though I have accomplished so many other things that I am proud of in basketball, I don't think anything means more to me than those Dunbar days. I might win ten NBA championships and make the Hall of Fame, and still I think my fondest basketball memories will always be of Dunbar High.

Of course, it doesn't hurt that for two years we never lost a single game.

My first game as a Poet was at the annual Poet/Laker Invitational Tournament, at Lake Clifton, Maryland, on December 4, 1981. We routed a school called Edmonson, 90–36. The *Baltimore News American* wrote that the 1981–82 Poets looked "slick, quick, and powerful," and that the team had added two outstanding transfers, center Tim Dawson and me, "Tyrone Boggs." It also said, "Boggs, only 5-6, displayed remarkable quickness and savvy en route to 15 steals, 12 assists, and 4 points."

Well, at least they got the score right. Actually, that first year, I got all kinds of press, a lot of it wrong. I was listed at anywhere from five-two, to five-four and five-seven. I was called "Boggs" and "Boges," "Mugsy" and "Muggsie." But that was all right, as long as we kept winning and the fans kept coming out.

Dunbar was the first place where I really experienced what a crowd can do for a basketball team. Our rec league games drew a lot of people, but nothing like high school games. You couldn't get a ticket to our games, what with the students and faculty jammed in there. It was a big thing. We'd go on these huge runs, outscore the other team 20–2 or so, and everyone would be screaming, "Go, Muggsy! Go, Russ!" Oh, my, it was so exciting.

I am telling you, high school was the best basketball experience of my life. We were winning. We were *it*. I mean, playing in the NBA is fun, and it's a lot more fun now because we are winning, too. But it's different. In high school we couldn't lose. We couldn't even *imagine* losing. Sometimes teams would challenge us for a little while, but by the end of the game we'd win by ten, twelve points. We never had an overtime game, never had a one- or two-point game. We'd hold teams to only two or three points in a quarter while we were scoring twenty or thirty. We killed everyone.

We won that first tournament, playing Lake Clifton in the championship game. They had a big, ball-handling guard named Thommy Jefferson at the point guard. I stripped him of the ball three possessions in a row to start a game, and the crowd went wild. I threw alley-oops to 'Gate, to Reg, and we rocked. We won by thirty-one. And we were on our way.

Early in the year, we went to New York and won the Harlem City Tournament at Madison Square Garden. I was the tournament MVP, and Russ was high scorer.

We cruised the rest of the way, and in February we were 24–0. Then came our toughest test. We had the biggest high school game of the year, maybe the biggest game of many years. We went up to Camden, New Jersey, to play the Camden High Panthers. At the time, they were ranked number one in the nation. We weren't even number one in Baltimore, despite our perfect record (Calvert Hall, also undefeated, was).

Camden had a tradition as strong as ours. They were a city school in a bad neighborhood, like us. They had lost only one game in five years on their home court. That year, they had some great players, like Billy Thompson and Kevin Walls, both of whom went on to play at Louisville, where they won the NCAA National Championship in '86. We knew we were good, and we could match up well with them, but they had the bigger reputation. And you could see they were pretty cocky. We were ready, though. Coach Wade was giving this big speech to get us pumped up, but I cut him off. I said, "Mr. Wade, if you don't mind, can we just go upstairs and play the basketball game? We understand what you're saying. You can finish your talk later."

Now, by this time in my career I was well known around Baltimore, and my size wasn't ever a factor. Most people had seen me play enough to not even notice that I was the shortest guy out there. But every time I went out of town, people were always surprised when they first saw me. Of course, they tried to hurt me about it to get me off my game. I always took a lot of trash from fans and players about my height, until I started playing. Well, Camden was no different. When they announced the starting lineup and I ran out onto the court, I could see the players and the fans laughing and joking. Kevin Walls came out, and when he came near me he laughed and pointed at me and then at himself, as if he was telling the crowd, "Hey, I got the little one." He thought I was a joke or something. When he pointed at me the entire crowd laughed at me.

As we came back to the huddle, I had my head down for just a second. Coach Wade grew worried that they had gotten to me. He asked, "Are you OK, little man?" Well, with that, my head sprang back up, and I got this big smile on my face and said, "Mr. Wade, I am just fine. And when the game is over, I'm gonna have the last laugh. We are gonna have a party here tonight."

That was just the kind of situation I love. Anyone who underestimates me is in for trouble. I had been taking it to guys like Walls my whole life, and I couldn't wait to show him what kind of joke I was, and what kind of joke our team was. As I look back on it now, it was the culmination of everything I had been learning up to then about turning my anger to motivation, using humiliation as a weapon. I think it was a big moment in my basketball career, maybe the biggest, because this wasn't the playground. This was on a national scale, and if I could perform here, I would change people's perceptions of me all around the country. There was no way this kid Walls was going to show me up.

We huddled up: "One, two, three, defense!" They get the opening tip, bring the ball up . . . steal by Bogues, to Williams for the slam! They bring it back up . . . turnover, to Bogues, alley-oop to Wingate. Slam! It was all over.

We trashed Camden. By halftime, we were up 50–21, and by game's end, with all our starters already on the bench, we won by twenty-five, 84–59. I held Walls to around nine points, and caused something like seven turnovers — including three possessions in a row. I dropped into the paint and stripped the six-eight Thompson four times as he moved in for baskets. Late in the game, when we slowed things down, I just dribbled the ball around them all like I was Curly Neal, and they couldn't touch me except to foul me. They were so frustrated, we could hear them fighting with each other.

Wingate was unbelievable, scoring thirty-one points; he made eight baskets in a row. Reg Williams had nineteen in the first half, then got into foul trouble and finished with twenty-two. I had my best game ever, with fifteen points, twelve assists, and six steals. By the end of the game, the same people who were laughing at me before the game were chanting "Muggsy! Muggsy!" I was never so pumped up in my life. Afterward they came onto the court asking for my autograph. David Wingate couldn't believe that — fans who had laughed at me now wanting my autograph. He told me later, when we were older, that all the guys on the team knew right then that I was something special. I was happy we had won the game, but I also admit I was happy that I had shown those people who I was and what our team was made of.

Camden's coach, Clarence Turner, said, "Dunbar's the best basketball team I have ever seen. . . . No team has ever beaten us like that in this gym or any damn place." Earlier in the year, Camden had been beaten by Calvert Hall by five points on a neutral site. Calvert was still ranked ahead of us in Baltimore, but having seen us both, Coach Turner knew who was really number one.

"Dunbar is twenty points better than Calvert Hall," he said. "And if the game's properly officiated, Dunbar might beat 'em by twenty-five or thirty points."

After the game, Coach Wade told the press we had won because I had controlled the game, and that I had upset everything they tried. Well, they had upset me first. They had it coming.

We entered the Baltimore City Public Schools Tournament undefeated at 23–0. And we just kept cruising, winning the opening game of that tournament by forty-seven points. Wingate and Williams had fifty points between them. But by the final game, which we won 63–47 against Lake Clifton, I was named tournament MVP, even though I only scored two points in the final. In the last game, I personally held the ball for three minutes to kill the clock, and Lake Clifton scored only four points in the last period. Their coach, Woody Williams, told the press: "Bogues was the key.

We couldn't even foul him. I sent a kid in with specific instructions to foul him, and he couldn't catch him. Melvin Mathis [a six-eight center] came back and said he was worried Bogues would go through his legs and really embarrass him."

The crowd gave me a standing ovation, and my teammates carried me off the court on their shoulders. It was Dunbar's sixth consecutive Baltimore City Schools championship. And a week later, we beat Lake Clifton again to win the Maryland Scholastic Association A Conference title, Dunbar's fifth state title in Coach Wade's seven years as coach.

Winning championships might have been nothing new for Coach Wade, but both titles were a first for me, and being a part of it was the most thrilling thing I had ever been a part of in my life. The year ended with us at a perfect 28–0.

The only sadness I felt after the season was at David Wingate's and Gary Graham's graduating. 'Gate was going to Georgetown, and Gary got a scholarship to the University of Nevada–Las Vegas. We'd miss those guys, both as players and as friends.

But we had a lot of talent coming back, and a perfect record and two titles to defend. We really looked forward to our senior year, to see if we could keep the streak going.

The Greatest High School Team Ever

He never brought pens and paper to class. He always got the
girls to give him paper. He thought he was so cool. But he did
his work.
— Carolyn Damon, Dunbar math teacher

DUNBAR WASN'T JUST ABOUT BASKETBALL FOR ME. I got an education, too. My teachers at Dunbar made a big difference in my life because they cared about me. Not just as a basketball player; they cared about me as an individual. It was obvious they wanted to make us better people and prepare us for life outside of school. Even though my teammates and I spent most of our time on basketball, we were always challenged to perform in the classroom as well. These challenges were always positive and constructive. Some teachers resent athletes and give them a hard time for no reason. Sometimes it's the opposite — teachers cut athletes an unfair break, and then the other students resent them. But at Dunbar, the athletes were treated just like the other students. We had to do the work.

Carolyn Damon was my favorite teacher. She was friendly with my sister, and she would often walk me home after games because she thought I was younger than I really was. She'd also complain to my sister about me and some of my tricky ways. But she respected that I did the schoolwork, and she worked with me when I had problems with math. Plus, I think she liked me as a person.

She likes to say that I had the personality to make friends with other kids. Some athletes stay within themselves and the team, but I liked to be part of the whole school. I could hang out with all the different groups, the brainy kids, the artistic kids, and of course the jocks. I could make even the shyest students talk to me, and teachers like Ms. Damon respected me for that.

I also liked my history teacher, Mr. Cubs, and Miss Hawkins, my business teacher. She worked us, boy. Her class was dreadful. But she opened our eyes to the realities of the business world. Mr. Green, my economics teacher, made sure we knew our debits and credits. He taught us to balance our checkbooks correctly.

My English teacher, Mrs. Kelso, was a big help, too. And I needed help in English. Public speaking always made me nervous, and one time I really embarrassed myself. Coming from the street, I had a lot of the street slang in me. It's still in me now, but I am able to control it and speak in a more articulate fashion when I have to. Back then, though, I was still learning.

There was a local television show called "City Line," and because our team was so successful they were looking for some Dunbar basketball players to interview. Coach Wade asked us to volunteer, but no one wanted to do it, so I just shot up and said, "Shoot, I'll go."

It was the first time I had ever been interviewed in street clothes, outside a locker room, and I was very nervous. My heart was racing. All my teammates were in the audience. I was on the show with Tim Dawson, who was a smooth speaker, and that made me even more nervous. I was stuttering and stammering my answers, which was bad enough, but the worst came when I was asked a question and my slang came out. I wanted to say the words "out there," but it came out of my mouth as "ow-chair." I couldn't believe I had said that. Then, later in the show, I was asked another question, and instead of saying, "No, I don't," I said "No, I doesn't." I thought to myself, Oh, man, now you've done it. Coach Wade and all the players were laughing at me, and when I got back to school, everyone was all over me.

Well, I was walking the halls with Coach Wade, and Mrs. Kelso saw us. She walked right up and said, "Mr. Wade, we have to get this boy some help. He can not be going on television talking that way." She was not joking around. I got defensive: "Hey, I can talk! I was just nervous!" But I was embarrassed, and I felt truly awful. I knew I had to improve my speaking, and when I went to college I studied communications. Now I am completely confident in interviews and when I speak to groups of kids or adults. But Mr. Wade still has a ball over that incident. He'll tell that story to anyone, anytime, just to get me mad.

Of course, Mr. Wade was the teacher I most looked up to. He was more than a coach to us. He was our second father. He taught us so much about life, about conducting ourselves, about being the best possible people we could be. He taught more than basketball skills. He taught life skills. There is no one in the world I respect more than Bob Wade.

Topping it all off was our principal, Mrs. Woodland. She was the best principal I ever knew. I can't imagine a better one. She supported the whole school, from the sports teams to the honor societies. She was there for everybody, and she was everybody's mother. Everybody was her "baby": "Hey, baby. How you doing? You having any problems? Let's get together and air this thing out."

She had total control of that school. There was never any fighting, never any hostility, never any suspensions. It was so disciplined. I never saw that kind of control, before or since.

I was not as good a student as I should have been. I graduated with a C average. Now, I wasn't the worst student by any means. My mom always made sure we went to school. She was never on our case about homework, but she let us know the consequences if we didn't do our schoolwork. No grades, no job, no life. So I did the work, but really no more than was necessary, and that hurt me when I got to college.

The teachers tried to prepare us for college, especially us athletes who might wind up at tough schools. They would constantly tell us it was going to be a lot different there. In college, you'd have much more free time on your hands, you'd have to make your own schedule, and your material would be a lot harder and come a lot faster. Of course, I never listened. I pretty much coasted through high school. Once I got to college, and all their predictions came true, all those teachers flashed through my mind. I always went back to Dunbar and told them, "You were right."

If I could tell any kids reading this one thing, it would be this: If you hear someone giving you good advice, please follow it! People are trying to tell you things they've already experienced. You may think you have to find out for yourself, but you don't. That's why they are giving you that advice — so you don't have to learn the hard way. Life doesn't change that much. You will experience the same things they did if you don't listen to them. If you respect the person, listen to him or her. Be prepared to accept what these people are giving you, whether it's a parent, a teacher, a relative, a friend, a coach, or even someone like me.

Our senior season at Dunbar was one of the most special times of my life. Our junior year team was great, and we missed Wingate and Graham, but that senior year we were so close we were like a family. We were fifteen guys who hung out together, who did everything together. We really loved each other, traveled together, and knew we were accomplishing something special, sharing something precious. We treasured that. We had a bond that has lasted forever. Even though we grew up and went our separate ways, we are still tied together. We may not speak to each other as often as we like to, but we are always in each other's hearts.

Of course, Reggie Williams and I were closest of all. I was so fortunate to play with Reg. He was a true superstar as a kid, high school player-of-the-year his senior year, one of the most highly recruited kids in the country. He was famous. But he needed me, both as a teammate and a friend, and he appreciated what I did for him the way I appreciated what he did for me. We had a connection on and off the court that was unique; we complemented each other perfectly. I have that now to a large degree with Larry Johnson and Alonzo Mourning. But it started with Reg. He couldn't do what he did without me, and I couldn't do what I did without him.

I remember a game against DeMatha, in Washington, when we put on a highlight-film show. I was driving the lane and went into the air. For a split second it looked like I was stuck, and no one in the gym knew what was going to come next — no one except me and Reg. I was in the air, just hanging around, when I did a full 360 spin and flipped the ball behind my neck. Only Reg knew what was coming, and he was right there to take the pass and throw it down in a monster dunk that tore the house down. Reg knew exactly what to expect. He never took his eyes off me, because he knew the ball could come to him at any time. We had that kind of understanding. L.J. and 'Zo understand that now, and we have almost as close an understanding. But there will never be anything in my life like the times I had playing with Reggie.

Off the court, we shared some great times as well. Reg was always a quiet one. I was a joker, along with Wingate. I remember one time when Reg and 'Gate were throwing water around in a hotel room, and they blew out the television set. Coach Wade went through the roof over that one, because that wasn't like Reg. He was so clean-cut, never initiated things, never got into trouble. Even his game was quiet; he'd get his twenty, thirty points without you even knowing it. No one ever said anything bad about Reg. His game and his personality never change. Even today, when we get together, I want to go out on the town, but Reg would rather stay home, barbecue on the grill, be with his family, and just relax quietly. If I ever get him out, he has a couple of soda pops, and leaves before you know it. That's just his way, and it's part of why I love him so.

We also got to know Reggie Lewis really well in those years. We had competed against him for a long time in the rec leagues, so we knew his talent, but we didn't become good friends until high school. He was a quiet guy like Reggie Williams, never caused any problems. Truck wasn't starting, even though he was good enough to be. (It's still hard for some people to believe that a guy who became the captain of the Boston Celtics didn't even start on his high school team. But that's how good we were.) He went out and got his minutes and did his best, and when he went on to Northeastern University he really blossomed into a national star.

I think he was eager to prove what he could do, and when he got the chance he just exploded. His teammates at Dunbar were the only people who were not surprised. We knew the talent he had. I mean, on any other team in the country besides Dunbar, he would have been The Man. And he was a huge part of our success. His not starting made no difference to us — though I know it did to him, and as a result he had some problems with Coach Wade at the time. But that was understandable, and over the years Truck and Mr. Wade became as close as the rest of us.

To see him develop from our quiet sixth man to captain of the Celtics was so gratifying for me. I personally felt every success he had. First taking over at Northeastern, then taking over for the great Larry Bird when Bird went down with injuries. Man, that was so special. There was some star quality inside all of us who played at Dunbar. Wingate and Williams and I were able to get it out earlier than Truck, but we were just lucky to be in the right place at the right time. Everyone needs his chance, needs to wait for his time, and when Truck's time to shine finally came, we were all so unbelievably happy for him.

We rolled through our senior year the same way we did the year before. We were ranked number one in the nation before the 1982–83 season by *Basketball Weekly*. Wingate's spot was filled by Keith James, and Graham's spot was taken by another transfer, Derrick Lewis. (Some of the other schools started calling us an all-star team, because we had so many transfer students.) Otherwise, we were the same team: Reggie Williams and Tim Dawson up front, me at the point, Reggie Lewis and Mike Brown (another transfer!) off the bench.

We started the season blowing away powerful DeMatha, who

had Danny Ferry at center, by twelve, and then Archbishop Carroll by twenty, and winning the Beltway Classic, the season opening tournament in the Washington-Baltimore area. And the country really took notice. People like Morgan Wooten, the legendary and great DeMatha coach who had coached against teams like Lew Alcindor's Power Memorial and James Worthy's Gastonia High, began praising us, and the word spread.

"Dunbar is as fine a high school team as I've ever seen," Wooten said. "I've never seen one better. The thing that Dunbar has that none of those other teams had is Bogues. Monty Towe was a better outside shooter, but Bogues is better at everything else."

It felt so great to be singled out by Coach Wooten. Hey, I have an ego, and I like to hear praise as much as anyone. But when it comes from someone with as much respect as he has, it makes it truly special.

In that DeMatha game I made that 360, over-the-shoulder pass to Reggie Williams, and afterward people started to call me "The Human Assist." What is so funny to me about that game was the circumstances that led up to it.

It was a Friday night game up at Towson, Maryland. Before every away game, everyone met at the Dunbar gym at a certain time to take the bus. That night we were supposed to meet at 6:00. On my way over to the gym, I ran into the cheerleaders. Their coach told me that Coach Wade and the team had already left. I thought no way they'd leave me behind. But I looked inside the gym, and sure enough, all the lights were out. I didn't know what to do, so the coach said I could ride with the cheerleaders — which wasn't so bad. But when we got to the arena, no one was there.

They were all back at Dunbar, still waiting for me, but they were in the locker room instead of the gym. And Coach Wade was going crazy. He had always stressed being on time. He used to say he didn't care who it was, if a player was late the team left without him and he didn't play. But he was waiting for me, and my boys were getting a kick out of that.

All the fellas were wide-eyed, wondering what Coach was going to do. There was a guy who always followed our team who was a county sheriff, and Coach sent him over to my house. The sheriff put his red light on and drove over to the projects, right up to the front door of the house. People thought it was a raid or something. My mom said I had already left for school. The sheriff went to the rec center and to other apartments, but couldn't find me anywhere. He reported back to Coach, who had no choice but to leave without me.

There was complete silence on the bus. Every once in a while Coach would hear a kid whisper, "I wonder what Coach is gonna do?" He had never had to leave without anyone before, and they wondered if he'd really bench me.

The bus got in to Towson, and pulled onto the campus. Coach turned to his wife and said, "I wonder if someone kidnapped Muggsy." One of the kids heard that, and right away they all started whispering, "They kidnapped Muggsy! Someone at De-Matha kidnapped Muggsy!" This rumor spread like wildfire.

But as they climbed out of the bus and headed to the arena, someone spotted me and yelled, "There he is!"

Normally Coach would be like a father finding his lost son. He'd probably tell him how much he missed him, and that he loved him and was glad he was safe. And I expected that from him. Instead, this time he reacted like a stern father. He started hollering at me: "Where the hell were you? I ought to take my fist and go right upside your little head!"

I was shocked that he was questioning my loyalty. I got so upset I started yelling back at him, "Mr. Wade, you know I wouldn't let you down! They told me you had left already. It ain't my fault." We went at it for a while, him giving me hell, me getting madder and madder. Finally Tweetie Bird Lee, who helped Mr. Wade, yelled down from the bus, "Bobby, punish him after the game. He's here now, so let's go inside and win the damn game."

But I was still mad. "I don't want to play!" I yelled.

"Get your little butt inside and get your clothes on!" he yelled back.

When Coach tells this story now, he likes to make it seem like I was sobbing, tears running down my face, snot running from my nose, but I wasn't that bad. I was heated, though. In the locker room I was still yapping, "He didn't have to yell at me like that, it wasn't my fault, what was I supposed to do, he knows I wouldn't leave you guys, I'm always there for you all. . . ." Finally Reg said, "The hell with him, man. We knew you were here. Forget about it."

Before the game I saw my mom and sister, and they calmed me down and wiped my tears away. So when Coach asked if I was all right to play, I told him, "Yeah, I'm fine. Let's do it." And that's when I did my 360, a move I couldn't do again if I tried. I guess it paid off to get me so upset.

From there, the season was like a dream. We won the prestigious King of the Bluegrass tournament in Kentucky, blowing out three teams by thirty or more and winning the final by seventeen. We beat everyone in Baltimore by twenty-five or more. We beat my old Southern team by seventy-one, 120–49, and beat two other teams by forty-eight and fifty-four points. And remember, high school games are only thirty-two minutes long. That's not much time to build a lead like that.

We were number one in the country all year, and we felt that our second team could have been number two. In fact, our practices were usually more competitive than our games.

We won the city championship game, our seventh straight, by twenty. We won the state title for the sixth time in eight years. We finished 31–0, and combined with the previous year, we had won fifty-nine straight games. Some people began calling us the best high school team of all time. I have no doubt that we were and always will be.

Reggie Williams averaged twenty-four points, thirteen rebounds, and four assists per game, and was called the most wanted player in America. Tim Dawson had twelve points, twelve rebounds, and five blocks per game. I averaged straight eights — eight points, eight assists, eight steals. And Coach Wade called me the team's most valuable player.

That meant so much to me. To be respected like that, when guys like Reg were getting so much attention, was special. Here we had guys who ended up going to great colleges — Reg and David Wingate to Georgetown, Gary Graham and Keith James to UNLV, Mike Brown to Clemson, Reggie Lewis to Northeastern — all of them great players, all of them scoring more than me, but Coach Wade knew the part I had played in our success.

"Tyrone made those teams go," he says. "He set up the offense and controlled the defense. He was the playmaker. Everyone looked to Tyrone. Even though Reggie and Wingate did the bulk of the scoring those years, Tyrone got everyone into position. Those teams had such great chemistry. While I was there I just thought I was blessed with some outstanding student athletes who wanted to excel and do their best against local talent, and more important, wanted to shine on a national level. I thought both teams were outstanding, especially the second one. Now, after a few years have gone by, and people keep talking about it, I can safely say it probably was the best high school team ever assembled."

I certainly agree with that.

We were such a tight team, we had all thought about going to the same college together if Mr. Wade got a college coaching job, which was being talked about. But it didn't happen, so we all went our separate ways.

For guys like Reg, all that was left was the national all-star games and camps, and then deciding which of the many schools recruiting him would get him. I played in the all-star games, too, but I didn't have to worry about college. I had already committed to Wake Forest.

I had signed early, during my senior year, because I didn't want it hanging over my head. I wasn't that heavily recruited as a junior. People were still concerned about my size. North Carolina–Charlotte, Pan American, and Drake showed some halfhearted interest. P. J. Carlesimo wanted me to come to Seton Hall and recruited me heavily. He told me straight out that the ball would be in my hands. But this was before the Big East Conference and Seton Hall became national powers. I had my heart set on going to a well-known conference like the Atlantic Coast Conference, which I truly loved, and playing on a team that got some heavy coverage. I figured that was my only chance at getting noticed by pro scouts, and while I wasn't thinking that much about the pros, it was something I still believed I had a chance at — even though most people didn't think I even had a chance at college.

I knew my only shot at a full commitment from a good college program would come at the various summer scouting camps, where high school stars from across the country gather to play in front of the major college recruiters. I knew it wouldn't be good enough just to compete at these camps. I had to excel, I had to be noticed.

After my junior year, I had played in all the all-star games and had torn them up. I was named MVP of two of the best all-star camps in America, the McDonald's Classic in Washington, and the B/C camp in Georgia. I had been a star at the Dapper Dan game in Pittsburgh. But people still weren't paying much attention to me. They had all come to scout the better known kids like Reg.

It was at Howard Garfinkel's famous Five Star camp in Pittsburgh that I began to be noticed for my ability. Bob Wade was a coach at the camp. Before camp started, all the coaches rated the players in order to help pick evenly matched teams. When Coach Wade selected me as the number one guard in the camp, Garfinkel went crazy. He told Mr. Wade that the whole camp was messed up by taking a five-three player as the first guard. But Coach Wade knew what I could do. "Garf," he said, "I'll bet you dinner we win the league with Muggs as my horse." (A horse was a player who was allowed to play as much as the coach wanted him to. Each team got one horse. All the other players could play no more than two quarters.)

Well, my team blew through the Five Star camp undefeated. Garf bought Wade dinner at Denny's.

At the time, I understood the importance of these camps. But looking back, I now understand that they were more important than I had imagined. I knew there would always be doubts about whether I could play at the college level, but I didn't realize how strong those doubts were. People just had never seen anything like me, so they couldn't imagine me being successful. I had to show them. They had to see it with their own eyes. Back then, a school like Wake Forest would never have signed me if I hadn't proven myself on the court.

Ernie Nestor, who is a Wake Forest assistant coach, remembers watching me at that camp and thinking, "I wonder what school is going to have the guts to recruit a five-three guard to play big-time college basketball." After I pretty well dominated the whole camp, he thought, "Hell, I wonder if *we* have the guts to recruit him." He went back to Wake's head coach, Carl Tacy, and told him about this little guy who could really play but was only five-three. Coach Tacy, though, didn't care about my height. He only wanted to know about my ability. When he saw me play with his own eyes, he was sold.

I was also recruited a bit by Georgetown, but at the time they had some great guards already lined up, and Coach Thompson was honest enough with Coach Wade to admit that I wouldn't play much. Scouts and recruiters always had to go through Coach Wade first. He set up everything, and never let you talk to a scout alone. He was always there to make sure everything was clean. He looked out for everyone on his team, from the starting five to the last guy off the bench. It's a lot to ask of a high school kid, a lot of pressure is involved in recruiting, but a person like Coach Wade, who is so respected by all the college coaches, made things much easier on us.

Even though I really would have liked playing with my boys David Wingate and Reggie Williams, Coach Wade convinced me it would be better to go somewhere else, where I could be on my own and prove what I could do. It was hard to imagine not being with Reg, but I knew he was right. I asked what he knew about Wake Forest.

He talked with Ernie Nestor directly. "Ernie," he said, "don't mess with me. Don't pull the kid's leg. Are you sincere about recruiting him and playing him? Is this for real?" Nestor said he was very sincere, and Coach Tacy was sincere. When Tacy came up to talk with my mother, Coach Wade knew he was committed enough to offer me a scholarship. He told me right then that Wake Forest was a great choice. He knew I loved the competitiveness of the ACC, and that the academics at Wake, although they would be tough for a kid like me, would prepare me well if basketball didn't work out as a profession. He gave me his nod of approval. That was more than good enough for me, and I signed a letter of intent.

After our senior season, I played in a couple of all-star games, including the Dapper Dan tournament in Pittsburgh. There were some great players at that one: the Pennsylvania all-stars had Dallas Comegys and Dave Popson, and the U.S. all-stars had guys like Ricky Winslow, Steve Alford, Mark Jackson, Pearl Washington, Curtis Aiken, Reggie Williams, and me. I got a lot of the press attention at that tournament, because suddenly everyone realized that here was this little fella, just five-three, who was one of the best players in the country and was headed to the ACC. It was as if people just woke up from sleep and there I was.

My final high school games came at the Capital Classic, an all-star tournament in Washington, and I won the MVP award. And that was it. My Dunbar days were over. The feelings I had were bittersweet. I knew that I would miss Dunbar, miss playing with Reg and Truck and all those great guys. I'd surely miss playing for Coach Wade. I knew even then that we would look back on our days at Dunbar as some of the best days of our lives, and it hurt knowing that those days were now in the past. And I knew I'd miss my family so much.

There was another complication as well. During my senior year, my girlfriend had gotten pregnant and given birth to my first child, a daughter, whom we named Tyisha. That was a difficult time for me to have a child — I was still in high school, I had no money, and I was just seventeen. I knew I didn't want to marry her mother. I had to grow up quickly.

I never ran away from my responsibility, and I truly loved my daughter from day one. I took care of her. I made sure she had everything I could give to her. My mom agreed to help take care of her while I was at college, and I always had her in mind.

Having Tyisha really helped me so much. It kept me going, knowing I had this precious little girl back home. It made me not want to quit whenever things got tough. Thinking about her helped me get through any difficult situation I experienced at college. She added so much to my life when I went away to Wake Forest. I saw her as often as I could, every time I went home over the holidays. Her mom and I made sure Tyisha never saw a lack of love between us. We kept our problems with each other away from her. As difficult as all this was, I was so glad she came into my life. It wasn't the best time to have a child, but it was one of the best things I ever did, and it has all worked out very well.

All these things made leaving Baltimore very painful. But I had a new challenge ahead of me, proving that I could make it at a very tough school academically, and proving that I could be an impact player in the ACC, even as the smallest player in the conference's history. There is nothing I like better than a challenge. I had loved being a Dunbar Poet, but now I couldn't wait to get to Winston-Salem, North Carolina, and become a Wake Forest University Demon Deacon.

A Long Way from Home

*All kids have to make adjustments at the next level. But
in this case I think the next level will have to make
adjustments to Tyrone.*
— Bob Wade

I SHOULD HAVE KNOWN that both Wake Forest and I were in
for some adjustments from the very beginning. When I first
showed up at the athletic dorm on campus, during my recruiting visits, the other players thought I was someone's little
brother. Once they realized I was their new playmaker, you could
feel the tension around me. When we got on the court, of course,
and they all saw that I could play, the tension broke immediately.
I was accepted right away by the guys on the team. In fact, for my
first year or two the team was the only place where I felt comfortable.

Wake Forest University sits peacefully on 320 beautiful acres in
Winston-Salem, North Carolina. The school was founded by Baptists in 1834 near the town of Raleigh, and moved to its new
campus in 1956. The campus looks much older than that — people tell me there's an Ivy League feel to it. But it is also very
southern. Located in the heart of tobacco country — it is adjacent
to R. J. Reynolds's world headquarters — and within North Carolina's high-tech Triad area, Wake Forest is still a Southern Baptist
school at heart. (The Demon Deacons were for a while known as

the Wake Forest Baptists.) In fact, in many of the school's bro-
chures and media guides Wake is called "The Gem of the South."

It is truly a gem of a school, one of the finest academic institu-
tions in the country. Its undergraduate enrollment of thirty-two
hundred (out of six thousand total) makes it among the smallest
Division I schools. Yet, along with turning out its share of professional and business leaders, and celebrities like Senator Jesse Helms
and actor Carroll O'Connor, Wake Forest also has a great reputation athletically. Wake was a charter member of the ACC, and
Demon Deacon alumni include football's Brian Piccolo and Norm
Snead, and basketball's Billy Packer, Frank Johnson, and, more
recently, Rodney Rogers. Its most famous athletes on the whole
might be golfers, though. Curtis Strange, Jay Haas, Jay Sigel, and
Lanny Wadkins all attended Wake. And so did a pretty fair linkster
of the 1950s and '60s named Arnold Palmer. In recognition of its
most famous alum, the school annually presents the Arnold Palmer
Award to its best male athlete.

Wake Forest is the kind of place where a young, gifted student
can thrive. It can also humble the best and brightest kids, especially
those who don't come from the same background as the majority
of the enrollment. Like many private schools, Wake Forest is pre-
dominantly white, and many of its students come from economi-
cally well-off — OK, wealthy — families. Its religious influences
remain, and so do feelings of southern aristocracy and conserva-
tism.

For many inner-city, disadvantaged students like myself, this is
different from anything we have ever encountered. Kids coming
from struggling families and impoverished school systems are suddenly face to face with a school full of walking J. Crew models from
the most exclusive prep schools in America. Before classes ever
begin, these students are behind academically, socially, and eco-
nomically. They are often scorned by many people on campus and
in the community — not all, of course, but many — who feel they
don't belong in this environment. Some students and teachers and
faculty actually resent their presence just because they are good

athletes. In the blink of an eye, these kids have gone from being stars and heroes of their hometowns to being near outcasts. It is something they hadn't expected, and for many new students, including a little fella from the projects of Baltimore, it is the education of a lifetime.

My first weeks in Winston-Salem were very difficult. Culture shock is an understatement. Here is a little kid who hasn't been much of anywhere, who has never been on his own, now left alone in a white world in what to me was a hick town. I have to say that I love Winston-Salem now. I met some wonderful people and made friends I still stay in touch with, and I go back there every summer to run a basketball camp for kids. But back then, a city kid from Baltimore could see this place only as a small, out-of-the-way town.

The cars the other students were driving were amazing. Being a city kid, I always could hold my own in the clothes department. You don't need a lot of money to look good. I had them in that area. But seeing all the little boys and girls in their convertible Mercedeses and Corvettes, while I'm walking to class with my backpack — these cars were worth more than my folks made in a year!

And it was so quiet, it freaked me out. I was used to sirens, police cars, ambulances all hours of the night, people screaming and yelling on the street, gunshots, the constant noise in the city. Here I'd be walking to The Pit — the student hangout — to get something to eat, it's late at night, and it's *silent*. A few crickets maybe in the fall. Absolutely nothing during the winter but the stars over my head. I could only think to myself, Man, I am a *loooong* way from home. If the boys could see me now. There were no curbs, no sidewalks. You needed a car to get anywhere. We walked across soccer fields, across commons areas, through woods — it was a real education outside the classroom for me. Those first few weeks, I was just trying to survive.

Plus, from the beginning, I felt like I wasn't welcome there by a lot of people. Wake Forest had high academic standards, and athletes were thought of as just dumb jocks. I'm not saying I would have gotten into Wake without basketball; of course I wouldn't. But students bring all sorts of abilities to a university. Athletes bring their talents, musicians bring theirs, artists theirs, studious types theirs. We all come with a lot of different abilities, and it's the whole package that counts. As a package, I felt I belonged at Wake. Others didn't think so. No one ever said that to me directly. It was just a feeling. But it was a feeling a lot of other athletes had as well. I wasn't alone. And it wasn't long before I knew this feeling was justified.

I have to say that I never experienced any racism, either on campus or in town. I want to be clear about that. Whenever I had problems with some of the professors or other students, whenever I felt they weren't giving me a fair deal, I never thought it was a racial thing so much as it was bias against athletes.

I felt more pressure on me there than I ever felt in my life. On the court I was safe. Off the court was the pressure. I was trying to maintain my studies, reading forty chapters in a week or two, working with tutors in every subject — not just one subject, every subject. I had practice two hours a day, study hall after classes, tutors after study hall — it was intense. My schoolwork was devastating. I had just never experienced the amount of work they required — so much reading, so many papers and exams. The professors covered more in a day than I had covered in a week in high school. I thought back on all my high school teachers who had tried to warn me. I wasn't prepared for this. Some of it was my own fault for coasting through high school. Some of it was simply that city schools aren't capable of competing with rich prep schools. But placing blame isn't the issue; the bottom line was, I struggled.

I never felt comfortable that first year. I really had to get my head together, because it was tough every day. Plus, as a freshman ballplayer I wasn't playing much, and that was certainly new to me. These days, I look back on my first year at Wake and just wonder, "How did I ever get through that?"

I was lucky that my teammates were a great help. Guys like Delaney Rudd and Anthony Teachey and Danny Young were good guys to learn from. They were older, and they talked about how they were treated coming up. Delaney Rudd was my roommate at the time. He was two years ahead of me. He was a Carolina boy, so he fit in at the school and understood how it worked. Anthony Teachey was also a kid from the area. In fact, most of those guys were from the area. I was in pretty good hands.

As a high school recruit, I was pledged to Kenny Green and Delaney Rudd. They showed me around for a day or two on my visit to the campus. I had asked them a lot of questions. Is there racism on campus? Is the coaching staff straight with you? Will they sign some other guard over me? They were straightforward with me and told me Coach Tacy had never been known to recruit two players at the same position. The guys told me that if the coaches said they would commit to me, they would. It is hard to judge people just over a weekend, but these guys seemed like down-to-earth people, and I felt I could be happy there. I felt comfortable with them.

Danny Young was the senior point guard, and he had the starting job. He deserved it — as a senior, he had paid his dues and it was his time. I knew that coming in. The coaches had all told me straight up that Danny was the starter, and I would back him up. I would get my chance after he graduated. I understood. But it didn't make it any easier that I wasn't playing. Understanding and accepting are two different things.

Danny and I used to go at it every day in practice. I was very competitive, always challenging him. I felt I was good enough to start, too. So I was tough on him. I wasn't mad at Danny, I was mad at the situation. I had a little anger in me, because it was the first time in my career that I was a sub. Anthony Teachey was Danny's roommate, and I can recall Teach getting on me, yelling, "Stop hacking Danny all the time!" I, of course, responded in some way I shouldn't repeat now. It was good-natured ribbing, but there was an edge to it, at least on my part.

It's not that I didn't like Danny. He was a quiet guy, laid back, went about his work on the court and in the classroom. As a veteran, someone who had gone through a tough institution and succeeded, he gave me hope for my future at Wake. He was a role model for me in some ways. It was just that I had to earn these guys' respect. I did that by going hard at Danny. I believe strongly in working hard in practice. If you perform well in practice you perform in the games, and your teammates know they can count on you.

Mark Cline was the only other freshman that year. I had met Mark at the McDonald's all-star game, and talked him into coming to Wake Forest. We were on a bus going to practice, and Mark asked if I had committed to Wake. Now, the Wake coaches had told me to work on Mark a little, so I said, "Mark, you come to Wake, we'll be the thing. I'll get you the ball, you'll take that sweet shot of yours, we'll be *it*."

And I was right. In later years, we *were* it. In fact, we were all Wake had. But as freshmen, we were not it at all. And that was disappointing, because we were one of the top ten teams in the nation at the end of the year. Little did we know that we would never see those heights again.

When I got down about not playing, the other guys kept me going. But it seemed like I had a meeting every day with Coach Tacy, complaining about my playing time. He did most of the talking, though. Sometimes he took a little too long to say what he wanted to say. It would take him twenty minutes to get his words out. I'd sit there, thinking, "I'd better pretend I'm happy, so I don't have to spend all this time in his office."

I learned right away that college coaching is totally different from high school and rec league coaching. I was always extremely close to all my coaches. Coach Wade, Coach Howard, even Tweetie Bird, were more or less father figures to me. I didn't have that feeling with Coach Tacy. Maybe it was my fault, because I wasn't playing. I'm not saying he wasn't interested in me. He knew the game. He knew how to win. And he kept his promise and gave me the opportunity to play the next year. But it wasn't what I was used to. It felt a little distant, a little cold.

*   *   *

We had a lot of talent on the team in my freshman year. We had an opening stretch where we went 10–0, which meant that, counting my high school record of 59–0, I had a streak of sixty-nine straight wins going over three years. The streak was getting hyped a lot, and even though I wasn't out on the court that much, it felt so good knowing I hadn't had a loss in such a long time. I was very proud of that.

But there came a time when it had to end. Georgia Tech beat us when this redheaded kid hit a jumper from deep in the corner, right in front of the bench, at the end of regulation. Our jaws just dropped. But I'm glad the streak ended like that, in a good game that we had a chance to win.

I don't remember much of our other games, because I wasn't really a part of it. I do remember playing against Michael Jordan — he was still at North Carolina then, and led the ACC in scoring that year. He was something to see even then. He was always outstanding on that team. Even though Carolina was in something of a rebuilding phase — James Worthy had left, and Kenny Smith was just coming in — Mike led the team to a 14–0 conference record, although they lost in the ACC tournament. He was *it*. You could see that he was going to be great. Some people were surprised that he became as dominating as he did, because under Dean Smith's conservative coaching style he never really got to show his stuff in college. Not me. I knew the game of basketball, and I could see what Mike had in his game.

I got into every one of our games, but never started one. I averaged 9.8 minutes a game and just 1.2 points, but I was still among the team leaders in assists and steals. I filled my role as a spark plug off the bench, giving the team an energy lift, making some steals, breaking the press, getting my dimes. My job that year was to give us a real gear-shift. Danny Young was a control guard, a solid player, nothing fancy. I came in when the coaches wanted to explode the game. I think I shook things up in a couple of games. I remember a game at Marquette: It was right before the Christmas break, just after exams. It's zero degrees, and a lot of us had already mentally gone home for the holidays. We were struggling. Coach put me in the game, and immediately I stripped this kid and went in for a layup. Next possession I hounded the same kid so bad he dribbled right out of bounds. He was more concerned with me than where he was going. It was just two plays, but it really turned the tempo around and got us the initiative to win it in overtime and get out of town.

The fans and press noticed my game. I was getting publicity. Everywhere I went, crowds would cheer for me whenever I got into the game, and the media at the various places we played all did a story about me, usually about my being the smallest player in ACC history. They often paired me with Spud Webb, N.C. State's five-seven point guard. Even though we have two completely different games, people concentrated just on our size. I hated that. I wanted to be covered for my game, not for my height.

For example, early in the season, we went to a tournament in Jacksonville, Florida. We were undefeated then, 6–0 or 7–0. But all the reporters wanted to talk to me. I knew it was going to be a problem. Here we had this great team, a lot of players playing really well, and the media is interested in one of the reserves. I was very reluctant to do the interviews. I told John Justus, our sports information director, "I'm not even playing that much. Let them talk to Danny or Delaney or those guys." He convinced me I should do the interviews, but I knew I hadn't earned it. I wanted to do interviews because I was a basketball player, not because I was five-three.

All in all it wasn't a bad freshman year as a learning experience, but I was still unhappy. I always want to play every minute. Sitting on the bench is tough for me. The best thing about that year was getting a berth in the NCAA tournament. We lost in the ACC tournament that year to Maryland, but we got invited to the NCAA tournament because of our 21–8 record. We beat Kansas in the regional tournament in Lincoln, Nebraska, and then played De-Paul, with their great coach, Ray Meyer. We knew he was retiring that year, and we wanted to take him out. Of course, they were the heavy favorites, and we were the Cinderella team. In the locker room, we all felt we were going to do it. "Retire Meyer" was our slogan. And we did. On national television.

My big moment was stealing the ball from Kenny Patterson, DePaul's great ball handler. But I only played a total of six minutes in that game. Against Houston in the Final Eight, I only played two minutes.

That year Houston had Hakeem Olajuwon, Clyde Drexler, Ricky Winslow, the whole Phi Slamma Jamma gang. They were a great, great team. Being one of the Final Eight, and almost beating them, was amazing. We lost to them, 68–63, but our boys from the ACC, North Carolina State, took them out in the final. I felt great about that, because ACC teams pull for each other — when they aren't competing against each other, of course. No one had given them a chance, but Jimmy Valvano and his crew pulled off a great upset.

The NCAA tournament is big time, boy. All your friends back home see the tournament. It feels so special, like the season is over for everyone else, but you're still playing. The tournament was about the only highlight of the whole year, really. I was upset about not playing much, but I figured we'd be back. We were losing three starters, including Anthony Teachey and Danny Young. But we had Delaney Rudd, Kenny Green and Mark Cline coming back, along with myself, so it seemed a sure thing we'd see a lot more NCAA tournament action in the years to come.

That's what I was thinking after the games had ended. However, my biggest challenge was waiting for me as soon as I got back to campus.

While we were at the NCAA tournament, we were missing classes. When we got back, I had a final exam in history. I knew I wasn't prepared, and told the professor I hadn't had enough time to study. He told me, "Come in anyway, look the test over, and do what you can. If nothing comes, just sit there until it's over and hand it in. I'll give you a makeup test later." Well, I couldn't do anything, so I just sat there. I handed in my exam and figured I'd take a makeup.

I went home for the summer. A week later the coaches called me and said I had been accused of cheating on the exam.

"I didn't even take the exam," I said.

They didn't see it that way and were threatening to suspend me. I was so frustrated I almost quit. The whole year had been so difficult for me. I was away from home, in this white private school, and felt very alone. Basketball was where I had always gotten my feelings of security, but I wasn't playing and I couldn't get into my world. Now they were accusing me of something I didn't do. It was the only time I really thought about giving up. I was so lost and confused. I felt defeated. I was crushed, I was scared.

I had truly tried to do my schoolwork, tried to get help. It was difficult, because the school didn't have a great support system set up to help the athletes. Wake Forest went through a rough stretch when many athletes didn't graduate. They have since built up a much better academic support program and are doing a much better job of graduating athletes, but when I was a freshman we were pretty much on our own. It seemed like they almost wanted us to fail.

I was so upset I wanted to transfer. I picked up the phone to call my mom, but hung up. I couldn't tell her. She would have been so disappointed. I called Dell Curry instead. We had met when we played Virginia Tech, and even though I didn't know him that well, I felt that he was someone I could talk to. I asked him about Tech. He said he really enjoyed it, and told me to come on over.

I called Coach Wade. "I gotta get out of here, Mr. Wade. People here don't like me. They accused me of something I didn't do."

"Well," he said, "you tell me what you want and I'll do what I can to help. Where do you want to go?"

"I don't know. I just want to move on. It's not what I expected, maybe it's time to go."

"Well," he said, "I'll tell you this. Wherever you go there's no guarantee it'll be any different. Your problems might follow you. But if that's what you want to do, we'll do it."

I was so confused at that point. But I calmed down and I thought about it for a couple of hours and changed my mind. Coach Wade was right. I just had to fight through my problems here, not run away from them. I decided to stay.

Then I talked to my mom. I told her what was going on at school, but that I was going to stick it out. I think she was really proud of me.

I had to face the school's honor council, which was made up of other students, many of whom had a deep prejudice against athletes. One of my teammates lived in a fraternity with a student who was on the honor council, and this guy told my teammate, "Muggsy shouldn't even be in this school." With that kind of prejudice, what chance did I have? I was found guilty of cheating. But I appealed to a higher court, and the case was retried by the dean's office. In my defense, my teammate testified to what this guy on the honor council had said. After some more hearings with the dean, I got cleared of cheating and wasn't suspended, but I was put on probation for having a grade point average that was too low.

The whole incident put a cloud over my summer. But it made me more determined to prove myself. I wanted to come back for my sophomore year, get my game together, get my schoolwork caught up, and show everyone what the little fella could do. Within a few weeks, I was my own self again, trickin' as usual, feeling good about myself.

I was back at it.

Making History

This is history, folks. We're looking at a little man simply taking charge of a Division I game. History, folks. He's an all-American. I mean, he's controlling a game more than Patrick Ewing controls a game, more than Wayman Tisdale controls a game. . . . He's the most impressive player I've seen in forty years of watching basketball.
— Al McGuire, NBC commentator, February 2, 1985

N MY SECOND YEAR AT WAKE FOREST, Coach Tacy pretty much gave me the ball on the first day of practice, and from that moment on I was happy that I had decided to stay. All I ever asked for was the chance to show my stuff, and now that I had that chance, I knew I would succeed. I thought that over the next three years, Wake was going to put on a show.

We did, but it wasn't the kind of show I had expected. Frankly, we stunk. We stunk even more in my junior and senior years. In my sophomore year, we were fair to mediocre. We got off to a decent start, going 5–4 over the first nine games. I was playing more than thirty minutes a game, which felt great, averaging about six points and eight assists. I really felt like I was getting things together, and so was the team. From there we won seven straight games and caught a lot of people's eyes. We won conference games against Clemson and Georgia Tech, and I shut down two of the ACC's best guards, Tech's Mark Price and Clemson's Vincent Hamilton. I had eleven assists against North Carolina, and eight steals against Davidson, two of my better efforts.

Coach Tacy was happy with my game, but he told me to take more shots. I had a reputation of being a bad shooter — I had only shot about thirty percent as a freshman — and teams were laying off me, daring me to shoot. If they gave me shots, Coach said, I've got to take them.

I knew I could score. I just didn't think it was as important as playing tough defense, running the floor, and getting my dimes. But he was right, and I did shoot more. I scored in double figures six times that year.

But my year really came together during a two-week stretch in late January and early February. We had two big games, in which I first became well known around the country.

It began on January 17, 1985. We were in the middle of a long winning streak, having won five in a row, and were 10–4 overall. But our next opponent was Duke, then ranked the number two team in the nation. And it was at Duke, one of the toughest gyms to play in. They had a great team, with Mark Alarie, Tommy Amaker, Jay Bilas, and David Henderson. Their best player was probably Johnny Dawkins, a superstar guard who came into the game having scored in double figures in fifty-one consecutive games. He had scored thirty the game before, and would score thirty-four the game after, and overall was averaging more than eighteen points per game.

Coach Tacy made the decision that I was going to play Dawkins, who was their two guard, instead of Tommy Amaker, their point guard. Coach asked how I felt about that.

"Hey, I *wanna* play him," I said.

I was geeked up to play that game, boy. I was loose, joking — that's how I relax. I don't sit and think about the game; that makes me tense and nervous. To relax, I'm joking, talking, kidding around, getting everybody happy. I don't want anybody tense. I want people loose and relaxed because that's when you play your best. You can't worry about making mistakes. Make a mistake? So what. That's what the game of basketball is all about.

Well, that night was my night. I never let Dawkins out of my sight. He couldn't move. He scored only eight points, on four of sixteen shooting, breaking his streak of games in double figures. He was so tied up by me that he turned the ball over five times. Afterward, Dawkins told a reporter: "When you are playing against Tyrone you are playing against a great player and a great competitor. He comes at you offensively and defensively. He's listed at five-three but he plays like he's seven-seven. He's everywhere."

I don't know about being seven-seven, but I *was* everywhere he looked that night.

Delaney Rudd hit a seventeen-foot jumper with three seconds left to tie the game at 73–73. We outscored them 10–2 early in the OT, but they battled back and pulled within two, 89–87. Late in the OT, I made an important steal and one of my best assists ever. They had a fast break, but I caught up from behind and knocked the ball loose, and as the ball was going out of bounds, I grabbed it and made a behind-the-back pass to a teammate.

With nine seconds left I was fouled, and made both ends of the one-and-one. That put us up 91–87, and we held on to win, 91–89. It was the biggest upset of the season, and I felt like I had a big part in it. I had twelve points, seven assists, and four steals, including the big one in OT.

For that one game I got named ACC player of the week, which was the biggest thrill I'd had so far in college. I really felt like I had proved I belonged. With all the great players in the ACC, I was considered the best — at least for one week.

Of course, the Duke crowd — a notorious crowd for getting on other players — was all over me the entire game, yelling "Stand Up!" every time I had the ball. And the band always played "Short People" whenever I was introduced. I don't mind getting busted on by opposing fans. It just motivates me, gets that internal fire burning a little bit hotter. And by the end of this particular game, even the tough Duke fans liked me.

They liked me even more when they learned later that I was playing the game under a death threat.

There was a well-known local nut in Winston-Salem, a guy who was associated with right-wing extremists and had earlier been committed to ninety days of mental treatment because of other threats. He had called the secretary of the Winston-Salem Board of Aldermen. He told this woman, "Make sure Tyrone Bogues doesn't play Thursday or Friday. On Friday morning, if the aldermen go to the morgue, they will see Tyrone stretched out there." He said he would "make sure that Tyrone Bogues doesn't ever play basketball again. If he is smart he will get sick and miss the game."

Why did he pick me? He said I was "a sacrificial lamb."

The coaches told me and the rest of the team about it before the game. The funny thing was they didn't want to tell me. Before we left to go to the game, they brought me into a meeting with all the coaches. There were also some policemen. Of course I'm thinking, What did I do wrong now?

They said, "Muggs, we just received word of a death threat on you. They say if you play the Duke game we'll find you in the gutter."

Who would want to threaten me?

"It's an older gentleman," they said, "who has been sending these kinds of threats for a long time. But this is the first time he identified anyone in particular. We think he figured the only way anyone would take him seriously is if he attached a name to it. We understand if you want to sit out the game; that will be all right with us. We don't want to take any chances. We don't know what this guy's gonna do."

Well, that was something. Now I have a death threat against me and I don't know why. But it didn't worry me much. "I want to play, Coach," I said. "Where I come from, I hear gunshots all the time. If it's gonna happen it's gonna happen. I'd rather it happen on a basketball court than anywhere else."

I traveled to Duke with the rest of the team. They all knew about the threat. There were a few jokes, but we all took it pretty seriously. I really wasn't worried, though at one point when I was at the free throw line someone in the arena stomped on a paper cup and it went *Bang!* I instinctively ducked and started looking around the gym. My teammates were cracking up on the bench. I'll never forget that.

The Duke game was a very good game for me in spite of all the commotion. But my best game came two weeks later. We played Spud Webb and N.C. State on national TV as NBC's game of the week.

That was the first time Spud and I met. People made a big deal out of us, of course, him being five-seven and me five-three. But we have totally different games. He's a scorer, and he can dunk, as everyone found out when he won the NBA Slam Dunk contest a few years later. He was the bigger star at that time, he had the publicity. I was still just getting it going. I felt good to finally meet him. I like to meet the guy I'm about to go to battle against.

It was exciting playing against all those great ACC guards. I knew the only way I would get respect was to have great games against guys like Mark Price, Tommy Amaker, Kenny Smith, Johnny Dawkins, Keith Gaitlin, Spud Webb, Grayson Marshall, . . . the list went on and on. The ACC is a great league for guards, and that's a big reason I wanted to play in that conference. The only way I would make my mark was if I stood out against guys like that. Then things would work for me. If I didn't stand out, people would just say, Oh, that's to be expected, and I'd be forgotten.

Spud and I talked a little, and we respected each other's games. We complimented each other, too. "Nice pass, honey." "Nice shot." "I liked that move, honey." To this day, we still act that way toward each other.

I stuck to my game, as I always do. Even though he was the guy everyone knew, I felt that I was every bit as good as he was. And that night, for some reason, I felt great. My confidence was high. Of course you never know until the game starts and things begin to happen, but I stole the ball on State's first two possessions, and I made my first shot, and that started it. Then I made a good pass, and that kept it going. You build on these things, and pretty soon you know you have it going. I got my big fellas running hard down the floor, I made a few more steals, my jumper was on, everything was rolling. And we were on national tube!

We were up by twenty just thirteen minutes into the first half, and we never looked back. It was a rout. We crushed the Wolfpack, 91–64. I was having the game of my life. I was really putting on a show.

Later in the second half, when we were up by about twenty-five points, NBC was thinking of leaving us to go to a closer game. Al McGuire wouldn't allow it.

"I never get involved in these things," he said later. "They want to leave, that's fine. But this time I jumped in and said, 'Do what you want, but this is history here. A five-foot-three player is completely dominating a basketball game.' "

I heard later that McGuire was as surprised as could be about my play. Apparently, he didn't know much about me or my game. When he showed up on campus to research us before the game, he didn't even know how to pronounce my name. He kept calling me "Bogus." I hoped he didn't think I was a bogus player!

By the end of the game, I had made nine of eleven shots, and my twenty points — my career high — were more than half of what I scored all season as a freshman. I also had ten assists and four steals. I have to say, it was the best game of my college career, and considering the competition — State had guys like Nate McMillan and Chris Washburn to go along with Spud — it was probably the best game of my life. It couldn't have come at a better time.

A lot of people thought I really arrived that day as a legitimate big-time player. McGuire interviewed me on national TV after the game, and the media crowded around me for the first time as a player and not as some oddity. It was a treat, and kind of embarrassing. (I was so caught up I forgot to say hi to my mom on TV, and I felt bad about that.)

I didn't know at the time how much Al had liked my game. Hearing his comments afterward made me feel marvelous. I have to admit, my ego enjoyed hearing those things.

For the first time, I felt like a regular — not some role player, but a contributor. My teammates were accepting me as well. Everything changed. They had confidence in me as a shooter and a defender, as a complete player. Delaney Rudd told me he thought that as soon as I learned to stay in the Wake Forest offense and defense, to stop gambling so much and play more within the team concept, then I'd be a better player. With this game I felt like I finally had the whole thing down, and the rest of the team responded. I felt like a true point guard again, leading my boys into battle.

Unfortunately, just as my game was picking up, the team was sliding. After the State game, we lost six of the next eight games and finished next to last in the ACC.

I just worked to improve. I was learning to play more under control. Coach Tacy got me playing solid defense to generate the offense. And on offense I was making smarter decisions. He taught me that it does no good to make a sensational play one out of five plays if we lose the ball the other four times. I wasn't losing the ball that often, of course (in fact, my assist to turnover ratio of 3.34–1 was the best in ACC history), but I got his point. I got it into my head not to try to make spectacular plays every time down the floor. I learned that if you're more in control you can make the simple, good play. That's the most important thing.

By the end of the season I set school records in assists, with 207 — an average of 7.1 per game — and steals, with 85. My scoring average was up to 6.6, but more important was my shooting percentage of exactly 50 percent — an improvement of 20 percentage points over my freshman year.

We finished the regular season 15–12, and met North Carolina in the ACC tournament. We were huge underdogs, but we played a great game and led most of the way. We were up by five with a minute or so to go, but they tied it up, and we ran out of gas in the overtime.

We still thought we had a shot at the NCAA tournament, but when we didn't get an NCAA bid, we just fell out. We had to settle for the NIT (National Invitation Tournament).

I used to call the NIT the "Not In Tournament." It just isn't the big one. I shouldn't have felt that way. It's still a good experience. Nevertheless, our hearts weren't in it then, and we lost in the first round to South Florida. I had a bad game — their point guard scored twenty-five points against me. No one really showed up for that game.

All in all I was pleased with my sophomore year. I had led the conference in assists and steals. I had had some big games, especially on television, but also against some top ACC teams and some great ACC guards. I had gotten some recognition around the conference and the nation. People started respecting my ability, thinking "Hey, the little fella can play."

That summer I kept my game in shape by playing in the Urban Coalition League in Washington. Our team had me, Dwayne Wood, and former Maryland star Ernest Graham. The league had guys like Sleepy Floyd and John Duren from Georgetown, and Duke's Danny Ferry. It was wild, pro-style basketball. We won the finals 146– 142. Ernie Graham averaged more than forty points per game. I even scored a point or two.

I wanted to continue improving my scoring. I spent a lot of time at the gym, both in Baltimore and back at Wake Forest, playing in any game I could find or just working on my own. Let me tell you, those gyms in North Carolina can get hot in the summer, but I knew I needed to spend as much time as possible in there. After my strong season, I wanted to come back strong as a junior. My competitive juices were flowing.

The highlight of the summer was at the annual Dunbar reunion game. All the old fellas were there — Russ, 'Gate, Gary Graham, and I.

That year's Poets had gone 29–1 and were named national champs. So Coach Wade called up some of us from the last championship team. They gave us a game and were leading by eleven with five minutes left. But the old guys wouldn't let that stand. I put the thing to bed with a full-court drive and a score in the closing seconds, and we won 131–128.

There was some serious trash talking. It was jam packed, wall-to-wall people. It felt like I was back in the rec league days. Even though Russ and Wingate were at Georgetown, Gary was at UNLV, and I was at Wake, it felt like the old Lafayette-Cecil rivalries: "Check out this move." "Let me show you what I learned at college." "I got this in my game now, honey." It was great.

But the best part about it came after the game, when I met the lady I would eventually marry. After the game I ran into Miss Kim Lee. Meeting Kim that summer turned my life around — even though she doesn't have the story quite right:

KIM BOGUES: My godsister was dating one of the players, Mike Brown. I went with her to the alumni game, and we were waiting around afterward for Mike. Muggsy happened to be with him. Now, I had no idea who he was. I grew up in the suburbs, so I was sort of familiar with this Dunbar team, but I didn't know that much. He couldn't believe I didn't know who Muggsy Bogues was, so of course he had to prove himself.

MUGGSY: Here's the true story: Coming out of high school I was one of the more recognizable guys on the team. I was well known throughout the city. Her uncle was a Poets fan, and she was close to him. He was in the booster club. I'm sure he'd tell them all about Reggie Williams and David Wingate and Muggsy Bogues. But she claims she didn't know who I was, even though everyone in the building had to be mentioning me. She claims she was just there for the excitement, because it was a big old party, and we were entertaining them.

Anyway, her friend was dating Mike Brown. And *still* she claims she didn't know who I was. I'm not buying it. They were waiting for Mike after the game, and I got introduced to Kim. She continued to pretend she didn't know me. But I swept her off her feet. I was talking so much stuff to her, that I was the man of her dreams, that she had to fall in love with me. In a couple of hours she *was* in love with me.

KIM: We were introduced, and right away I knew I wouldn't like him. I thought, He's too short, he has a big head — not that he's cocky, but the actual size of his head was big — I just wasn't attracted to him. We went out to eat and I thought he was really nice, but I knew there wouldn't be anything between us.

The next day he called me. He said he was going back to school but he wanted to see me before he went. I said OK, and invited him over.

MUGGSY: She took me to meet her parents, and they loved the little fella. They told her, "Kim, you got a good man there." Her parents, Mister Ray, Miss Gloria, are great. I told them I was doing them a favor. Kim was dating all kinds of crazy men, suburban guys trying to be city guys, doing things they had no business doing. I told her parents to be happy I was taking her in a different direction.

KIM: As a suburban kid, I had always wanted to date someone from the city. I liked that they seemed so hard and rough, but he wasn't any of that. He had a hard side, but he was soft and gentle. I thought he was so interesting.

Muggs likes to say that I grew up in the country, but it was really the suburbs. It was quiet. It was a white neighborhood when I was growing up — we were one of the only black families there. Now it's mostly black. But it wasn't a sheltered life. My dad made us work for things. He's a cardiac surgeon at Johns Hopkins. He started off working the elevators there. He was one of nine kids growing up poor in the country in Virginia. He moved to Baltimore and got that job in the elevators, and one of the doctors there liked him and gave him a job in his lab. From there he went on to medical school. My mom was very protective, but my dad never set any rules, he let us decide for ourselves. Muggs would always bust on him: "You shouldn't let your daughter hang out on the streets like that; she's too soft."

For a long time Muggsy wouldn't let me come to his house, because he didn't want me parking my car in his neighborhood or walking alone. He was protecting me. People can sense when you're not from the area. I was scared going down there. Being black didn't make a difference. Once people knew who I was and who I was with, it was fine. But at first I was scared.

MUGGSY: She loved me right then and there. I just had that effect on her. She couldn't get enough of the little fella.

KIM: I was dating a guy who was six-nine. My mom said, "What are you doing, going from one extreme to the other?" He'd tease me that he would win me away from a six-nine guy and he's only five-three. I thought he was funny. We kept in touch, and he started calling so much it got on my nerves. I told my parents to tell him I wasn't in.

MUGGSY: She'll tell you I was calling her, and her mom would have to say, "Kim's not home now," like I was bothering her. That's what she says. I don't remember any of that. I remember *my* phone ringing off the hook. She stayed on the phone constantly.

KIM: Well, the next summer he was back in town and I met him at a nightclub. And now I thought, you know, he looks good. So I started calling him, and he started ducking me. We both were playing a little hard to get. This went on for another six months, and that was all she wrote. I was hooked, and so was he. His mom told me he had never come home from school that much.

We got married a couple years later. That was the best day of my life. It was the first time I ever saw him cry. I was walking down the aisle, and I don't know if he was crying for fear or because he was marrying the best girl he could ever marry. While he's crying, all his friends and homeboys and coaches are laughing. He couldn't help it. And then his best man, Reggie Williams, this big tall guy, is crying, too, and then my dad starts crying. I thought, What's going on here? and I started crying, too. When it was time to exchange vows, at first I couldn't do it; I was stuttering and sobbing.

MUGGSY: Getting married was the best thing I ever did. My family is the most important thing in my life. Kim is a terrific woman — even if she can't remember details.

We thought we had a pretty good team going into my junior year. To this day I don't know how it fell apart. I do know that after my sophomore season was over, Coach Tacy called a meeting with all the players, and said he had resigned.

He told us it had nothing to do with us, that he enjoyed coaching us and watching us develop, but he was at a point in his career where it was time to move on. It was best for him and his family. We supported him, and wished him well.

That was the second blow to our chances. Just before that, Kenny Green announced that he was leaving school early to enter the NBA draft. He and Coach Tacy had had some problems over the years. Kenny pretty much did whatever he wanted. He also missed some practices. Coach had had to deal with Kenny's habits and had suspended him a couple of times, including for the NIT game at South Florida. Kenny felt he had had enough of school and was ready to go.

We knew we were losing three seniors that year. Two were important guys off the bench, Lee Garber and Chuck Kepley. The third was my old roomie Delaney Rudd, our team captain and MVP. But with Kenny also leaving, we were suddenly losing more than half our scoring and almost half our rebounding.

And when Coach Tacy quit, we were stunned. In all we lost six lettermen and our coach. We had six freshmen coming in. It left the three returning starters, young veterans Mark Cline, Charlie Thomas, and me, wondering about the future.

"He'd Steal the Ball from Houdini"

*I know better than to try to bring it up against Muggs. I saw
him in high school. He'd steal the ball from Houdini.*
— Lefty Driesell, former Maryland coach

*He activates a primal fear in guards he faces. They know that he
can strip them at half court in front of God and the whole world.*
— Ernie Nestor, Wake Forest assistant coach

If you don't see Muggsy, he's about to steal the ball.
— ACC saying, 1984–87

WITH COACH TACY GONE, the speculation as to who would
be the next coach started right away. There was a lot of
talk about Gary Williams, who was at Boston College then.
He was the guy they truly wanted, but when he turned the
job down, they hired Bob Staak out of Xavier University in Cincin-
nati.

Coach Wade knew about Staak and had told me he was a good
coach. Coach Staak sat down with all of us before the season and
told us what he expected. He was straight with me. He told me that,
with the loss of our top two scorers, Kenny Green (who averaged
17.0 points per game) and Delaney Rudd (16.7), I'd have to take
on some of the scoring. Coach Staak favored an up-tempo game,
which suited our team, and me. Running, pressure defense, fast-
paced offense — that's Staak's style, and mine.

Coach Staak and I got along well. From the first time we talked I knew we'd have a good relationship. He's the type of coach I want to be with: he's open. If I had a problem I'd tell him. If something bothered him, he'd tell me. If I let down in a game, he'd get on me. It was a much closer relationship than the one I had had with Coach Tacy.

No one expected much from us. We were picked to finish last in the ACC. One so-called expert said we were "a five-three guard away from being a Division III team."

Things went sour quickly. Charlie Thomas hurt his ankle and was out most of the year. Mark Cline suffered a bad shooting slump. A freshman center named Mike Scott left school, so we recruited a six-eight premed student named Alan Dickens out of intramurals to play for us. One day he's playing against fraternity teams, the next day he's on the varsity to help out in practices, and two days later he's in the lineup against Virginia. Two weeks after that he started against Duke on national television. It was quite a story, and was covered by the national media. Dickens was already getting an academic scholarship, and after starting four games for us he also got an athletic grant. He did a pretty good job for us. But — without disrespecting him or the other guys on the team — we weren't putting quality ACC players on the floor. At one point we were so banged up, we had a football player who came out and played. In one game, against Duke or Carolina, I had nine assists at the half, but I had also fed eight layups that we either missed, or dropped, or had blocked. It was frustrating. But I couldn't blame my teammates; they were trying their best.

The good thing about our team was, even though we weren't winning much, we had a lot of fun, and that made it better. We competed every night. That was my main job every game, to keep us motivated. What we lacked in ability we weren't going to lack in hustle. We were going to give ourselves an opportunity to win every night. I wouldn't settle for anything less. If I'm going to bust my butt, the next person better do the same. We weren't talented enough to win many games, but we gave other teams a hard time. And that's something I can hold up my head about.

I was also proud of my own play. Through twenty-two games I averaged 11.6 points. I led the ACC in steals, and was in the top ten in the country in assists, minutes, and fewest turnovers. By mid-season I was averaging 8.4 assists, even though the team was scoring only 61.8 points a game and shooting only 46 percent. And I was pulling down rebounds — some games I led the team in boards, and was among the top two or three point guards in the conference in rebounds all year long.

When you combine assists and points, I was producing an average of 27.4 points per game, about 45 percent of our scoring. Only Mark Price at Georgia Tech was producing more total points, 28.8, but his team was outscoring ours about 80 to 60, so I was the most productive player for his team in the country.

But my personal accomplishments didn't give me much pleasure, because the team wasn't successful. This was the first time I'd played on a losing team. It affected me more than I admitted. But I tried to be positive. I've always believed that for everything negative, something positive has to come out of it. I think everyone on the team had that attitude. No one dwelled on the bad things that happened. You can never adjust to losing, but you don't have to accept it, and you don't have to dwell on it. You have to get it out of your mind and move on.

Against North Carolina I set a school record, with seventeen assists — also a conference single-game record — but we got killed, 91–62. Dean Smith, the legendary North Carolina coach, paid me a real compliment. I learned later that he had told his big men never to bring the ball to waist level. Whenever I was on the court, if they got a rebound or caught a pass, they had to hold the ball over their head. It didn't matter if they saw me or not — in fact, he was more worried when they didn't see me, because that's when I am able to sneak in and make a steal. Coach Smith had some good things to say about me in the papers the next day, and that made me feel marvelous. Coach Smith is, after all, one of the greatest coaches of all time.

There were a lot of great coaches in the ACC. The conference had the best coached teams in the land, if you ask me. Jimmy Valvano, at N.C. State, always had good things to say. Playing at State was always wild. Their fans were so loud, during timeouts we would have to go into a hallway just to hear what our coach was saying.

Coach Valvano was an inspiration. Not only did he have a lot of talent on his team — he had great recruiting years when I was at Wake — his bench players could easily have started elsewhere. Players wanted to go to that university because of his personality. The way he communicated with his players was special. All his guys, Nate McMillan, Spud Webb, Kelsey Weems, Quinten Jackson, always told me how great Coach Valvano was. He looked out for his players. He cared about them. And it showed on the court. His players busted their tails. You can't ask for a better coach than that, a coach who gets the most out of his players.

Bobby Cremins at Georgia Tech was another terrific coach. When he was recruiting Reggie Williams while we were at Dunbar, he used to come in and make funny cracks. I got to know him better at the World Basketball Championships the summer after my junior year, when he was an assistant coach. His Georgia Tech teams were always tough. They had that grittiness, that New York toughness, that he brought to Tech. They represented him well. Guys like John Salley and Mark Price killed for Coach Cremins. Every year they had great runs, and that reflects his coaching.

Then there was Coach K, Mike Krzyzewski. I didn't have many dealings with him, but he said positive things about me. He gave me my "propers." In fact, no coach in the ACC ever said a bad thing about me. Lefty Driesell at Maryland, Coach Smith, Coach Larry Ellis at Clemson, they all gave me my propers. And that's something that feels special. To have opponents and coaches who gave me that respect, who constantly told the media to look beyond my height at me as a basketball player, felt great. I knew that they were beyond the size thing, and I'll always respect all of them for that.

I met many important coaches outside the ACC as well. Coach John Thompson at Georgetown is a hero of mine. To this day he always tells me he messed up by not recruiting me more strongly. I wanted to go to Georgetown, to stay with Reg. But they already had Michael Jackson at the point, and he was only a year older than me. They had committed to him, so there was no place for me. Still, Coach Thompson always tells me, "I don't know why I let you get away."

He was a true hero because he reminded me of Coach Wade. I saw how Reg and Wingate reacted to him — they loved Coach Thompson. When my friends get a certain feeling about someone, I get that same feeling. That's how I felt about Coach Thompson. He was looking after my boys, and they were playing hard for him. That told me all I needed to know. He did so much for that university — he literally put it on the map in terms of basketball. He continued to recruit in the cities, and the black community owes him a lot.

Playing at Maryland was special, because I had rooted for Maryland when I was a kid. It was extra special because they had a special player, Len Bias. He was a *player*, boy, he had a game. There is no doubt in my mind he would have been a sure all-star in the NBA.

Lenny was from Maryland. I knew him from the summer league games. But before my junior year, I had never covered Lenny Bias personally. Unfortunately, there was no one else to try, so the coaching staff decided on a little experiment. In our first game against Maryland, they had beaten us 77–55, and Lenny had scored twenty-one points. We knew we needed a new strategy for our second meeting.

The coaches had been talking about me covering him during practices that week. I thought they might be joking. You know, "Hey Muggs, you'll be guarding Bias." "Yeah, sure." But when it came to game time, going over the matchups, Coach Staak said,

"Muggs, you got Len Bias." I remember thinking in the locker room before the game, Coach just gave me the duty of guarding Len Bias! Man! I got Lenny tonight.

We used a defensive scheme called the "box and one" against Bias. On the box, you put two guys at the elbow, where the foul line hits the sideline of the lane. Two guys are down low, so it looks like a box. And the "one" was me. The coaches kidded around and called it a "box and none."

My job was to follow Lenny everywhere, even though he was a powerful forward/center who went six-eight — almost a foot and a half taller than me. The idea was to slow him down and harass him all night. My strategy was basically to be a pest, to be in his stuff all night. I knew he wasn't going to try to dribble against me. The only way he could use his height was to post me up, catch, and shoot. But we had it so that if he did post up, one of the other guys could slide over and help out.

Bias was shocked to see me on his jock. He kept bugging me: "C'mon, Muggs, get away from me. Go guard the guards. You're being a pest."

"Sorry, big fella," I said. "I got you tonight. Coach gave me the duty, now I gotta stop you."

"Hell, Muggs, I got to have a good game tonight."

"Too bad, big fella. I got to play you tough tonight."

Lefty Driesell couldn't figure out what was going on out there. He was hollering all game long, "C'mon Lenny, move, *move.*" But I was with him every step.

And it almost worked. They still won, but it wasn't easy. He scored about sixteen points, but it wasn't his normal twenty or twenty-five. (He led the ACC that year with a 23.2 average.) And the points came hard for him. I really made him work. He couldn't put the ball on the floor. I just chased Lenny anywhere he went. We lost by eleven, but it was a tight game most of the way. We stayed close. That was something to see, me on Lenny. People who saw that game still talk about it.

I knew he was going to be a sensational NBA player, which is all the more reason Lenny's death that summer was such a tragedy. I didn't learn about his drug problems until I was in training for the World Championships. I got a call at six in the morning saying that Lenny had overdosed. I thought, This can't be true. I never would have thought he was using drugs. Then I turned on the news and it was all over the TV. I was shocked. Lenny Bias was gone. There were a lot of ACC guys trying out for that team, and none of us could believe it. At practice the next day there was a cloud hanging over us all, a silence in everybody's heart.

By the end of the year we sometimes had as few as eight players dressed, what with injuries and defections. We finished 8–21, 0–14 in the ACC, and shot 50 percent or better only five times. Still, I had a good year. I led the ACC in assists and steals the second straight year, and in minutes for the first time. I was fourth in the nation in assists (8.4 per game), and set a new school record with 235, breaking the old record of 207 I set the year before. With 128 field goals added to the 235 assists, I accounted for 52.8 percent of our field goals. My 3.1 steals per game (a school record total of 87) led the ACC and were eighth in the country. I also averaged 11.5 points, which proved that I could pick up some of the scoring slack. I finished the year as the all-time steal leader at Wake, and was second all-time in assists. I was voted the team's MVP, which was quite an honor.

The word about me also continued to spread around the country. Whenever we would go to a place for the first time and we ran out on the floor, there would be a buzz. Usually when the visiting team runs out, there's silence. When we ran out, there would be a two- or three-second delay, and then a buzz would start through the crowd. It wasn't applause, or booing, it wasn't hollering or anything derisive, just a buzz like something is going on that people can't believe. There would be two or three games like that every year, nonconference games where we'd never been before, where they'd never seen the little fella. But by the time we left town, those people knew that the little fella could do the job.

I think I really made my mark that year. I was called upon to do more things for the team, such as scoring, and I did them. People gave me respect as a basketball player, not as a five-three basketball player.

That year, the NBA became a realistic goal for me. I proved not just to the ACC but to the whole country that I could get it done. We lost so often, I walked off the court with my head down so many times, that my neck began to hurt. But on a personal level, I was happy with how my career was progressing.

I was fortunate, too, in that my season didn't end there. After the year was over, Coach Staak called me into his office and told me I had been invited to try out for the United States team that would compete in the World Basketball Championships in Europe that summer. I had never heard of this tournament, but Coach Staak told me it was very big. I would be playing against some of the best talent in Europe — if I made the team — and it would be a great learning experience.

In April, I was among about fifty players at the U.S. National Team trials in Colorado Springs. The trials were held from May 15–19, and on May 21 I was chosen to be among the eighteen finalists. Three weeks later we were in Tucson at the University of Arizona for twelve tough days of practice under head coach Lute Olson.

I wanted badly to make this team. I knew it could help make my reputation to play well against so many great players, especially against players I had never seen before, guys like Sean Elliott, David Robinson, Armon Gilliam, Derrick McKey, and Charles Smith. I knew it was a great opportunity. National exposure can't do anything but help you.

There were a lot of players, big timers, who didn't make it. With guys like Mark Jackson, Kenny Smith, Steve Kerr, Tommy Amaker, Curtis Aiken, Jeff Lebo, they had some big-time guards. I had to perform, I had to prove I belonged.

We had some great practices. I had a very consistent camp, strong every night. Playing with these guys was special. Many of them had never seen me play, guys like Robinson and Gilliam, and gaining their respect was something I really enjoyed. All these guys from different programs from around the country came together like a family. There was great chemistry on that team.

To get to know guys like Kenny Smith, David Robinson, Charles Smith, and Tommy Amaker was a wonderful experience. To this day I still kid David Robinson about a cologne he used to wear. There is nothing like meeting people in person to truly get to know them. Television sometimes gives people an image, but they're not like that at all in real life. I saw Robinson on television at Navy, and I thought he was talented, but he seemed more or less aloof, distant. But when I met him at Colorado, he was joking, friendly, fun to be with; you enjoy being around him. He's very intelligent, but he's also very warm, has a nice sense of humor about himself, and doesn't have a big head. His television image was totally wrong.

Those were some intense practices, but I surprised a lot of people. I think they didn't expect me to play so well. There were so many great guards at camp, I'm sure they expected to cut me. But I made the team, and it was one of the happiest days of my life.

As usual, I didn't play much at first, during our exhibition season. Coach Cremins was an assistant coach, and he was great then. He would keep me going. In the beginning I felt I should be starting, and every time I went into the game positive things happened. I was disappointed, but Coach Cremins was great at keeping me patient. He told me I was on the team because the coaches knew I would contribute, I was good enough to make it. "Whatever you do," he taught me, "don't show your sadness. It only brings negativity to yourself and the rest of the team. That's one thing you don't do. If you're unhappy, don't show it. Keep it to yourself. Enjoy things, because you have a lot of talent and you deserve to be here. If you didn't we wouldn't have kept you."

I really appreciated that. Players have to think about those things. I learned something special from Coach Cremins: Things are not going to go well for you all the time, and you have to accept it when they aren't going well. It keeps the other guys going, and it brings out the character in you. It's called being professional.

Eventually I started, and I was running the team well. I really understood what he was saying then. Coach Cremins was a big part of my success in Europe, and I've carried those things with me to this day. He caught me at the right time.

It took a while for the players on the team to get accustomed to my style of play, but soon I could sense that they were looking for me, that they knew what I was capable of. They never took their eyes off me again.

We played exhibition games in Paris and Lyon, France, then went to Malaga, Spain, for the first round of the twenty-four-team competition. We beat teams from the Ivory Coast, China, West Germany, Italy, and Puerto Rico. At 5–0 we went on to the second round in Oviedo, Spain.

The atmosphere was tense. There was a lot of terrorism going on at the time. Steve Kerr was on the team, and his father had been assassinated two years earlier in Beirut, where he was president of American University. So everyone was on edge. In Madrid there was a bombing of a police van just down the street from the hotel — we all heard the explosion. We had guards with machine guns outside our rooms, there were soldiers with rifles on the roof of our hotel the first few nights, and helicopters were always flying overhead and even following the team bus wherever it went. It was very distracting.

Kenny Smith and I were roommates, and we had a funny experience with this kind of distraction. (Kenny got over to Europe later than the rest of the team, and didn't know who his roommate was. When he got to the room and began to put his clothes away, he saw these little pants, and he thought they were shorts for a big guy. When I walked in and put them on, he couldn't believe it. He still kids me about that.) We overslept for one game, and we were late for the bus. My alarm clock said it was 1800 hours, and that tripped me out. I had no idea what that meant. Military time was a mystery to me.

Now because of the terrorism, Americans weren't well liked over there. When we missed the bus we had to run a mile and a half down the street, wearing our big USA warmups. I was afraid we were going to get shot. I'm not sure which scared me more, that terrorists would shoot us or that Coach would kill us when we got into the locker room. Neither happened, but Coach Olson did ignore us. He wouldn't let us take our warmups and made us sit at the end of the bench. I was mad, but Kenny said, "It's all right, Muggs; we'll just treat this like a paid vacation." I said, "Boy, you're sick."

We were playing Argentina, a team of all these old guys who looked to be forty with twenty kids apiece, and they were kicking our butts. They just stood out there at the perimeter shooting jump shots all day. Kenny and I are relaxing, thinking, Well, we're on a European vacation. All of a sudden, in the third quarter, we're down about fourteen, and Coach Olson says, "Kenny, Muggsy, you're in."

Well, we were *working*. Kenny got about twenty points, and I had something like ten assists. We came back, took the lead, and Coach pulled us back out. He congratulated us though — "Way to stay focused."

We got to the quarterfinals, against undefeated Yugoslavia and their great player Drazen Petrovic. We heard all kinds of talk about this Petrovic — a big-time scorer, all-everything. We knew we had to win this game. Coach Cremins comes over and says, "Hey, Muggs, how would you feel about playing Petrovic?"

"You know me, Coach. I'll play anybody."

Sure enough, come game time I was on him. I'm on him like glue. He didn't know what hit him. At first all the players in Europe reacted like all players do the first time they see me. They laughed, thinking I was a joke. They all wanted to cover me, and thought they were about to have a big game. Heck, according to the program I was only 160 centimeters tall. (At first I thought that made me sound taller, until I saw that David Robinson was listed as 213 centimeters.) But I had the last laugh.

Petrovic was averaging twenty-seven per game, and I held him to twelve — well below his average. I was in his stuff all night, and he made only four of seventeen field goal attempts. Their coaches couldn't understand it; the fans couldn't understand. They had never seen Petrovic slowed down, let alone by a five-three guy giving him all kinds of heck.

We won 69–60.

In the semis against Brazil I had twelve points and game-high five steals and four assists in a 96–80 win. That got us into the finals, against the powerful Soviet team.

Their big star was Arvidas Sabonis, a seven-two guy who could really play. But the guy I remember most was an even bigger, seven-five, guy. He was a funny-looking fella. There was a common area where all the players had lunch. Derrick McKey and I walked in and saw a big guy with a big head and droopy mustache, and we just laughed. When he warmed up, the basketball looked like a little apple in his hand. He didn't play much, but seeing this guy on the bench, big head and hairy face, sitting all slouched over, was too much. We called him "Sasquatch." He was a huge human being.

Sabonis was pretty big himself, but he could play. It was a big game, the game for the gold medal. We were eager to go home, but first we wanted to take that gold. We were all geeked up. High fives in the locker room, lots of chatter.

Comes the tip, we are all over them, running, pressing, stealing, laying it up. The Soviets appeared pretty uninterested early on, and twice we had ten-point leads in the first half. David Robinson and Charles Smith were having big games, and I had shut down their point guard, Valdis Valters. With less than eight minutes left we were up by eighteen, 78–60.

But we got too relaxed. We slowed things down to try to run out the clock, but that was a mistake. The Soviets came roaring back. They made a game out of it and brought it close — in fact, they had an opportunity to win it. Sabonis had two vicious dunks, to close the lead to 81–73 with 4:41 left. And over the next four minutes, a guy named Valdemaras Khomichus scored the next ten points for the Russians, and we were only up by two, 85–83.

We went into a four corners, and with twenty-five seconds left Kenny Smith saw an opening and scored over Sabonis. The Soviets then scored, and when we messed up the inbounds play, the Soviets had a chance to tie. My man Valters tried the last second shot, but I was on him tight, and he never had a chance. He was way off balance as he shot, and I thought, No way that's going in.

We won 87–85, the United States' first world title since 1954. I didn't score a single point, but I had ten steals and five assists.

Man, when we finally won, all the pressure was released. We all fell to the floor, laughing and cheering. And standing on the podium, with a gold medal around my neck and the anthem playing, I had tears in my eyes. Looking at the king and queen of Spain up in their private box, man, I was showing all my pearly-whites.

I finished the tournament with twenty-one assists and thirty-seven steals in ten games and averaged 4.2 points per game. Fans clapped every time I had the ball. The crowds were pretty anti-American, but I think I helped turn that around. I really became a fan favorite. Every time I went into a game they whistled, stomped, clapped, and got outrageous. It was great. Here I was, a city kid, in Europe, playing in these old smoke-filled gyms crammed with people cheering for me.

One Spanish newspaper, *El Pais*, called me "La Chispa Negra"— "The Black Spark" — and said, "He is a spectacle to see. He has nerves of steel and superflexible muscles, and on the court he appears to be a little brother of his teammates, but it is he who orders, commands, and directs."

I was also written up in the Soviet press, by *Pravda* and Tass, and featured in Spanish and Italian newspapers. In the town of Oviedo, where the medal-round games were held, they wanted me to be grand marshal of a parade during their city festival, the Feast of St. Matthew. But the NCAA wouldn't allow them to fly me over, so I couldn't do it.

That entire experience really added to my career. It got scouts to look at me differently, to see that I could play with NBA-caliber

Myself at age eight.

My publicity photo for the Wake Forest media guide. (*Wake Forest University Sports Information*)

At my high school prom. The little fella looks good in *any* uniform!

Coach Bob Staak really helped me blossom at Wake Forest my last two seasons, even though our team struggled. (*Wake Forest University Sports Information*)

Is it Bogues or Bogie? I love this shot, taken when I was voted most respected player in the ACC. I wish I still had the car! (Charlotte Observer)

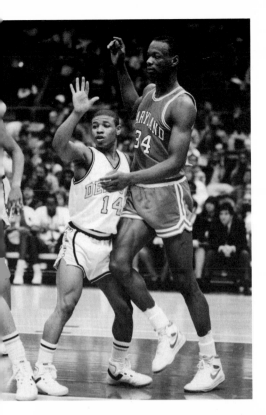

Above left: I guarded Maryland's late, great Len Bias, which was a huge challenge for me — and a total shock to Lenny, who kept telling me, "C'mon, Muggs, get away from me. You're being a pest." (*J. Grogan Photos*)

Above: Score two points for the Demon Deacons. (*Wake Forest University Sports Information*)

Looking for a big man to pass to, so I can get myself a "dime" — an assist. (*Wake Forest University Sports Information*)

My big fella, Larry Johnson (2), didn't get the ball this time, but he knows I'll get it to him next time. (*Tim O'Dell*)

To shoot over a bigger man, I have to rely on timing, intelligence — and my 44-inch vertical leaping ability. (*Wake Forest University Sports Information*)

I love working with kids — it's the only time I'm the tallest one on the court! (*Louis Shaffer*)

I try to teach the skills I learned as a kid — like dribbling — whenever I'm at a basketball camp. (*Louis Shaffer*)

A wedding toast, from Reggie Williams, my best man. *(J. W. Kerins)*

With my favorite ladies: my mother-in-law, Gloria Lee (left), and my mom, Elaine.

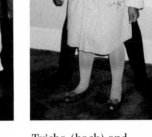

Stepping out with (standing, left to right) Dell Curry, Alonzo Mourning, and Kenny Gattison of the Hornets, and our good friend Henry Underwood (in front).

Tyisha (back) and Brittney Bogues.

Kim and Tyrone Jr. (The Big Red Boat, *Disney Cruise Line*)

The world's greatest kids (left to right): Tyisha, Ty, and Brittney.

The two Tyrones,
at a Hornets game.
(*Tim O'Dell*)

Working hard off the
court: this ad layout
for a clothing company
showed me promoting
a few of my favorite
things. (*Chip Simons*)

MUGGSY BOGUES
PRO BASKETBALL PLAYER

guys like Robinson, Smith, Elliott, and McKey. It was a rare opportunity.

And for me to be in Europe was an unbelievable opportunity, as well. We didn't have a lot of time for sightseeing, but we saw some old churches and museums and the Eiffel Tower in Paris. And I got a chance to see how other people live. What struck me most was seeing how the poor people lived. I saw real poverty over there that was far worse than the poverty I had experienced. It was totally different — I saw kids begging for food, kids with no shoes, wearing old torn clothes, never going to school. The slum areas over there were so different from slums in the United States. I appreciated the United States more, and looked back on my own upbringing in the projects with more perspective. It is one of the reasons I say the projects were not so bad, because compared to Europe, we had it made. It was a real education.

I also ran into my Spanish teacher from Wake Forest, who was from Spain and had come home for the summer. She looked me up and we chatted in my hotel room. That was great. It felt good to know that at least one of my teachers was following my career and cared enough about me to keep in touch outside the classroom.

The whole experience was great. Well, not all of it. The food was bad. The meat always tasted wrong to me. And I could never understand why they didn't have French toast in France. How can that be?

A Final Showcase

He's the only player I've ever seen who dominates a game and is smaller than the referees. His senior year he altered every team's game plan. You got ready for Tyrone Bogues. You pay all this attention and then you turn to your assistant and say, "What am I, nuts? This isn't Kareem Abdul-Jabbar or Magic Johnson."
— Jim Valvano

We spend more time discussing Bogues — about the same as [former all-America center Ralph] Sampson — than anybody we've played. It's better not to say, "Watch out for this, watch out for that." You get nervous. It makes the problem bigger than it is. That's why we don't spend much time talking about other players. But once in a while, you have to make concessions.
— Dean Smith

O N A TRIP TO HAWAII for the Rainbow Classic tournament, the team went to an amusement park, and at one of the games I won a huge stuffed rabbit. I carted this rabbit around the whole trip. I was determined to bring it home. One of the assistant coaches, Jerry Wainwright, turned to Coach Staak and said, "He's the only guy in Division I basketball who wins a stuffed animal bigger than he is. You know the program's in trouble when your best player is smaller than a stuffed animal."

The program was in trouble, there was no denying it. But I was determined to make the best of things. After my successful junior year, the NBA became more and more of a realistic possibility, but I needed to have an outstanding senior season to make that dream come true. In some ways it is hard to be successful when you are on a bad team — you can't do everything yourself; you need help from other talented players. On the other hand, though, I knew the focus of attention would be mostly on me. I wasn't going to be overshadowed by anyone, so everything I did — good or bad — would be noticed.

My senior year began with two great honors for me. Before the season, a local newspaper polled conference players, and I was named the most respected player in the ACC. That was a great honor. The newspaper dressed me up like a gangster, in a pinstripe suit, with a tommy gun, a fedora, and an old car. I loved that. It was more or less how I saw myself. I was a tough kid, and I didn't take any stuff from anybody. That picture really captured a part of me.

I was also honored to be selected for the cover of the Wake Forest basketball media guide. They put me in my USA team jersey and warmup suit, with my gold medal around my neck, and had six kids looking up at me. I almost felt like a little kid myself that afternoon. Everyone was ordering us to stand here, stand there, smile more. . . . It was fun, though. I love being around kids. It was exciting just to be considered for something like that, to be on the cover of the team's book. I had always hoped that someday I would receive recognition for my basketball, and this was very meaningful to me.

(One of the kids on the cover was a young boy — ten or eleven years old — named Jeff Capel, the son of an assistant coach at Wake. Jeff is now attending Duke, and he's playing basketball for Coach K. I saw him recently, and he is now a big, strong young man, about six-two, and he can play. I thought, Man! I am getting old!)

That senior year was fun, the best of all my years at Wake Forest. I finally felt like I had a handle on the off-court pressures of life at Wake. I understood how to handle the schoolwork better, and I felt like a part of the school community. It became a little easier to find the time to have fun away from basketball. I still spent most of my time at the gym or on my studies, but I was out on the town a lot, too.

My social life at Wake was at times pretty wild. I admit I was living a bachelor's life. Kim and I were becoming very close, but I was also dating some other women at school. People wondered how a little fella like me competed with the big guys in that department, but let me tell you, women *love* the little fella. I can always work that smile. I never had much problem getting dates and going out. I knew how to party, believe me. I never drank much — I never developed a taste for it, which is just as well — but I love to dance, I love to eat well, I love to get dressed up and strut around a bit.

One time, though, Kim busted me. She came down to visit me as a surprise. She showed up unexpectedly, and I had these pictures of other girls lying around. I quickly hid them and put pictures of Kim up, but my roommate decided he was going to be a wise guy. He said, "Hey, Muggs, I've never seen *these* pictures before." Plus, I was getting a lot of phone calls, and I had to keep telling these girls I couldn't talk just then. Well, Kim and I got into a big fight, and she ended up leaving. I wasn't being very respectful to Kim, I know, but we weren't engaged, and I considered myself basically a single guy living a single life. I didn't see anything wrong with that. It is something everyone has to get out of their system, and I was only twenty-one years old. I wasn't ready to give up my fun just yet.

That was all about to come to an end, though. Kim called me not much later and told me she was pregnant. By the end of the school year we had a daughter, who we named Brittney. She was a beautiful little girl, and over time she really helped bring Kim and me closer together. It didn't happen immediately, though. Over the next year or so, I still wondered about which life I wanted to lead — the carefree single life of a college star and, later, an NBA player, or the life of a family man. I knew I wanted a family, I just wasn't sure if the time was right.

For a while I chose the single life. But I got tired of it. I really thought hard about it and tried to put everything in perspective. It took some more time, but I eventually came to realize it was time to settle down. And it was the best thing I ever did. When you are successful, the best thing you can do is share it with others. That is the ultimate feeling in the world. Doing things for your wife and your kids, not just financially, but by spending time with them, that is what's most precious in life. You can get tired of "Me, me, me." I know I did.

My two daughters helped me grow up that way. Tyisha was living with her mom, and I still felt responsible for her. When Brittney was born, she stayed with Kim in Baltimore. Suddenly I had two little girls to think of. "Me, me, me" became less important. I didn't know at the time where my basketball career would take me, whether I'd get drafted by the NBA or go play somewhere else, but I knew that wherever I went, Kim and Brittney would come with me, and Tyisha would get a lot more of my attention.

As for basketball, my goal that year was to stay healthy, be consistent, and not leave anything out on the court. I never wanted to feel disappointed by not doing everything I could. That transferred to my teammates. That's why even though we weren't that good we had six overtime games that year — one of them a double OT in the ACC tournament. That's all I asked of my teammates. Let's compete. We will determine whether we win or lose, not someone else. But no team waltzed in and said we were an easy game. We lost five of those overtime games — a conference record — but we made it difficult. Our guys really busted their butts. That team had a lot of character. We could have just gone through the motions, but I made sure we never did.

I always went all out, every second of every practice. Coach Wainwright thinks I went too hard. We had very young guards, and he says I totally destroyed their careers.

"He so thoroughly demoralized our guards in practice that he set our program back several years," Coach Wainwright says. "There was no mercy. They had to face him every day in practice, and they lost a lot of their creativity, a lot of their confidence. One of them, Cal Boyd, is now a high school coach. Cal knew he had a great learning opportunity. He really absorbed it, even though he was being crushed by Muggs every day."

Coach Wainwright took me aside once during a practice and said, "Hey, Muggs, you gotta let up here. You're killing them. There's no reason to burn out."

I told him, "Coach, it's the only way I know how to play, because someone is always trying to replace me." I don't know anything else but hard. When you are five-three, you can't let up for a single second.

But I wasn't totally without mercy. I tried to help my teammates out. We were so bad, guys would miss passes all the time. I broke one kid's nose with a pass. One minute the kid is standing in the lane, and the next minute he's on the floor bleeding and moaning. Still, I tried to be patient with them, telling them, "Just do your best."

Every game was big for me, from the nonconference games like William and Mary to the big rivalries with UNC and North Carolina State. In one game I scored twenty-three points and assisted on thirty-seven more (from a school record seventeen assists), in a 91–88 overtime loss to Clemson. That gave me 68.2 percent of our points. The next week *Sports Illustrated* called it "the most points per player inch ever produced."

I held Kenny Smith to three points one night. Playing with him all summer got me knowing his game well, and I was all over him.

I was having a good season, averaging almost fourteen a game, shooting 49 percent from three-point range, even averaging five boards a game. Through ten games I was averaging forty-one minutes per game — not bad for a forty-minute sport.

In early January I broke the school's assist record of 579, set by Skip Brown. It came in a win against Maryland–Eastern Shore, on a pass to my teammate Tony Black across the lane. It was one of fourteen assists that night (along with thirteen points), but it was certainly the most special.

One of the highlights of the season was playing against my old coach, Bob Wade, who was now the new head coach at Maryland. It was special in several ways. I talked all kinds of mess to him. I hit a jumper and said, "Coach, you better get somebody out here to guard me!"

And he gave it right back: "Oh, little man, that ain't in your game! You can't shoot! You ain't never had a jump shot!"

"Coach, this kid can't check me. I am gonna have a field day."

Every time I passed the bench we had something to say to each other. I didn't want my old coach to lose, but I didn't want to lose either. I am sure he felt the same way. We understood it for what it was — competition.

He had a guard named Tion McCoy on me, and he told him, "Now Tion, let someone else bring the ball up on Muggs. Don't try to be a he-man on Muggsy." Tion took it as a slap in the face and said, "I can bring it up on him." Coach Wade said, "Tion, I have seen this kid for a long time. I know him better than you do. Don't try it." Well, he tried, and I stripped him a couple of times. Every time I would look over at Coach Wade and wink. When the game was over I went right over to Mr. Wade and said, "I love you, baby." He said, "I love you, too."

That game was also special because we won, our first win in the ACC after twenty-four straight conference losses. After we won, we celebrated by dumping some Gatorade on Coach Staak, for getting his first ACC win. And the crowd at our gym was so happy, they wouldn't leave until we all came back on the court from the locker room.

We beat Maryland again at their place a few weeks later — our only two ACC wins that year. Coach Wade and I continued our trash talking, too. My mom and family and friends were all there, and I put on a nice show, even though I had a bad wrist at the time.

Coach Wade and I talked after the game. He had come into a tough situation, taking over for Lefty Driesell. He had a couple of good years there, then things fell apart and he got fired. I think he got a bum deal. Knowing Coach Wade, I can't see him as anything but positive. I don't remember what the problems were, but I know they were ridiculous. I'm sure it was nitpicking. Knowing that a lot of coaches do much worse and always manage to keep their jobs or get even better jobs, to see Coach Wade forced out like that was a sin. With all he had done at Dunbar, he had the credentials to coach anywhere. He could have gotten a lot of talent to come to that university, a lot of city talent, and that might have scared the university some. I won't say it was prejudice, but I won't say it wasn't, either.

To this day, I think they let something good get away. Coach Wade was perfect for that program. He could have turned Maryland into another Georgetown. He could have been another John Thompson, if they had given him a chance. I truly believe that.

But he's a strong man, and he's happy now, working for the city of Baltimore Parks and Recreation Service, working with the youth in the city. He's helping a lot of young kids get the opportunity to make something out of their lives. I've never met anyone more qualified for that job than Mr. Bob Wade.

After we beat Maryland the first time to end our conference losing streak, Coach Staak spoke to John Feinstein of the *Washington Post* about me: "I think Wake Forest should retire his number. How do you measure something like that? I would say this: Did he contribute to the basketball heritage of the school? Was he a leader? But more than all that, will we ever see anyone like him again? Think about that last one. Tell me when we'll see another Muggsy Bogues."

Coach Staak had told me a couple of weeks earlier that they were considering retiring my number. To see that in the paper was really wonderful for me. But I never thought much about it actually happening. Only four other Wake Forest basketball players had had their numbers retired. I tried not to think that I might be the fifth.

I felt so proud just to be considered, and when the day actually came it was truly emotional for me. It happened at our last home game, on Senior Day, when Mark Cline, Alan Dickens, and myself all said good-bye to the Wake Forest fans. During the pregame ceremonies they retired my number 14, and showed me the jersey and pants in a big glass frame. I guess the jersey itself was too small to fill up the frame, so they needed the pants, too. Seriously, it was a great honor to be recognized in that way. After 119 college games, it's nice to know you'll be remembered, because your jersey is hanging in the trophy case at the school gym and no one will ever wear your number again.

My mom was there, and my sister and brothers, and when Coach Staak held up the big frame with my jersey, the tears rolled down my face. And now I had to go out and play!

Well, I put on a show for those fans. We were playing N.C. State. I scored a career high twenty-nine points, and with about a minute left in regulation I hit Mark Cline for an open jumper and broke the ACC career assist record, set by N.C. State's Sidney Lowe. I made two free throws with five seconds left in regulation to give us a lead. I was out of my mind. Billy Packer was calling the game and giving me all kinds of praise.

Unfortunately, like so many games that year, we just couldn't hold on.

That in itself was unbelievable. Five seconds left, we're up by three, and Vinny Del Negro hits a wild, off-balance three-pointer to send it into overtime. He never should have gotten that shot off. We should have fouled him, anything to keep that shot from going in. But we didn't, and ended up losing in overtime once again, which kind of told the story for our team those last few years. A lot of heart, but just not enough talent. That loss was painful. I was so hurt inside. Everything was going so great, and all I wanted to do was leave the fans with a victory in our last game.

Even though we lost, I went out the way I wanted to. I gave everything I had to the Wake Forest fans and to our team. That's the one game I will always remember. In fact, I have it on tape at home, and every now and then I watch it. I still can't believe Del Negro hit that shot.

*   *   *

The ACC tournament that year was memorable. The tournament was at the Capital Center in Washington, so all my family and friends were around. Our first game was against Clemson, with the ACC player of the year, Horace Grant.

That was a lot to think about. I got my mom and everyone there, I'm back home at the Cap Center, on an NBA floor, lots of scouts in the stands, playing Horace Grant (he beat me out for player of the year, and I was pissed off about that).

They came out smokin'. We were down by fifteen, with only ten or so minutes left. We called a time-out and Coach Staak told me, "Little fella, you got to go to work."

I went berserk, hitting J's everywhere, getting steals, making passes, and next thing you know we're back in the ball game. In the space of three and a half minutes we went from down fifteen to a tie. When I am on my game I can start a frenzy that totally rattles the other team. The crowd couldn't care less about Wake Forest and Clemson, but the majority were pulling for us. It started with me making a couple of steals. Clemson puts in a freshman guard — well, Coach Wainwright called it "beyond a felony. You can't have a mass murder on one guy, but not only did Muggs kill him once, he kept killing him."

And when we pulled it out and won at the end, the place went wild. Even though the arena was filled with other fans — there were Carolina fans, N.C. State fans, Duke fans — everyone became a Wake Forest fan that day.

After that game I was laying back in the locker room with an IV in my arm. I was so dehydrated I nearly collapsed.

But who do we have to play the next night? N.C. State.

Boy, that was a good game. I got in foul trouble and missed most of the first half. I was upset that we were out there losing, and I couldn't help. We fell behind by a dozen or so. In the second half, I tried my best. I pulled us back close, then got my fourth foul. I looked at Coach Staak and said, "Don't you take me out. Leave me in."

I hit what I thought was a three-pointer to win it in regulation, but they only gave me a two, so we went to overtime for the sixth time. We're down by two, six seconds left. I drive the lane, everybody collapses on me. I dish it off to A.J. — Antonio Johnson. Layup! Tied again! Second overtime! Crowd screaming, "Go, Wake! Go, Wake!"

Second overtime — well, they won it. We lost on a controversial call against me, a block/charge call that was my fifth foul. I drove to the hoop and made contact with one of their big men inside. I made the basket, and if I had gotten the call and made the free throw, we would have been up by four. One official called it a blocking foul on the other guy, but the outside official overruled it and called a charge on me. Just like that, I fouled out, and we lost.

I knew full well that I was done with college basketball. I guess you could see the pain on my face, because all the coaches tried hard to console me. But I couldn't handle it, and I just walked off the court.

The next day, John Feinstein captured my feelings when he wrote in the *Washington Post:*

> If Virginia–North Carolina was a classic — and it was — then Wake Forest–N.C. State was a final showcase for as memorable a player as this league has seen.
>
> He is only 5-3, but Bogues transcends height. The only shame in Wake Forest's loss yesterday was that there was no chance for Bob Staak to take Bogues out of the game for a final standing ovation, one he richly deserved.
>
> It is fair to say that he has graced this league for four years and everyone, not just Wake Forest, will miss him.
>
> If there was a sadder sight than Bogues walking off the floor last night, head down, not even wanting to stop for a final handshake, it does not come quickly to mind.

Losing in the semis, I felt cheated out of not playing in the finals, on national TV, against North Carolina. It would have been an ultimate send-off for my college career. Other people thought so, too. John Justus said, "I felt so bad he didn't get that, considering all he had done, not just for Wake Forest but for the ACC. It would have been a great story. That's one of the big losses I've felt here. That really hurt."

It hurt me, too. In fact, my head was killing me after that game. I felt so sad. But I was proud of what we had done. I was the leading vote getter for the all-tournament team, and I didn't even play in the final. That's unprecedented, I think. If you don't get to the finals you usually don't even *make* the all-tournament team. Besides, State was a better team. We were the seventh seed, after all, so being competitive at all was a big upset. We felt whoever won the game would win the tournament. And State did, beating the favored Tarheels.

I sat in the locker room, and was a bit tearful about the end of my college career. But I was also excited. I knew good things were going to happen for me. I had new challenges.

I finished my career strongly. I made the all-ACC team and the all-tournament team. I finished with an ACC record 781 assists, including a record 276 my senior year. I had 275 steals over four years, which most people believe is a league record (steal stats haven't been kept for very long). I led the league in assists, steals, and minutes played three straight years. I proved I could score, leading the team with a 14.8 average, shooting a respectable 50 percent and 80.6 percent from the free throw line, sixth-best in the league. If you counted baskets I assisted on, I "produced" 35.7 points per game. By scoring 159 baskets and assisting on 276 others, I produced 435 of our 779 team field goals, or 56 percent. I was the ACC's second-leading rebounder among guards with 3.8 per game. I was Wake's leading scorer in sixteen games, and reached double figures twenty-three of twenty-nine games. Twice I registered a league-record seventeen assists in one game, vs. North Carolina and Clemson. I retired with seven school records.

I also received a great national honor, the 1987 Frances Naismith Award, presented by the Basketball Hall of Fame to the nation's most outstanding college basketball player under six feet tall. I was disappointed at not making any all-America teams, but that award made me feel a little better.

But I think the award I liked best was the Arnold Palmer Award, which Wake Forest gives to its top male athlete. It is special because it is voted on by all the varsity lettermen. Getting that honor was terrific, because it came from my schoolmates and teammates.

All in all, I had done everything I had set out to do in college in terms of basketball. The only thing I didn't accomplish was graduating. At the school sports banquet in the spring, I made a serious promise that I would be back at school.

After the season, I worked hard to get myself in a position to graduate. I attended classes, which is more than some guys do. With a lot of athletes, after the season is done they are gone. But I owed it to myself and my mom to keep working for a degree. When I first got to Wake, I thought I'd be satisfied just to play four years and make a stand academically. The idea of earning a degree, well, as I got adjusted to college and saw what was required, seemed pretty far-fetched to me. People were always telling me, Get a degree, Get a degree, but no one ever explained just how I was supposed to do it. It sounded good, I knew it was good, but I just didn't see any way. I struggled, as many student athletes struggle. Wake Forest is a small private school, and your choices of requirements are tough: biology, chemistry, physics. I didn't have the easy course choices you have at other schools. And as I said earlier, the school didn't have as good a support system for athletes as it does now.

Plus, the prejudice against athletes didn't disappear. In my senior year, there was a controversy about some work I had done on a paper. The professor said I had gotten too much help from my tutor. There were no grammatical errors or spelling mistakes, and he couldn't believe I could do that without help from a tutor. I couldn't understand that. What are tutors for, except to help? My academic advisor, Gil McGregor, was talking to one of the professors about this, and the professor said to him, "You know, Muggsy doesn't belong here anyway, and I guess I don't blame him. I'd cheat, too." Gil was furious. He immediately called the admissions office and said, "You have a professor on your campus who tells me that the admissions people who decided he should be admitted here are wrong. This professor has the nerve to say this young man doesn't belong here. How can this young man be expected to perform in the classroom with that kind of attitude against him?" He was outraged about them not being fair. "The same professors who came to the game to cheer for the athletes were the ones to talk about their limited academic abilities," he said.

Gil was a great help to the athletes. Not only did he fight the administration on our behalf, he also battled with us, too. He really challenged us to do the work. He said that there are certain things you have to do to have success. If you go to every class, if you work with your tutors, if you attend study hall, if you ask for extra help, your professors' attitude toward you will improve, and your grades will more than likely improve. I tried to follow his advice. I let my professors know when I was going out of town, I asked when tests and papers were due, and just by my showing that extra interest, some of the professors tried to work with me. I think I adapted pretty well to the academic side of Wake Forest, especially my last year. I did whatever Gil McGregor asked me to do. I could have just blown off anything he suggested, and believe me, there were several athletes who did just that. But I never did.

One day Gil told me, "You'll do a lot of things for classes, work hard, really sweat them, and the results still might not be there, and you're going to question me and what you're doing here. But even if the numbers aren't there, the effort will be a lesson in itself. You'll work hard, and that's the only way you'll make it in anything."

I can identify with a situation where an athlete gets used by a school. I've seen it happen. But if the student doesn't give himself the chance and comes away with nothing, then he's the one who failed. What I think has to happen is that the school and the individual have to come to an agreement. Both have to give a little. The school has to acknowledge that the athlete is under pressures that the normal student doesn't have. But the athlete also has to work with the school to make sure he does the required work.

I never thought it was possible for someone like me, but I learned that if you want to you can get yourself up near the level of other students. Maybe not above them or even the same as them. But right up close, and you can do solid work. I wasn't the best student in the world by any means, but I knew what to do to stay eligible to play basketball. If I could survive four years at Wake Forest, then anyone can.

I didn't get my degree — I'm twelve credit hours short in communications. I will get it, though — I just need to find the time to go back. It seems like every summer I get busier. And Wake has a lot of restrictions about taking courses off campus. But I will find the time. That's the only thing I haven't accomplished yet. Once I get my degree (and win an NBA championship) I can sit back and say, I've done it all. Until they happen, there are missing chapters in my life. I want that diploma to hang on my wall. I want to be the first kid from my family to graduate from college. That will be the biggest thrill my mom will ever get, way beyond making the NBA. I know I am going to do it. It might not happen soon. But it *will* happen. When it does, my life at Wake Forest will truly be complete. But even without my diploma, I know my years at Wake were happy and productive. I got more than I could have asked for. And the school got a lot in return, too.

Coach Wainwright has told me that since I left school seven years ago, every player in the country under five-five writes to Wake Forest. They always say, "I watched Muggsy Bogues play at Wake Forest when I was growing up."

That is something I am so proud of. I am pulling for every small player to make it. I hope someday there's a kid even smaller than me playing at Wake Forest. I will be his biggest fan.

CHAPTER

11

How I Do What I Do

He's so annoying you want to slap him.
— Sherman Douglas, Boston Celtics guard

He's your worst nightmare.
— Alaa Abdelnaby, Boston Celtics forward

He's a damn pest, a damn pest, a damn pest.
— Arvidas Sabonis, Russian basketball star

NOW THAT WE'VE REACHED the midway point of my career—the half, you can call it—I'd like to do a little halftime analysis of my game.

There are two questions I am asked most often. The first is, can I dunk? The answer to that is no, but not because I can't touch the rim. I can jump over forty inches high, which gets me up to the iron. I can't dunk because my hands are too small to palm the ball, which is crucial to dunking. I can dunk a volleyball, which is smaller, but not a basketball. Believe me, I've tried.

The second question I'm asked, or others ask about me, is this: how the hell does a guy who's only five-three play in the NBA? I know that the question is not meant to be mean. It is not meant to ask, "Can he *really* play, or is it some kind of trick?" That is no longer an issue. In my seven years as a professional, I think I have more than proven myself. True fans know that I can play. My opponents certainly know I can play. But to all of them it is still unbelievable that the little fella can compete in the land of giants. They all want to know how I do it.

Well, here's how.

Back in the first chapter, I mentioned that people often ask what the game looks like from my point of view among all those giants. Like I said then, I've always been the shortest guy on the court, so I have no idea how a seven-footer sees the game. I only know that the ball's on the floor more than it's in the air. And down there is Muggsyland. That's where I rule. But it is more complicated than that. I usually have a hard time answering questions about how I play, because I don't think about it consciously very much. Most of it is instinct, natural ability, and gut reactions. It comes from having played the game for so long, from knowing and understanding the game as well as I do. But let me try to break it down a little.

First of all, to know what I do you have to understand the position I play. I am a point guard, also known as the "one" guard or just the "one." For those of you new to basketball, positions now are more often referred to by numbers. The point is the one. The off guard, or shooting guard, is the "two." The small or shooting forward is the "three." The power forward is the "four." And the center is the "five."

Now the responsibilities of these positions might change a little among teams, and different plays might have guys doing different things, but basically each position has certain duties. For the one guard, the basic duty is running the team on the court. The point guard is the quarterback.

Just like a football quarterback, the point guard is the guy who handles the ball and distributes it to the other players on the team. He has to survey the opposing team's defense and decide the best way to get the ball in for a score. He also has to try to break down the opposing defense, penetrate into the defense when necessary, and take a shot when it is available. The object is to get a high-percentage shot, either from a teammate or for yourself, every time you bring the ball down court.

On defense, the point's job is to harass the other team's point guard, to prevent him from doing all those things I just mentioned. He has to prevent penetration, he has to try to force the ball in a certain direction, away from the other team's best players and toward the less dangerous ones. He has to run through all the screens and picks that are set to block his way, and stay close to his man so that guy doesn't get an easy, open shot. He has to look for opportunities to steal the ball, break up a pass, or grab a long rebound.

And then he has to start the transition game, which means turning from defense to offense in a split second and getting everyone on the team involved and running the other way.

The point guard is also like a coach on the floor. He has to understand his teammates' emotions, egos, and personalities. You have to know who is happy and who is not, who is hot and who is not. A point guard has to reward the big men with a good pass and an easy basket if they run the floor hard and keep their eyes open and their heads up. And yes, sometimes he has to look them off if they are not working as hard as they can. The big men want to be rewarded for working. If they run hard and I see it, I will acknowledge it. If they don't get the ball then, it is for a good reason, probably because someone else is in a better position. Even then, I still tell my teammate, "I saw you this time, big fella. Keep running and I'll get it to you next time."

I think point guard is the hardest position on the floor to play. It's very complex. Every possession involves making dozens of decisions: Do I pass here, or here? Do I cut this way, or that way? Is he open or not? How much time is left on the shot clock? What's the score situation? Who is in foul trouble? There is a lot of pressure involved in running the show, but I love that kind of pressure.

Of course, on top of having to think about all those things, I have my so-called disadvantage, my height. I feel it is just the opposite. I think my height is actually an advantage. But more on that later. First, I want to talk about my game. As I said, all point guards basically have the same job. Some, though, try to score more points. Some try to create more. I try to do whatever comes naturally.

Knowing the skills that I have — passing, dribbling, creating — my first goal is to get my teammates involved. That's how I get the best out of everyone on the floor. Each guy has a certain role, and I have to understand that. I know when a guy likes to get the ball, and where he likes to get it.

For instance, Larry Johnson is an all-star who can do many things with the ball himself. But when you give it to him, you have to be sure to give it to him where the other team cannot double- or triple-team him. He is often double-teamed, so I have to wait sometimes for guys to give him a little bit of room. Then the big fella can go to work.

We were playing Detroit one time, and Johnson had twenty, twenty-five points, all layups. I would pass it, and he would have a full second to lay it up. I can't remember who was guarding him, but Larry told me later that the guy had said to him, "Larry, I am playing the hell out of you, playing *the hell* out of you, but that little mother keeps getting you the ball. We can't stop that little fella."

For a second example, take another of my teammates, Dell Curry. Dell won the NBA's Sixth Man Award as best player off the bench last season, mainly for his scoring ability. Dell is one of the greatest pure shooters in the league; if he's got the slightest crack of an opening, he can catch, square up, and shoot, and he rarely misses. So I try to get the ball to him when he's got that opening. If he's stuck in traffic, I just have to wait a second until he finds that crack. Then I give him the ball, and he fires. Nobody in the league can catch and shoot the ball quicker than Dell.

Our offensive scheme in Charlotte is perfect for my game. Here we play mostly what is called a passing-game offense. That means we don't run many set plays. Instead, everyone on the floor is constantly cutting and slashing and moving the ball around in a more or less freelance fashion. It's like a run and shoot offense in football — you make it up as you go. Guys look for open spots on the floor, run through screens, constantly try to shake loose from their man. Eventually, the defenders get tired or screened out, and someone is likely to get open for a good shot.

I love that offense. It keeps everyone involved, head up, eyes focused. The faster the better, for me, anyway. I try to read all the different angles on the play, try to visualize how the play will end up and who will get open for the easy bucket.

When we do run a set play, the point guard has to know how to execute it, how to direct the traffic and move the ball so it ends up in the hands of the open man. Each play is designed with a certain guy in mind to take the shot; he's called "the first option." But if he can't get open, or the play breaks down, you have to look for the second or third option. That's what I meant by making decisions every minute you're on the floor.

Now the biggest criticism people have of me on the offense is that I can't shoot, or that I don't take the shot when it's there. Don't think that I don't hear that criticism, from the fans, from the media, from my own coaches. Heck, even my own family dogs me about shooting. My sister, Sherron, calls after every game — "Shorty, you got to shoot the ball more!" she yells at me. (I just say, "OK, coach.")

I still say that I am one of the best shooters on the team. I know I only shoot about 45 percent for my career, but in practices I always beat the other guys in shooting games. We play a game called O-U-T, which is just like H-O-R-S-E but with less letters, and I win all the time. I said, All the time! Ask Dell. Ask David Wingate. Ask Larry. I am the champion of O-U-T.

But in game situations, I still believe it's my job to give the ball up. If I have the open shot I will take it. But if I am open and Dell Curry is also open, you better believe I am going to swing the ball to him before I am going to take the shot myself.

I could shoot fifteen times and score twenty points per game, but it won't help us win every time. (Sometimes it will, but not usually.) There's only one ball out there, and if I take fifteen shots, that means guys who need those shots, guys who are getting paid to take those shots, aren't getting them. Shooting is their role, their game. It just makes sense for me to pass the ball rather than shoot it. I know I have to shoot when the shot is there, or other teams will play off me, making it harder for us to get rebounds and second shots. And believe me, I love to shoot. I can score as well as any guard. But it always comes back to my role, and how I can best help the team win.

People have had one more problem with me for a long time. Everyone thought that I would be easy to post up. That means the other guard could slide down into the post position, under the basket, and since the NBA is strictly man-to-man coverage, I would have to go down there with him. Then, the theory goes, since he is so much taller than me, all the other team has to do is lob the ball over my head where he can catch it, turn, and score an easy layup.

Well, I've been in the league six years now, and that hasn't happened. Allan Bristow, my coach at Charlotte, has said he can't think of one time I've been taken out of the game because I wasn't tall enough to be in there.

Why not? Well, for a couple of reasons. First, point guards aren't comfortable in the post. They don't belong there. It's not their game. They belong out on the perimeter, quarterbacking their own team. By bringing the point guard down low, that takes the other team out of its offense. Now, their two guard or small forward has to run the offense and make the passes, which they don't like to do. Advantage for us.

Second, guards don't like to bang bodies, but I do. Remember, I was a wrestler. I may only be 145 pounds, but I am a *strong* 145 pounds. Not many guards can move the little fella around without paying a price. And not many guards are willing to pay that kind of price. So they don't. Advantage, us.

Third, I've got some friends to help me down low. Their names are Larry and Alonzo. Once the ball comes inside, the big fellas can leave their man-to-man coverage and help me out. How many point guards in the league do you know who wouldn't be intimidated to see Big L. or Big 'Zo flying at them, arms outstretched, ready to block their shots into the third row? Advantage? Take a guess.

So you see, we don't mind at all if teams try to post me up. Sure, they may get a few points off it. But in the long run, we'll win every time if they do.

People used to question my defensive ability a lot as well, but I think that has subsided. I truly believe I am one of the best defenders in basketball. I am always among the league leaders in steals, but that's only part of it.

It starts the minute the other team gets the ball, and I get right into the other point guard's face. I press all the time, on every possession, trying to slow the guy down, disrupt his rhythm, mess up his timing, destroy his dribble. Other guards often don't like to be physical. They just want to play loose and relaxed. Pressure worries them a lot. That's what I love doing, giving them something they don't want. Even when I don't get the steal, I have given the guard something to worry about. He can't be thinking about setting up a play when he has to worry about getting to half-court. I am his only thought, his only concern. And I can see it in his eyes when he's worried.

Pressure defense, turning the other guard back and forth all the way up the court, is important in another way. By pressuring him, I'm taking time off the twenty-four-second shot clock. Normally, teams want to get to half-court and set up their offense with nineteen, twenty seconds left on the shot clock. But by pressuring them, the clock gets down to fifteen . . . fourteen . . . thirteen seconds before they're even set up. Now they've got to hurry. It throws them off rhythm a little bit.

Once the ball crosses half-court, the press is off. Now, your team defense wants to prevent easy baskets, so you don't want to gamble unless you're behind and time is running out. Mainly, my job is to cover the point guard, to prevent him from getting open or making the easy pass.

I also look for the chance to "collapse" down on a double-team. When the big fellas get into the post they like to look around, see where everyone is, then make their move. If they don't see me, that's when I can make *my* move. Once I'm out of their sight, they think I'm out of the picture. That's when I like to sneak in and pop the ball out.

If a big guy grabs a defensive rebound and is holding the ball loosely and looking down court, I know he's about to make a pass. He's not paying attention to me if he can't see me. He's forgotten I'm even there. Boom! I slap the ball out of his hand.

When the ball goes inside to a big guy on offense, he's not usually aware of me. I can often race in from the off side, and when he puts the ball on the floor, I can reach in and pop it out. Man, you should see their faces when that happens! I can see them thinking, Dang! Where did the little fella come from?

I love it when guys can't see me. That's using my height to an advantage. Guards are all told always to "front" an opponent, get between him and the basket, but I like to play behind guys, or to their side. If I'm between a guy and the basket, they can throw it over me. But if I'm hiding among the trees, I can jump out and make the steal.

Doc Rivers, the New York Knicks guard, knows how I work. "When you get in front of him, you can't find him," he said after our playoff series with the Knicks in 1993. "With most big guys, you turn around, you glance, you see them. With Muggsy, you turn around and he's under you, and you can't find him again. I try, even when I'm pushing the ball up, to keep him on my side. I don't want to go by him. There's no telling where he's going to come back at."

When I make my opponents work hard, and they know they have to work on every single possession, it not only hurts them, it helps my team. It motivates them in ways you don't see in the box score. When I am working, they will work, too. If I coast or lose focus, I can see everyone else lose focus, too. Like I said, the point guard is the quarterback, and he leads the way.

It's an unbelievable feeling when you can sense that the other team is rattled. In the '93 playoffs against both Boston and New

York, I could definitely sense it. Boston's Sherman Douglas got so rattled he had twelve turnovers in four games. He never actually slapped me, but I knew he wanted to!

But let me get back to my point, which is that defense is a big part of my game. I love defense as much as offense. Not just because all offense is generated by defense. Coaches have been saying that for as long as I've been playing. And you know what? They are exactly right. But more so, when you constantly create havoc on defense, it brings out the best in everybody. You'll probably notice that whenever teams go on big runs, outscoring their opponents by fifteen or twenty points over short periods of time, it usually comes not because the offense is so hot, but because the defense has taken the other team completely out of their game. They become so unfocused that they commit turnovers, miss easy shots, and allow easy transition baskets. Again, defense is the key. And I feel I am great at creating havoc on defense.

I hate it when people call athletes "dumb jocks." Hey, we're always thinking out there. It's a thinking game. If you go out there light-headed, you'll easily get lost. If I'm coming down the middle and looking at a play, a play that's already developed in my mind, I have to carry it through so it develops that way in reality. No one else is thinking what I'm thinking. I see Larry Johnson going this way, I got Alonzo Mourning and Dell Curry setting up for the jumper. I'm waving this guy over here. I see Hersey Hawkins streaking, so I wave Dell over there, and Hawk makes his cut; and I know once he cuts, he's going to open it up for Larry, because their defender is going to react to Hawk.

You have to make choices, you have to make decisions, it has to develop in your mind before it ever happens on the court. You have to think. Could a *dumb* jock do that?

I study my opponent's rhythm, watch the guy's eyes, learn when he makes his move. I have to have a feel for my people on the break. I've got my head on a swivel; watch me coming up court on a fast break — I am always looking left-right-left-right. I have to know what's ahead of me and what's coming up behind me and make my decision — Do I shoot it? Do I drive? Do I pass? Who do I give the rock to? And I have to decide in an instant.

I know the game. I don't get much credit for that. But I know my job, I know my role. I can easily walk off the court without scoring a single point and be the MVP of the game. I understand that. I know what it takes to win: hard defense, creating offense off the defense, keeping everyone running, everyone looking for the ball, everyone loose. Keeping everybody happy.

I know I'm effective if I am playing hard-nosed defense, running down the rebounds, creating easy baskets, giving my teammates the ball at the right time where they don't have to put the ball on the floor or try to create a shot. When I'm down low, among all those giants, I feel great. I know something creative is about to happen. I love tricking people. I get a big thrill out of assisting a basket; that's just how I am.

Along with all this thinking, success comes from hard work, practice, and studying the game. It's hard to steal the ball from me, but that's not because I am small. It's because I know how to dribble the basketball. Just being small isn't enough. It's ability that takes over. Ability comes from practice and working hard on your game.

Keeping from getting my shot blocked is something I've learned from childhood. Knowing when to put a little more arch on the ball, when to shoot and when not to shoot, comes from years of practice. Playing against tall guys isn't new to me. I used to practice shooting over guys standing on chairs, guys holding broomsticks over their heads. A seven-footer can't block my shot if I am smart about it.

Beating your opponent involves more than just who is better. You have to know him. You have to study him. Guards are routine-oriented. They get into habits, and you can study them. You look at a lot of film and you can see their timing; you know if they like the crossover dribble, if they dribble the ball high, if they like to turn their back toward you or come right at you. Again, thinking all the time.

Sometimes it goes even beyond thinking. I told you earlier about a great play I made with Reggie Williams when we were in high school, a 360 spin and pass without even looking to see if he was there. I just *knew* he was there, I could feel it, and I didn't have to look. I tried to explain the move to a reporter, but I couldn't find the words. I jump, I spin, I'm in the air, and I flip it over my head. Who knows how it happens? It just does. Sometimes thinking ends and something else takes over. I call it magic. I can't tell you where that comes from.

I can tell you that I love a challenge. Any challenge. That's my game: always trying. That's where I generate all my energy. I play each possession like it's the last one of a tie game. I exert everything I have till I am exhausted. I can play that way for forty-eight minutes. In fact, I *have* to play that way. If my mind wanders, and I'm just going through the motions defensively, my offense suffers. I can't get complacent. I have to stay active, focused. I've played that way my whole life.

My game is also to make people laugh. I'm always joking. I'm small but easily heard! That's who I am. Being quiet works for some guys, but not for me. I am an emotional fella. I remember what Jim Valvano said just before he died of cancer in April 1993. He said that if you laugh, cry, and think every day, that's a heck of a day. Every time I hear that I realize that it's so true. For some reason some things just stick with you. And that did. I went through a very tough time recently, when my dad, my friend Reggie Lewis, and my wife's uncle all died within a few days of each other, and I often thought of what Coach Valvano had said. Because every day I'd laugh, I'd cry, and I'd think hard. Boy, he hit home on that one.

Anyway, emotion is important. I'm the type of person who needs to like the people I am associated with. If I'm going to spend a lot of time with people, I have to enjoy being around them. That's so important on any team. The guys on the Hornets all have a love for each other. When we step on the court together, we will go to war for each other. We care about each other's families and kids; we want to make sure everything's going all right for everyone. It may sound strange at this level, because there's so much money involved and it's such a big business, but we're beyond that. That's why we're so close, we have so much fun, we laugh and joke. That's important anywhere, inside or outside of basketball. You're sharing the same problems. You're working for the same goals. It's important to be close to the people you work with.

I look on that as part of my job as the point guard, leading my troops to battle. The point guard has to keep his guys together. I take a saying from my old academic advisor Gil McGregor. Gil was a basketball star himself — he still holds some Wake Forest records, he played in the NBA and in Europe, and he is now a color commentator for Charlotte television as well as working with the front office in community relations — so he knows what he's talking about. He says that players on a team are like five fingers. Extend them all out there alone, and they break easily. But bring them all together in a fist, and it's tough to break. No one can come between them. Something fragile becomes something solid. I heard Gil say that, and I love it to death. It makes a lot of sense.

Confidence is an important part of my game, too. I know my confidence is crucial. If I've got my confidence going I know it rubs off on the next guy and the next. In order for me to stay on top I need my guys confident. I also need to knock my opponents' confidence off. If I let him feel confident and relaxed, like he's got an easy night ahead of him and nothing will go wrong, it makes it more difficult for me. If I am out there causing havoc, putting pressure on him, distracting him from doing the things he wants to do, then I am in the driver's seat. I take that idea into each game I play. I've done it since I was a kid.

On paper I'm supposed to be the underdog. But on the court, I feel I'm equal to every great guard in the NBA, or at least I can get my opponent thinking he's got his hands full. There's so much talent in the NBA. You never get a night off. There are no slouches. It's a constant challenge. That's what I love most about the NBA. It gets me up, it's how I play my game.

And that's why the fans relate to me. I represent something to them, I guess. I stand in for them. I'm the guy they can look at eye-to-eye. Especially kids. I love the kids as much as they love me, and again it's because they can relate to me. I'm on their level — they can see the kid in me when I play the game of basketball.

And that's definitely the most important part of how I do what I do. More than anything, I've got to have fun. The enjoyment of the game brings the best out of me. When I'm out on that basketball court, I've got the smile. All the time.

From First-Rounder to
Bench Warmer

In the NBA they play a transition game with no zone defense,
and that opens the floor even more. It is his brand of basketball.
He has a great future with a club that has the foresight and
nerve to draft him.
— Bob Wade

FTER MY JUNIOR YEAR AT WAKE FOREST I knew I had a
shot at the NBA. I knew it was a realistic goal, and there was
a strong possibility I'd be drafted. I was getting a lot of
exposure. When I had the senior year I wanted to have,
some NBA scouts began to think that maybe a five-three player
could make it in the big leagues.

Not everyone thought I had a chance, of course. There was a
difference of opinions, to say the least. One NBA assistant coach
said, "I don't think he'd get a shot off in the pros, and defensively
he can't stop anybody." All I could say to that was, "Here I go
again." Every time I stepped up to the next level, whether it was
high school, college, the world championships, or the pros, I had to
prove myself all over again. All I asked for was a fair chance to
do it.

The only way to prove my talent now was at the tryout camps
that the NBA holds every year prior to the draft. It's the only time

scouts get to evaluate players from all over the country in one place. Coach Staak always told me, "No matter what you do in your entire college career, you are going to be judged more by what you do in these all-star games than anything else."

The first all-star game is held during the Final Four, and that year it was in New Orleans. I had a nice game there, and that got the ball rolling. From there I was invited to one of the big NBA tryout camps, the Portsmouth camp in Norfolk, Virginia. The NBA scouts invite the top seniors they want to look at. A lot of guys didn't go. They were afraid that if they showed up and played poorly, it would hurt them. They felt they had enough of a name that they didn't need to be looked at any more. The really big names often don't show up for these games, and it backfires for some guys. Steve Alford, for example, was expected to go very high in the draft that year and didn't attend these camps. I think it hurt his chances. He was drafted much lower than he expected.

I still didn't have that big a name, so I really had to turn it out. There were a lot of guards at camp, I remember that, but I put on the best show. The big scouts, like Marty Blake, the director of the NBA Scouting Service, were more or less shocked at what I could do. After that, they said, "Well, we better invite him to Chicago," which is the biggest predraft camp.

That camp was held at the University of Illinois–Chicago. Fifty-five seniors were invited to the four-day camp. It was really for quality players who for whatever reason had never got the recognition they might have deserved. At the time, I said I was just out there to have fun. But I thought I could improve my draft potential if I played well in front of all the NBA executives sitting in the stands taking notes.

Most of the big players were there, too, and again I turned it out. I won the standing jump test when I jumped 44¼ inches, which was 8¼ inches higher than the next-best guy. In the scrimmage games, Scottie Pippen and I were on the same team, and we ran that camp ragged. Scottie and I went undefeated. Many guys had more name recognition, but I proved I could outplay them all.

I always find a way when my back is against the wall. I make it happen. I always prove myself. Scottie felt the same way. He was projected to go late first round, and I was predicted late first–early second. After that camp, boy, our stock rose so much. Those were the chances I knew I had to take, going to camps and showing my stuff.

With the camps over, and several weeks before the draft, I needed to play to keep my game together. First I played with a team of touring ACC players. Every year they put together a barnstorming tour of all the ACC seniors. With our amateur eligibility over, it was time for us to make some money. We played all over North Carolina, and we all got paid some pretty good cash, sometimes up to $1,000 per game. I played something like thirty games, so by the end of the tour I had a nice little nest egg. I have to admit it was nice to see some financial results for all my hard work. Those were fun games, but they also really helped a lot of guys like me get started financially.

Then I played some in the United States Basketball League — the USBL — a professional summer league for lesser known college players on their way up and some older fellas on their way down. I played for the Rhode Island Gulls. That was the same team that Spud Webb and Manute Bol had played for before they joined the NBA. I was one of the first players drafted by the USBL, and I was making the most money in the league — $1,000 per week. I sent a lot home to my little girls and my family, and I spent some on myself. It was wonderful to be making a living.

There were some wild games in the USBL. I played against Nancy Lieberman, the great woman player. I'll tell you, she's got a game. She was competitive, and I tested her. She knew that she had to take whatever came at her, and she did. She held her own. I played against Micheal Ray Richardson, too. I had a lot of respect for him, even with all the drug abuse problems he had been through. He gave me many pointers about the NBA. Mainly, he told me to just keep playing my game, that I was good enough to make it. World B Free was there, too. He told me good things as well. It meant so much to me. These veterans kept my confidence up and made me feel like I belonged. They didn't have to say those things, and I appreciated it when they did.

After the tryout camps, people started talking seriously about me not only as a legitimate NBA prospect but as a definite first-rounder. The question was, who would take me? I had heard I might go to Utah, I might go to New York, Denver was trying to make a trade for my rights, Dallas was interested. I had taken physicals at all those teams. It was funny, though, that I never heard any interest from Washington.

The day of the draft was so exciting. The NBA invites all the guys who might be first-rounders, about twenty-five guys, to attend. Reggie Williams and I flew to New York from Baltimore together, talking about where we would end up, wondering how high we'd be drafted. Although we didn't talk about it, we were both thinking, "Man, look at us now! Two Lafayette kids, on their way to the NBA!" All our dreams were about to come true.

There was a lot of nervousness that day. I had on a new suit I had just bought, and I looked sharp. I was decked out. Everything was perfect, but I was sweating. I'll tell you, I was so nervous that I draw a real blank about that day. I don't remember much of anything except walking up to the seats, sitting down, and waiting for my name to be called.

The first pick, by San Antonio, was David Robinson. He was in the Navy, so he wasn't there. I knew I wasn't going number one, so I wasn't very nervous yet.

Second pick, Armon Gilliam, Phoenix. I was sitting with Mark Jackson, and he was just as nervous. "Where we gonna go, honey?" I said. He said, "I don't know. Wouldn't it be nice if we both went home?" I told him the Knicks were interested in me. He said the Bullets were interested in him. We thought maybe we could trade ourselves so he could go home to New York and I could go home to Baltimore.

Third pick, Dennis Hopson, New Jersey. We all thought Reggie

Williams was going to New Jersey. So did the crowd, so they started booing. They wanted Reg. That made me feel good.

Fourth pick, L.A. Clippers, Reggie Williams. I told the big fella, "Way to go. Good luck." We slapped five. I felt so happy for Russ. But I was dying. The suspense was killing me.

Fifth pick, Seattle, Scottie Pippen — he was traded to Chicago later that day. Sixth pick, Kenny Smith to Sacramento. Kenny didn't want to go there, and he was pissed off. He was happy to be drafted, but he thought he was going to Chicago. He wanted to be back with his old Carolina teammate Michael Jordan. He was very disappointed.

Seventh pick, Kevin Johnson to Cleveland. Eighth pick, Olden Polynice to Chicago (he was then traded to Seattle for Pippen). Ninth pick, Derrick McKey, Seattle. Tenth pick, Horace Grant, Chicago. Eleventh, Reggie Miller, Indiana. By now, I was too nervous to pay attention. I barely heard the other guys' names. I was just keying on hearing "Tyrone Bogues" or "Wake Forest."

Up comes the twelfth pick, the Washington Bullets. Mark and I were a mess. We knew they were going to take a guard. "It's you or me, honey," I said. "One of us is going now." But since I hadn't even talked to them, I didn't think it would be me. But right then, NBA commissioner David Stern said, "The Bullets select Tyrone Bogues from Wake Forest." I let out a little shout. Then I told Mark, "Good luck, honey. You're going to New York."

I took my walk to the stage with a little strut, walked up to the podium with my new Bullets hat on my head, shook David Stern's hand, and was grinning from ear to ear. It was a hell of a feeling. My heart was pounding and my palms were sweating. I could barely get through my interview.

Backstage, Reg and I hugged. A few minutes later, we were joined by Reggie Lewis, who was the first-round pick of the Celtics, the twenty-second pick overall. We didn't realize it then, but the three of us had just made history. Three players from the same high school team were drafted in the first round of the NBA amateur draft. No other team had ever done what Dunbar High did when we three childhood friends and high school teammates all became first-round draft picks. One newspaper said the odds of that happening were 4,037,639 to one.

I also set an individual record to go along with that team honor. I had become the smallest player in NBA history. To a lot of people, the odds of that happening were probably even higher.

After we all hugged, we went right to the phones to call home. I flew back to Baltimore that night, and everyone went crazy. People in the airport were cheering me. My family had videotaped the draft and they kept playing it over and over. Everybody in the neighborhood was out. There were banners everywhere. It was unbelievable. We were up all night long partying, and I had a few cocktails myself, which I almost never do. I am not a big drinker, never have been, but once in a while you have to celebrate.

What I didn't know was that while everyone in my family was hoping I would come home to play for the Bullets, Kim was silently thinking, "Please don't let it be Washington; please, not Washington." When it turned out to be Washington, my family was nothing but happy. Kim, though, didn't know whether to smile or cry. She thought we needed to be away from home for our relationship, and that being close to home might hurt me more than help me. She thought being back with all my old friends might get me more into my bachelor ways, and that I would leave her and Brittney behind. I wasn't thinking about that just then, but she was right to be concerned. At this point in time I was still unsure about this myself.

We decided to see how things would work out if we lived together, and once the season started we moved into an apartment. My girlfriend, my new baby, and I all in the same place — that was new to me. I have to admit, it took a while to adjust to it. It was not an easy time for us. I think any new young couple has to adjust to living together, and we were no different. If anything, we had added pressure, because now we were dealing with things that we had never experienced before, things like money and a certain amount of fame, and a lot of traveling — not to mention a little baby. And it got even tougher when things with the Bullets began to go sour.

A couple of days after the draft the Bullets held a press conference, which set some sort of record for short person jokes. It was held at the U.S. Capitol. I was introduced by Senator Chic Hecht of Nevada, who is five-five and was then the shortest male senator.

"I promised to keep this short, and I will," he said. "On behalf of short people everywhere, basketball fans nationwide, and Bullets fans in the Washington area, congratulations, Muggsy. I know we are going to hear a lot about you very shortly."

Then I dunked a ball through a lowered basket.

I thought it was all very funny. Funniest of all was that I almost missed my own press conference. I was stuck in traffic. I wanted to call ahead, because I knew all these senators would be there, including Senator Bill Bradley, the former Knick. But there was no phone in the car.

After that I went back to Wake Forest, played some more ball, and worked out. I just had to wait until my agent, David Falk, and the Bullets agreed on a deal. That took a while longer than I thought it would, and dragged right up to training camp. I was worried that I might miss some camp, which would have been a big mistake for me as a rookie. As the Bullets' coach Kevin Loughery said, for a rookie, missing a week is like missing a month of the regular season. Two weeks is two months. Miss all of camp and you're behind the whole year. But my agent told me not to worry, and he got the deal done just before camp opened. Signing felt great. I wanted to get started as soon as possible and get in shape. Holding out would not have allowed me to do that.

I thought it was a great deal — $1 million over four years. It was beyond my comprehension — getting that kind of money to play basketball. These days it is an insult for a first-rounder to get that kind of money. But I could not have been happier. The first thing I bought was a nice truck, and later, a Mercedes. That was always a dream car for me. For most of the first year I had a deal with a local car dealer to endorse the Ford Festiva, which they called the "Muggsymobile." They gave me a Festiva to drive as part of the endorsement deal, so I didn't have to buy a car right away. When that deal ended, I bought my dream car.

Before that, though, I bought my mom a house. I knew I had to get her out of the projects. That was my main priority.

It took a long time to convince my mom to leave Lafayette Court. The bad elements had really started taking over, and the neighborhood had gone downhill in the four years I had been at Wake. It was the mid '80s, and crack cocaine had exploded on the scene, with a negative impact on the streets. Crack turned many people into dangerous criminals and crazed addicts, making the inner city much more desperate. Most of my mom's friends had already moved away. But she still wanted to stay. After all those years, she was comfortable there. I practically had to force her to move, and even after she finally agreed to move into the nice big house in the suburbs I had found, it took her a while to get used to it. She says that every time she came home to that new house at first, she thought she was dreaming. She expected the house to be swallowed up into the ground, like in the movie *Poltergeist*. Now, of course, you can't get her to leave that place, she loves it so much.

The day she moved in, I had tears in my eyes. It was such a big step for us, getting out of the projects and making our lives better. That moment made all the hard work and effort so worthwhile.

My sister and brothers moved in as well. My brother Stroh is married and has his own place now, but Sherron and Chuckie still live with mom. It took all of us city folks some time to get used to the suburbs. I had been in the country of North Carolina for a while, so I was accustomed to it, but the others had never before experienced country life. (To me, anything that isn't the ghetto is the country!) Sherron couldn't believe the quiet — on New Year's Eve, the ghetto would sound like a war was going on, but out there it was silent. She thought, These folks don't even know how to celebrate. But we quickly adjusted. The quiet is better, country life is just a lot healthier — especially for kids.

Another thing I did right away with my new money was to hire an attorney to help get my father out of jail. He had already served almost twelve years in prison, and the lawyer helped get him paroled. We hadn't used a lawyer when he was arrested — my mom had thought, He's guilty, so a lawyer won't help. But I had learned a few things in college, and one thing I learned is that lawyers can make things happen. I don't know much about how it happened, though. Someone recommended an attorney, I hired him, and boom — Pops was free. It was an emotional time for all of us, and I know that Pops was very grateful for my help.

A few days later, my dad saw me play a basketball game in person for the first time. He and my mom came to a Bullets preseason game, and it was the best feeling I've ever had playing in a basketball game. Every kid dreams of having Mom and Dad there. Most kids probably take it for granted, but I had never had that experience before. Seeing them both sitting in the stands brought tears to my eyes and a feeling that will never leave my memory.

Going to my first camp was a big thrill. I wanted to take it slow. I didn't know how the other guys would react to me, the rookie, but Moses Malone, Jeff Malone, Bernard King, John Williams, Terry Catledge, and Manute Bol all took to me early. They talked to me, told me to play relaxed, not to worry about anything. They started kidding around right away with me, and that made me feel at home. I was quiet at first, which is unusual for me, but pretty quickly I got into being my usual fun-loving self.

That first practice was kind of a dream. It hadn't really sunk in that I was an NBA player. I tried to not even think about it. I didn't want to put pressure on myself and do all sorts of wild and out of control things. I just wanted to see how things developed. I worked hard and tried to earn the respect of the veterans. I figured this team had a lot of talent and only needed a guy to direct them from the point. And that guy was me. Or so I thought, anyway.

I started the preseason first game, against the Detroit Pistons. I didn't expect that. At first I just wanted to contribute, but now, as a starter, I wanted to take advantage of the situation and give it the best I could.

This was the pinnacle. It was what I had been dreaming about for years. I had butterflies galore, I was shaking — I thought it was because of the cold, but that wasn't it. It was nerves. I was anxious to see how I would do, especially against Isiah Thomas, Detroit's all-star point guard. I just wanted to play my game, make my mark, and make it difficult for "Zeke."

I had all kinds of energy, my mind was active, I was getting into the game. Afterward, though, I just felt, Man, I am glad that is over.

That first pro game, which we lost, I played twenty-six minutes, went one for five from the floor, two of two from the line, four points, two rebounds, six assists, two turnovers. My first NBA basket? I stole the ball from Isiah (I was thinking, Oh, man, I just stole the ball from the great *Zeke!*) and sped the other way, only to run into big Rick Mahorn. I pulled up, just inside the free throw line, and put up a high, rainbow shot over his hand. All net. At the time, it didn't hit me that this was my first NBA bucket and my first NBA points, because I was too into the game. But looking back, I know I was pretty excited. I just had to keep it inside.

Of course, everyone was watching me, the little rookie first-rounder. I thought that first game went about as I expected. I just wanted to be patient, to let the game come to me, to get comfortable with it and let things happen. I don't think Isiah embarrassed me. He scored only twelve points. I held my own against Zeke, who was the best guard I had ever played in my life. I could tell right away how good he was — he was intelligent and he had all the point guard tools — just by the way he carried himself on the floor and by how he made his teammates better. In college you can only do so much, because you aren't surrounded by as much talent. Up here, you can do anything. It was a sight to see all his talented teammates responding to him. I was going to school — graduate school in basketball. I don't give many guys their propers, but Zeke is one I give all the respect in the world.

Another exciting moment was an exhibition game we played against the defending champion L.A. Lakers, with Pat Riley and Magic Johnson.

I tossed and turned all during the night before the game, and I couldn't sleep at all the day of the game. Even though it was preseason it was a big thing for me. For my money, Magic was the best guard in the league, and at six-nine he had changed the way point guards were considered. No one that big had ever played the point before. And here I was trying to change things in the other direction. Six-nine versus five-three — even though we played different styles of games, we had the same vision about the position: that size didn't matter if you used it to your advantage.

It was the first time I had ever met Magic. Just before the tip-off I walked up to him and extended my hand. I tried to be cool. "Hey, Magic. How ya doin?"

"Hey, Muggs," he said, shaking my hand. "Welcome to the league."

Then he said, "Boy, I didn't realize you were that short! You *are* a little fella!"

I just smiled at him. He also offered me a lot of encouragement, saying, "All rookies go through tough times, but don't get down on yourself.

"And another thing," he said. "Don't you steal the ball from me!"

"Well, don't back me down low!" I said, and he laughed.

It was thrilling, Magic Johnson giving me respect. I felt like I was really in the NBA. And after the game — I had played a great game, and was very pumped up — Magic came over and told me to stick with it. "Keep pushing," he said. "You can play in this league. You'll be around a long time." Man, I can't tell you what that meant to me, to hear that coming from someone like Magic. I was on cloud nine.

More than fourteen thousand fans came out to the Cap Center that night. I didn't play the first quarter and we fell behind, 31–22, but in the second period I was on my game. I scored twelve points and had four assists, and we led 57–49 at halftime. It was important for me to start scoring, because in our first two exhibition games I was only one for thirteen in shooting.

I really wasn't intimidated playing against Magic or the Lakers. I was completely focused. I guess they weren't intimidated either, because they came back to beat us. But they were impressed by the little fella, and it made me feel good to read their comments in the paper the next morning.

Pat Riley: "Little son of a gun. He's great. Before the game we talked about how to defend him, and in the second quarter we couldn't stop him anyway. He just took over and rolled through us. He opened up the whole game for them."

Michael Cooper: "It's funny, because I remember when I first came here I was awed by Kareem because of his size. With Bogues it's similar in a way. His size really is awesome in its own way. A couple of times I thought I was playing against my [six-year-old] son on our one-on-one Dr. J. basket at home. I kind of wanted to put my arm around him and say, 'Nice play.' But then he'd blow by me and I'd forget that."

Magic Johnson: "I'll tell you one thing, if you let him get beside you, forget it. He's gone. The little guy is quick. No one will get it up the floor faster. He changes the whole game when he comes in. You have to be aware of him at all times. He's like a fly that gets in your face when you're trying to sleep. Every time you think you've slapped him away he comes buzzing right back."

All in all, I felt I had a strong training camp. I was ready for our regular season opener in Atlanta. What do I remember about my first real NBA game? Not much, to be honest. I know I was nervous. I think I had a pretty good game. I started off slow, as did the whole team. I was forcing things too much, trying to make a great play every trip down. I wasn't patient. I was a typical rookie, trying too hard. I felt this was how I had to play, to prove I belonged, and that was a mistake. I made some turnovers, forced my shot. Coach took me out, and I regrouped and had a better second half. But I went through that for the first seven or eight games. I was running the break and not finding anyone with me. I was trying to make great passes to teammates who weren't there.

The problem in Washington was that they had a lot of big, slow guys, so they played a slow game. They liked to walk the ball up the court, set up a half-court offense, and run set plays. I had never played that style before in my life. And I wasn't suited to it. I am a lot of things, but I am not big, and I am not slow. I need to run to be effective.

But I had to play the team's game. I got caught up in the half-court game, and I felt like a different person. I wasn't creating any more. I wasn't penetrating. I was just setting up and spotting up. It was the first time in my entire life I wasn't able to play Muggsyball. There would be an occasional fast break here and there, but no one else was running with me. I'd bring the ball up, then have to circle around and wait for my teammates to catch up.

I was in a totally different game. It didn't feel like basketball to me. I used to tell John Williams and Terry Catledge and Moses Malone that I felt like a robot out there. Moses really sympathized. He'd say, "I don't understand. They draft the fastest guy in the league and they got him playing half-court. With a guy like you, we *have* to play a running game."

We lost the opener in Atlanta, then lost in double overtime in Boston. Through my first four games I was doing all right. I was playing thirty minutes per game, averaging almost nine points and eight assists, and shooting 47 percent. I even made a sixty-footer to end a quarter at Milwaukee.

Then things started to turn sour. In a game against Chicago, an 84–82 loss, I missed my only two shots, and missed my two free throws, in twenty minutes of playing time. The team was struggling. Even though we had lost to good teams — Chicago, Boston, Milwaukee, and Atlanta were a combined 23–6 — that wasn't any excuse.

I was struggling, too. My game was suffering, and I started to slump. I was tentative, afraid to take a shot, afraid to make a pass. I didn't know who was out there at the point, but it didn't feel like the Muggsy I knew. That Muggsy had disappeared. There was talk of benching me for Frank Johnson, but that was delayed when he sprained an ankle. There was a lot of confusion on the team, especially among the guards. Frank Johnson had held out during the preseason and come to camp out of shape, and another guard, Darrell Walker, was new to the team, only joining us late in camp. Jeff Malone was more of a shooting guard than a point guard. Coach Loughery implied that I was starting by default.

Kevin tried to help me out. He told me not to get caught up in all the stuff I was hearing. I hoped he would work things out for the team. But the next thing I knew, he was fired. Here I was, only a few months into my pro career, and everything felt like it was coming apart. The mood on the team was terrible, something I had never experienced. Even when we were losing at Wake Forest, we still had a positive attitude and had fun. Here, I had a hard time finding anything positive at all. My teammates helped as best they could, but they were all as confused as I was.

Wes Unseld took over as coach, and we just never hit it off. He never talked to me about anything. Management there was all caught up in the problems of the organization and didn't connect with the players at all. I felt really lost.

By early December my game was way off what it should have been. I was confused and didn't know what to think. Some of it was from not getting the minutes, some was from playing this slow style, which just wasn't my strength, and some was the pressure of knowing if I missed my first shot, or my first two shots, I'd be on the bench. Most teams let their rookies work through their struggles, giving them a chance to find themselves. I never got that chance, and if there is any bitterness I feel toward the Bullets it is over that. They gave up on me too fast.

There were times I'd go home with tears in my eyes. It wasn't the competition, or the grind of the long season. My confidence had disappeared. Here I was a totally different person. I was a robot, hesitant about everything, about making passes, about making steals. When your confidence goes, no one can help you but yourself. No matter what they said, I had to get my confidence back myself. I was sure I was capable of eight or nine assists and ten or twelve points, NBA or no NBA. But it wasn't happening.

With four guards on the team, Walker, Johnson, Jeff Malone, and me, I knew I'd be odd man out. It's very hard to rotate more than three guards and get all of them enough minutes to be fresh and warm and involved. Something had to give. Unseld called me into his office and told me I was out of the starting lineup.

I was numb. With my game all shot, and the team struggling, this was just one more thing. I wasn't mad or depressed or anything. Just numb.

I had a lot to learn about the NBA that year. Of course, the NBA also had to learn about me.

Early in the season, we traveled to Milwaukee to play the Bucks. In Milwaukee, there's a skywalk that goes from the Hyatt hotel to the arena. I got behind the other guys, and was signing autographs on the way to the gym. By the time I got up to the door of the arena, everyone else was already inside. The security guard sees me with all these kids around me, and as I grab the door he says, "Hold on there, son. What do you want?"

"I'm going inside."

"Oh no you're not. That's just for the players."

"I am a player. I'm Muggsy Bogues."

All the kids around me started yelling, "Yeah, yeah, he's a player! He's on the Bullets! He's Muggsy!"

But the guy wouldn't believe me. I had to stick my head inside and call for someone to get me in. The big fella, Moses Malone, rescued me.

"Oh, sorry, Mr. Bogues," the security guy said. "It's just, you know, you're not . . . you're so . . ."

"Don't sweat it," I said. It really didn't bother me. I thought it was kind of funny, actually. And it wasn't the last time Moses helped me out.

I made a lot of friends on the Bullets, but Moses was the guy who carried me through my rookie year. He was a big inspiration, like my big brother. When I wasn't feeling good about my game or how things were going, he'd keep me straight. He would see me looking upset, and he'd tell me everything I needed to hear. He helped me keep focused and keep the hunger that I needed to make it in the league.

He'd tell me, "Little fella, you got to understand, you are in a situation you can't control. As long as you keep working, you keep the effort, you'll be a good athlete, but you have to get on a team that's keyed in to your game. Then you'll benefit." He talked to me a lot. He'd tell me to keep my mind strong, keep my pride. He'd say, "Once you realize what goes on in the NBA, you'll be able to play the game. It's politics, you know. A lot of guys, when they come to the NBA their first year, get coaches trying to change their game. When I first came to the pros they tried to change *my* game. You have to stick to what you do the best."

He knew that Washington was the wrong team for me from the beginning. Had it not been for Moses, I don't know what would have happened to my confidence, my self-esteem. Moses was the only one who said, "Little fella, come with me." He basically threw his wings over me and took care of me. My friends outside basketball couldn't understand what I was going through, and the other players were fighting for their own jobs. Only Moses had been in the league so long that he was above all that. I felt privileged to get advice from him. Whenever I needed someone to talk to, Moses was there.

I don't know if I ever thanked Moses enough for all he did. So, big fella, if you're reading this, I want to tell you I appreciate everything you did for me that year. I had many things to get off my chest, and you were always there for me. You gave me the encouragement and the desire to succeed that I needed. Thanks, big fella. You don't know how much it meant to me.

While I was glad to have Moses, another guy in particular was glad to have me around. Manute Bol had grown pretty tired of all the attention he got from being so tall. Now that I was around, he was left alone. Manute and I became good friends, too. I had first met him at summer games around Washington. I saw this big old fella in the stands, his legs draped across three rows of seats. Look at this guy! I thought. Can't weigh but a buck and a quarter.

Manute had gotten married in the off-season. Apparently he had been pretty lonely in his five years in America since coming over from the Sudan. He had wanted to find a wife, and had eloped with a girl in 1982, but his family dissolved the marriage after an argument over how many cows Bol's family would pay for her hand in marriage, which is a custom of his Dinka tribe. In the United States he had dated a lot, but he didn't really like American women, who are more independent than he was used to. In Dinka culture, the women serve their husbands, which sure doesn't happen here anymore. He also didn't like American divorces, where you split everything you own fifty-fifty. In Sudan, the man gets everything, even the cows he paid for the dowry. But over the summer, he had married a girl from his village and seemed very happy.

On buses or planes he'd tell me about growing up in Africa. He had these scars from lines cut across his forehead, and he'd tell us about how they cut him and the other kids at an early age. He told us about chasing lions from his village with a spear, but we'd get on him about that: "Aw, Manute, you know you didn't chase no lions. You just went up to the friendly lions, and you'd say, 'Hello, lion. How are you today?' " We'd all bust up, and he'd laugh along.

We had some laughs, boy, Manute and I. We would play each other one-on-one after almost every practice — the tallest and the smallest, going at it. Everyone would watch. I always beat him. One time I blocked one of his shots. He was pissed! Moses got all over him — Moses was a big instigator — yelling, "Hey, Manute, the little fella blocked your stuff" and punching him in the arm. Manute was so mad that he chased me around the gym, yelling,

"Come here, Muggsy!" in his heavy African accent. I was laughing so hard I almost fell over, but he never caught me.

One day, in the locker room, Manute bet that I couldn't pick him up. I made the bet, and then picked him right up. 'Nute was furious. He said, "No no no! I pick you up now." So I held on to a seat, and 'Nute struggled to pick me up. Everybody started laughing — seeing the big fella pulling at me but not getting me up.

Another time Manute and I were wrestling in an elevator, and I picked him up and lifted him till his head hit the ceiling. I had that big fella in the air and he was kicking like a baby. Moses was about to die.

The three of us would walk through the airport, with me in the middle between them. It was quite a sight — me, five-three, between seven-six Manute and Moses "only" seven feet tall. People would jump out of nowhere and try to take our picture, but Manute would scare them off by shouting, "Don't shoot! Don't shoot!" It was hilarious.

Manute and I grew very close. The press made a big deal about him and me, the tallest and shortest players in the NBA. But they never really understood our true relationship. The press could be very hurtful. The *Washington Post* called Manute and me "The Freak Show." That hurt both of us an awful lot, to be classified not as human beings but as freaks. I was very bitter about that for a long time. I still don't think much of the Washington media. A lot of them never saw what I was really about. They never got past my height.

Bernard King and I became good friends, too. He is a well-spoken, well-mannered guy, and I appreciated being around guys like him. I remembered Bernard when he was with New York, when he had both wheels working, scoring fifty points a night, dunking with both hands. I was a fan of his, and I learned a lot about professionalism from him. No one approached the game more professionally. He came to the gym totally focused, with his game face on, stuck to the routine, and competed as hard as he could. He kids around in practice and on off-days, but when it's time to work, it's time to work. Bernard's preparation and focus did a great deal for our team. It rubbed off on us. He wasn't much of a talker — neither was Moses — but they led by their experience. I learned so much from those guys.

I was lucky to have my teammates around; otherwise the year would have been a total loss. It was tough on Kim as well. It was very lonely for her. Most of the wives and girlfriends there were kind of into themselves, and everyone went their own way. The whole thing was all so new to us. I had someone to talk to, but who did she have? The team didn't help the players' families at all. There was no support. I think that helped bring us together even more. We needed each other pretty badly that year. My mind was quickly being made up. My single days were over, and I was ready for a full family life.

By the end of the year I was hardly playing at all. In the last eight games I played only six minutes per game, and twice I didn't play at all. There was nothing I could do but wait it out.

Statistically I guess you could say I had a decent year. My numbers were 20.6 minutes, 5.0 points, 5.1 assists (best on the team), and 0.6 steals per game. Of the nine other rookie guards taken with me in the first round, only Mark Jackson of the Knicks (13.6 points and 10.6 assists), Kenny Smith of the Kings (13.8 points, 7 assists), and Kevin Johnson of Phoenix (9.2 points, 5 assists) had better numbers.

But I considered my season a total bust. I was thrown into a style I didn't fit into and had never played before. It was clear that the team wasn't interested in me. I don't think they gave me a chance. They played me for a while to see what would happen, more as a sales thing than anything else. They didn't say, We believe in your ability. It wasn't that deep. I was a first-round draft pick, so I thought the organization would at least give me a realistic opportunity.

I learned that in the NBA, coaches don't talk to you. They don't tell you anything. I learned that the media is harsh. Reporters were always asking, "Did the Bullets make the right choice with

Muggsy?" It sends you. You've reached a level no one expected, you've succeeded everywhere you've played, and still no one believes you can do it. But that's what keeps me going. Through my whole life, people have had doubts about me. The only thing I can do is go out on the court and prove them wrong.

After that rookie year, I realized that Washington wasn't the place for me. And the team decided I wasn't for them. Once the season ends, you have meetings with the coaches. I met with Wes Unseld and he said, "Muggsy, next year it's your show. You got the ball. We're rebuilding the team around you." I said, "Fine. I will be ready." But I didn't believe him, and I was right not to.

A week or so later he called and told me the Bullets weren't going to protect me in the upcoming expansion draft. When Wes told me they were leaving me unprotected, I told him, "Thank you." Wes said, *"Say what?"* He was surprised that I was happy to go. But I was. Kim and I hated it in Washington.

I wasn't down at all about being released. I knew the NBA was expanding into Charlotte and Miami the next year, and I had thought about expansion a lot. From my little time on the court that year, I knew that with my head on straight I could play at the NBA level, and I thought I could start for a team that used me right. I had heard Charlotte was interested in me, and I prayed for the opportunity to start over again.

Looking back, I see my experience in Washington as a rookie-year thing, something I had to go through to get where I am today. I'll never regret my year in Washington. I needed it. Now I might even say, "Thanks, Wes, for not playing me."

But back then I couldn't appreciate what was happening. During that entire time, I was miserable. It was even worse than my freshman year at Wake Forest. At Wake, I was expected to wait a year. Here I was expected to be a starter, but I wasn't being given the chance. Unseld and I just didn't agree on what I could do or how to use me. It was his decision to get rid of me. He was the coach, and I couldn't make him play me. But I was determined to make Washington sorry they gave up on me.

CHAPTER

13

Thank God for Expansion

There have been only three important events in North Carolina:
the founding of the state, the Civil War, and the making of the
Charlotte Hornets.
— Max Muhleman, Charlotte sports consultant

ABILITY AND THE DREAM to play have never been enough to keep some truly gifted players from falling through the cracks and slipping out of the NBA. The Skip Wise story is never far from a Baltimore boy's mind. Sometimes, along with skill and desire, a little luck is involved. For me, that good fortune came in the form of NBA expansion.

In the mid-1980s a local rags-to-riches businessman named George Shinn wanted to bring pro sports to North Carolina. This area of the country had been a hotbed of college hoops for a long time, but many people saw Charlotte as a long shot for NBA expansion. The arguments were that the competition from the ACC (and from stock car racing, which is even more popular than basketball down here) would be too stiff, the population was too scattered, and the fans weren't interested in the pro game. These and other opinions led one out-of-town sportswriter to predict, "The only franchise that will end up in Charlotte will have golden arches." Still, Mr. Shinn kept trying, and in 1987 the NBA announced that it would be adding four new teams, two for the 1988–89 season, and two for the following season. Charlotte and Miami were the first cities selected.

The Charlotte team was named the Hornets, a nickname that came from a famous Revolutionary War militia that stopped British General Cornwallis on his drive through Charlotte. ("There's a rebel behind every bush," Cornwallis wrote. "It's a veritable nest of hornets.")

George Shinn hired his first front office: general manager, Carl Scheer, an ABA and NBA veteran executive; player personnel director, Gene Littles, a former ABA star player; and Dick Harter, an NBA assistant under Jack Ramsey and Chuck Daly, and a former college head coach. They began preparing for the expansion draft, from which they would select their first players out of the pool of all the players like me, who had been left unprotected by the established NBA teams.

The draft was held by conference telephone call and included the Hornets, the Miami Heat, and the NBA league offices. The Hornets' first choice was my old ACC buddy Dell Curry, a shooting guard who was released by the Cleveland Cavaliers. Their second was Golden State's Dave Hoppen, a center, one of the few big men available. In the third round, they selected me.

Getting drafted by the Hornets in the expansion of 1989 was the best thing that ever happened to my career. I tried to forget about my year in Washington. I now consider my first year in Charlotte as my true rookie year. I immediately thought, This is it; it's gonna happen here.

After they got the team, they began to make a list of players available in the expansion draft. Mr. Shinn had first heard about me from the president of Wake Forest, Dr. Thomas Hearn, and wanted his basketball people to get me if possible, not only because of my ability, but also because he thought I was a role model and inspiration to so many people. Mr. Shinn is a little fella himself — he's only five-five — and he had come from a very poor background and worked his way up from janitor at a business college to the college's owner. He then expanded it into a system of schools that made him very wealthy. He is a very religious man and is a motivational speaker, and he thought my story was a lot like his.

We had both overcome long odds to be more successful than anyone ever thought we would. In fact, he won the Horatio Alger Award, which is given to people who come from so little and achieve so much.

He felt that I was not only a great asset as a player, but that I would also help the new team from a marketing standpoint as a person who had succeeded against all odds. I didn't mind being marketed that way. I like being an inspiration. It's a lot better than being called a freak, that's for sure.

When they had the conference call, Mr. Shinn remembers, he just kept hoping Miami wouldn't pick me. When they got to the third round and they still had the opportunity to get me, they did. He was thrilled, because I was the guy he wanted the most. After my year in Washington I was so happy to be where I was wanted.

I couldn't follow the draft, since it was held by phone, but I knew Charlotte was more interested in me than Miami was. When it was over, I got a call from my agent that I had been selected third. Then I got a call from the new coach, Dick Harter. I went down for a press conference, and everyone was excited that I was coming back to Carolina. But no one was more excited than me. It felt like I was getting a fresh start, like I was being drafted all over again.

I spent the summer playing ball in the D.C. Coalition League. I wanted to come to camp in shape. I couldn't wait for the season to start, and I came to camp really geeked up. When I saw our first roster, I thought we could do some good things. I like to look at the positives, and we had some positives there.

I saw Kurt Rambis, the Los Angeles Lakers great who was signed as a free agent. I saw Earl Cureton, another veteran free agent whose game I respected, and Robert Reid, "Bobby Jo," who came in a trade from Houston. My ACC friend Dell Curry was there. So was Rickey Green, a nice guard from Utah.

Then there were the big guns. Rex Chapman, our first selection in the college draft that year, was chosen eighth overall. A six-six guard from Kentucky, Rex was going to be the team's first true superstar. He came out of college with a reputation as a great shooter, a hard worker, and one of the dunking-est white boys around. We were excited to get him into camp.

And Kelly Tripucka, the veteran scorer and former all-star, came over from Utah in a trade. He was coming off some bad years and had a big contract that Utah wanted to unload, but he still had a lot of talent — the kind of guy made for expansion teams.

In fact, we all were guys like that. We all felt we had been abused by our former teams, that we hadn't had the chance to prove our abilities for one reason or another. People call expansion teams "misfits," and I guess that is what we were. But we were talented misfits. We thought we could make some noise in the league right away. There was a feeling in the locker room and on the court that we all wanted to prove something. There was a lot of that attitude there, right from the start. We were hungry.

Dick Harter, the head coach, was straight with me at first. He said the point guard position was wide open. Myself, Rickey Green, and Michael Holton (an expansion draft pick from Portland) would all be competing. Harter said I could play anywhere from twenty to thirty minutes, depending on how things worked out. I believed him. He seemed like an honest guy. All I wanted was a chance to show what I could do.

That first camp was crazy. With all the attention we got you'd think we had already won a championship. There were a lot of inquiring minds out there in the Carolinas. The media, the fans, all the sponsors — everyone was enthused, anxious, and excited. And everything was up in the air.

That camp felt competitive. We all had guaranteed contracts, so we weren't really fighting to make the team, but everyone knew it was a new beginning. And we had professionals out there. This wasn't some CBA team. We had guys who had been all-stars and won championships, guys who knew how to win in the NBA. And the team's management all came from other organizations and had lots of experience in running a franchise. So it felt very professional right from the start. It was well run from day one. We did our work on time.

Outside, though, in the city and around the state, it was nuts. Everybody wanted a part of the Hornets. Everyone was interested. They had been waiting a long time for an NBA team, and they brought that collegelike enthusiasm to every game, even in the first preseason games. They loved us from day one, and they have been loyal ever since. They will give respect to the great players who come in with other teams, but once the ball goes up in the air, they are true to their Bugs.

The whole spirit was like a pep rally. Eventually, as the years passed, they started wanting a little more and a little more, which was to be expected as they grew more knowledgeable about the NBA game and the team got better. But at first they cheered us on no matter what, even though everyone knew we weren't going to win a whole lot of ball games. They appreciated our effort, and they felt a part of it. That made it all special. No matter what we accomplished or didn't accomplish, they were in our corner supporting us.

On opening night of our first NBA season, they had a black tie affair at the arena, and it was sold out. There was a symphony orchestra. Everyone was buzzing — twenty-three thousand people, all screaming for their new team. It was so exciting leading the team on the court that first night, I had goose bumps. Seeing everyone in tuxedos, everyone so geeked up, boy, it was something. There were speeches and videos, and it was George Shinn Day in Charlotte. Everything was wonderful. Until the game started.

We got stomped. We lost to Cleveland by forty points. We were completely destroyed. The Cavs were energized, they were smoking. Mark Price was hitting jumpers everywhere, Brad Daugherty was dunking, Hot Rod Williams was slashing, Craig Ehlo was shooting, their whole team was just rolling. I thought, "Man, this is gonna be a very long season."

But when we walked off the court, the crowd gave us a standing ovation. It was something I had never experienced before. We had just gotten our tails spanked, and they cheered us like we'd won the seventh game of the championship. We didn't talk about it much, though. We just showered and got on out of there, saying things like: "First one, baby. Yeah, first one. Can't get much worse than this."

The enthusiasm carried over from the Hive into the city. When some of the players went out to dinner after the game, they were given standing ovations — just for walking into a restaurant, after losing a game by forty points!

The crowds in Charlotte are more like a college crowd. In Washington it took a long time for the crowd to get warmed up. Here, they were used to college teams, they were college-oriented. Now, even though they are more knowledgeable about the pro game, they haven't changed. That's what makes such a big difference in the Hive. Everyone's enthusiastic, emotional. In the rest of the NBA, they don't celebrate until there's a reason to celebrate. Here, every game is a celebration.

That crowd helps, boy. It's hard to get geeked up for eighty-two games, but hearing our fans always gets us going. It's the only gym in the league that feels like a college gym. It gets loud in Chicago, and in New York, but the Hive is right there, too.

That first year we had some big wins, against teams we weren't expected to beat. We beat Chicago, on TBS, on a Kurt Rambis tip-in at the buzzer. That was a huge win, especially with Carolina boy Michael Jordan coming back home for the first time. (Mike got his respect from the fans before the game started, but once the ball was in play, they booed him like any other visiting player.) We won another one in Utah; again Rambis won it with a tip-in. I had a big game in a win at San Antonio, our first road win ever.

We won a huge game against Philadelphia, 109–107, when Charles Barkley was called for a charge in the final seconds on a basket that would have tied the game. That was our first win ever against a winning team, and after that game, the city went nuts. The papers started calling it "Hornet Hysteria," and from then on, you couldn't get a ticket to a home game. We've been sold out ever since.

That win was funny because, before the game, our assistant

coach, Ed Badger, had offered $50 to anyone who took a charge from Barkley. On that last play, both Rex Chapman and Tim Kempton fell backward when Charles drove, so they both got the fifty. Coach Badger was quoted in the paper as saying it was a legitimate business expense. I don't know if he wrote it off on his taxes or not.

Just before the all-star break, we beat Atlanta for our thirteenth win. After the break, though, we struggled. There weren't many memorable moments on the court that first year, but one special moment occurred when the Lakers came to town. This was the final year of Kareem Abdul-Jabbar's career, and every town had a little ceremony for him. The Hornets presented him with a custom-size rocking chair — that was one big chair, boy. He gave a nice speech, and said that he was moved that the East Coast thought of him so highly, like the West Coast did. I was always awed by Kareem.

Still, I stole the ball from him! He's an all-time great, but he had to learn: Put the ball on the floor, and you gotta watch out for the little fella. But they beat us anyway.

I never got the chance to talk to Kareem, and I am sorry about that. It was a missed opportunity, a chance to talk with a guy I looked up to as a kid. I always enjoyed those times that I could get a rap with one of my heroes. I had talked to one of my all-time favorites, Julius Erving, in Washington when I was with the Bullets. Boy, I loved the Doctor. He was the Six-Million-Dollar Man. I loved the moves of his I saw on television during his ABA days, with his big bush, dunking over big guys like Bill Walton and Artis Gilmore. Man, it was fun watching him. I don't get too hyped about meeting people, but meeting Julius was special. I easily could have asked him for an autograph.

It was weird those first few weeks and months. Everything was so new. We were the hottest thing in the city. I was suddenly going around the league, and a lot of people were inquisitive about me. But after the first time through the league, there was nothing else to say. They couldn't write about my basketball because I wasn't playing much.

It began to feel like Washington all over again. I was playing well, but Coach Harter couldn't get past my size. He just couldn't or wouldn't believe in me. It had started during training camp, with myself and Michael Holton fighting for the point guard spot. With Dick Harter, Holton always had the edge. You could see it. Harter could never be convinced that I was a legitimate starter, that he could win with me at point. That was enough to give me the drive, to get those fires burning inside me. There was no contest when I would put it into high gear. I think I outplayed Holton in almost every practice. But Holton still started the first sixty games or so.

There were times I got discouraged. Not only wasn't I starting, but Harter was being negative toward me and my game. I felt like it might be my rookie year all over again. But I fought hard not to let myself fall into the same mind trap. When I did get in the game I was playing pretty good basketball, and I just decided to stay with it. It wasn't that I wasn't playing well, like in Washington. Here I was on my game. If I was sitting, it was for different reasons. Specifically, it was because the coach didn't believe in me. But that was his decision. I just stayed focused. I never got too far down mentally that year. I was playing at least half the game, and the fans started to feed off it. They noticed that things happened when the little fella was on the floor, and they started calling for me. Pretty soon he had to play me more and more.

An expansion team's job is just to play hard and get some respect. We weren't going to win much, and we knew it, so all you can do is make a name for yourself. As a result there is a lot of freelancing going on. It's impossible to make good chemistry overnight. That comes from the coaches, by dictating the rotation of who plays when. But when you're out there you think about making your own mark, helping the team and playing hard.

It takes time to learn a team's chemistry. Once the season starts, you are off and running. There isn't time to work on things in practice, like in college. You play three or four games a week, and those first weeks of the season are almost like practices. Teams try to find the right rotation, the right chemistry. If you are lucky you find it quickly. Some teams don't find it all year long. An expansion team, without any history, is certainly going to take a long time to find that mix.

Off the court we got along well. We had some real personalities. That was one of the things that kept us going through a losing year. We enjoyed each other's company, and we had a lot of fun. There were no bad guys in the bunch. The organization really did their homework about that, drafting quality guys. They wanted to get players who were being let go from other teams because they didn't fit into their team's scheme, not because they were complainers or head cases or troublemakers. That really helped when we started losing a lot of games. There was very little bitching and moaning, everyone tried to maintain a professional attitude.

I used to hang with Dell Curry, Rickey Green, and Rex Chapman — they called us the "Strawberry Hill Gang," because that's the name of the apartment complex we lived in. Rickey Green we called "Goldie." (Everywhere I go we get nicknames.) Dell Curry was "Gomez" — he still is, actually. Earl Cureton was "Pretty Tony." I was "Willie." All these names came from a movie we saw, called *The Mack,* which is still my favorite movie, because it is more or less about the streets and the characters who live there.

We'd go to movies together, or play golf. At night we'd explore the city's restaurants and nightclubs, though there weren't that many. Charlotte has grown a lot in the past five years, but the first couple of years it was pretty much a small town. The city still closes up early, and back then it was even worse. After Baltimore and Washington, it was like being back in the country. But it sure kept us out of trouble, which was good.

Once Kim and Brittney moved down to join me, we got more into a stay-at-home life. I came down to Charlotte alone at first, because we thought it would be better if I wasn't distracted while the new team was being put together. I had time to learn the area, find a good place to live, and get things set up for all of us. Once that happened, Kim and I decided we would get married, and she and the baby relocated to Charlotte. She liked the apartment I had found — but she ended up changing all the furniture I got for it. Hey, at least I tried. I was still new at this homemaking stuff.

Along with my regular group, the other guys on the team were a lot of fun, too. Robert Reid was a total character. Bobby Jo — he was the liar of the bunch. Lies, lies, lies, everything he said was a lie. Whenever he was serious about something, we knew it was a lie. One day he's going off to Europe, the next day he wants to borrow $10,000 per player and he'll repay us $50,000, to invest in something or another. I recall Goldie saying, "Ten for fifty? Hell, that ain't bad. Tell you what, Bobby Jo, just give me the forty right now and we'll be even."

He'd say anything. We'd be in Washington, and he'd say he just met Nancy Reagan. We just laughed at him.

He'd wear the Jheri Curl in his hair to make it all wet and shiny. I call that stuff "juices and berries." Bobby Jo had it on all the time, and I'd get on him: "I know your pillowcase must be a spongy mess from all those juices and berries."

One time he told us his high school jersey, his college jersey, and his pro jersey in Houston had all been retired. I said, "Yeah, and each one is dripping juices and berries."

Rex Chapman was also a great friend. Even though he was a rookie, he fit in well and got along with all of us. He was good friends with Dell Curry, and I enjoyed being with Rex. But Rex had problems on the court. He was young and had come out of college early, and was so eager to prove himself that he struggled. He was so inconsistent. He'd have a good game here, then a bad game there. Dick Harter wasn't his biggest fan, either. Rex and Michael Jordan were friends and played golf together, but Harter would tell him that Michael was jerking him around. Harter would say things like, "He laughs with you on the golf course but he busts your ass on the court."

Rex didn't take that too well. He got down a little bit. But we talked him through it. He's also been injury-prone his whole career, and hasn't put a solid year together. But he's got a great game, and eventually he's going to show his stuff. In fact, he had one of his best years yet in 1994.

Kelly Tripucka was the team's big star, but he pretty much kept to himself. He was Dick Harter's man. I think Dick was the only one Kelly liked. They got along really well. We didn't have a problem with that. But we saw it. On the court he was a big-time scorer. He carried us many nights. But off the court, he wasn't a big part of the team.

Kurt Rambis was, though. I felt bad for Kurt. He had experienced all the highs with the Lakers, and now he was experiencing the lows, so to speak. But he had a lot to offer us. His competitiveness every night was an inspiration. He tried to lift us. People respected him, because he sacrificed his body every night.

Rambis was a crazy guy. He was the only guy I know who could go on a West Coast road trip, a seven-, eight-, nine-, ten-day road trip, packing one bag with one sports coat. I don't know if it was reversible or something, I don't know how he did it. In college I once freaked out when my bag of shoes turned up missing at the airport. I called my boys at Wake, and in Baltimore, and had them get on the case. I had to have my shoes. But Rambis wasn't a style guy. Everyone has his own personality. Some you can joke with, some you don't bother. We'd make fun of someone's clothes, their hair. But Kurt didn't care. He was laid back. He had his one sports jacket and went about his business.

One day, in Milwaukee, Coach Harter got on him: "Kurt Rambis, you need to start playing like old crazy Kurt again." So he went out all fired up. Third quarter, he goes to get a rebound, *crack!* Tears up his ankle. That'll teach you.

Earl Cureton was a big factor our first year. He had been around a long time, and had seen the league change from the days of Julius Erving to the days when Magic and Bird were just coming in, and then to Michael Jordan stepping in. He had witnessed the evolution of the league firsthand, and he had a lot to say about it. He talked about the guards of his day, how Andrew Toney was one of the unstoppable guards in the league, and about World B Free coming off the screen and shooting his skyscraper J. He'd talk about guys like Otis Birdsong raining jumpers, about Junior Bridgeman, about Sidney Moncrief, about Mo Cheeks "the Cookie Man" — he loved to eat cookies — running things in his prime, about Dick Vitale as a coach — a bit more laid back, but more or less the same character as he is now as an analyst on television.

Listening to Earl the Twirl — we called him "Twirl" because he did a finger roll the opposite way that most do it — was important for us. He brought some history with him. He was a link to the past for a team that didn't have any past.

All these guys had a big impact on me that first year, but none more so than Dell Curry. Dell and I just gradually became great friends. Our first year we got to know each other quite well. All of a sudden we were calling each other all the time. It took over somehow. We stayed around Charlotte during the off-season, and we spent a lot of time playing golf. Dell is the one who got me to try golf for the first time, and boy, did I stink. But I loved the game, and I've become pretty good. Sometimes I even give Dell a good game now, though he's still better than me. He says his next goal is to get me hunting and fishing, but that won't happen. I'll play golf, but you won't get this city boy in the woods with a rifle.

On a deeper level we started sharing things, not holding back, opening up about very personal things. We liked what we saw, and it just grew. Dell is a country boy, and his personality is a lot like Reggie Williams's. He's a quiet guy at heart. Reg is still my best friend, but Dell is a close second. I guess the quiet ones and the loud ones need each other. We respect each other, we aren't afraid to be who we are and let the other be who he is. I don't try to get him to be more wild, and he doesn't try to get me to be low-key.

Plus, he is an inspiration to me because he is totally devoted to his family. He's a big family man, and we did a lot of things together with our families. I have learned a lot from him about that. He is always with his kids, and his wife, giving them full attention. I do a lot more things outside of basketball, appearances and such, and sometimes I get caught up in all that. I might forget the important things. Dell always brings me back to earth, gets me focused on the important things. If there is one guy I use as a role model, it's Dell Curry.

Everything was so new to everybody the first year. Even the owner was a rookie. The front office really did a lot of work. They traveled to different arenas to see how other teams operated, how the fans were treated, to study halftime shows and marketing skills, just educating themselves about what it takes to be successful in the NBA. You need to keep fans entertained, keep them coming back, market your players correctly. They did their homework.

From day one they said they would be a playoff team in five years. And they did what it took to get there. They got the talent, and blended in players who could help. But the first year it wasn't like that. We had players who were fortunate to have a job in the NBA, myself included. That was a survival year. After the all-star break, we won a couple more games, including big wins in New York and Philadelphia. In April we won our twentieth game, against the New Jersey Nets, and five days later we lost our last game, at home, to Milwaukee. That was called "Teal Day," by the mayor, in honor of our first season coming to a close. We finished the year with a record of 20–62 — better than most people expected, and very respectable for a new team. I personally had a decent season, starting twenty-one of seventy-nine games, averaging 5.4 points and leading the team in assists with 620 and steals with 111. Not great, but not bad.

What was truly great was that we led the league in attendance, with more than 950,000 fans, more than 23,000 a night, which was 99 percent of capacity — the first time an expansion team ever led the league. At the time, it was the second-highest attendance figure in history, and it has been passed only six times since — five times by Charlotte fans themselves.

That first year was the foundation for everything that has followed. We had not only survived, we had been competitive. We had a nucleus of players to build on, and the front office was committed to improving the team and reaching its goal of making the playoffs within five years. George Shinn had seen that another expansion team, the Dallas Mavericks, had reached the playoffs in five seasons, and he had made a pledge that Charlotte would match that achievement.

And many of the guys on the team had gone a long way toward reviving their careers. For me, Washington already seemed like a long time ago, like some other person had gone through that experience. Here, the real Muggsy was back, playing the kind of ball I wanted to play. I wasn't playing as much as I wanted to, but the whole mood was different. I was completely positive that things would work out for the team and for me.

Every day I thank God for expansion.

CHAPTER

14

"Will a Midget Really Bother Patrick Ewing?"

Will a midget really bother Patrick Ewing?
— Dick Harter

P LAYING FOR AN EXPANSION TEAM is a real education. For an established team, change comes pretty slowly. They have created their identity, they have certain players they build around, and there is a consistency from year to year, with just small changes here and there. An expansion team is different. For the first several years, each season was almost like starting from scratch.

Each year presented different situations. The first-year Hornets looked like this: Rickey Green, Rex Chapman, Kurt Rambis, Kelly Tripucka, and Dave Hoppen starting. Michael Holton, Robert Reid, and Earl Cureton spot-starting, especially after Green got hurt. Dell Curry and myself off the bench, until I got more starts late in the year.

Like I said, that wasn't a bad lineup. But changes came immediately. In the summer draft after our first year, we selected J. R. Reid, the all-American six-nine forward from North Carolina, with the fifth pick in the draft. It was a controversial pick, because we really needed a true center, but there was pressure to draft a local product. Besides, J.R. was a great player. So the team wasn't sad that he was chosen. The Hornets traded the second pick for a center, Stuart Gray of Indiana.

More changes quickly followed. Next, Robert Reid was traded, and Earl Cureton was let go. Jerry Sichting was acquired, to give us another guard. And a month into the season, we added power forward Kenny Gattison, reacquired Bobby Jo Reid, and traded Rambis for Phoenix's power forward Armon Gilliam.

The result was that our lineup quickly looked almost entirely different from the year before: myself and Chapman at the guards, Gilliam and Tripucka at forward, and J. R. Reid as center, with Curry, Gattison, and Robert Reid off the bench.

That was an interesting lineup. We had some firepower. We still lacked an enforcer in the middle, a true center — Stuart Gray never worked out, and was traded in February — but we thought we were improved from the first year. We now had two young first-rounders in the lineup: Rex Chapman, the first potential superstar, and J. R. Reid, another potential superstar, who was supposed to fill our needs at center and was the guy who might take us to the next level. Our thinking was that Rex, J.R., and Kelly Tripucka might be a nice mix to start to build on.

We were wrong. We lost our first five games before beating the newest expansion team, Orlando. Our slide continued, and when we lost ten straight to fall to 3–18, we traded Rambis for Gilliam. But that wasn't enough, either, and we twice lost six straight games to fall way off the pace. By the end of January, we had won only eight games.

The mood was dark, boy. I was playing more, and starting more often than not, but I didn't feel at the top of my game. The whole team was struggling, and we started looking for reasons. I knew what I believed — the trouble was with Coach Harter. George Shinn may have wanted me to come to Charlotte, but Dick Harter wasn't so sure. He never took to me. I didn't know this until much later, but he was constantly disrespecting me to the press and the front office.

After one game a reporter asked him why he didn't have me "front" Patrick Ewing in a double-team. He dropped to his knees and asked, "Will a midget really bother Patrick Ewing?" When he was asked if I was having trouble scoring, he climbed up onto a chair, held his arms up, and said, "Try shooting over a building when you're only five-three."

Harter was a very negative person. The previous year, he had said to us during a game, "All their players are better than all of our players." He once said, when we were struggling, that he thought we'd lose every one of our remaining games.

During halftimes, he would let the whole team have it. Sometimes we almost looked forward to his halftime talks, because he'd go completely crazy. He got all over Tim Kempton to "stop daydreaming," he told Rex Chapman that Michael Jordan was jerking him around, and yelled at Kurt Rambis to start acting like "old crazy Kurt."

He'd go from one player to the next: "Kelly, we need forty from you to win, because your man is gonna score forty. . . . Dell Curry, I am trying to keep you in the league, son. They say you can't play defense. . . . Dave Hoppen, I am going to hire someone to chase you around with a baseball bat to make you tough." He'd go off like that. It was pretty ugly stuff.

Then one day, Harter said to me, "And Muggsy Bogues — quit trying for all those damn assists. Assists don't mean shit in this league."

I couldn't believe it when he said that. An assist means a basket. If I was generating offense, it didn't matter to me who scored the points.

I was really upset at the time. Here I was performing well in the NBA, and still my own coach doubted me. Added to the fact that we weren't winning much, this was frustrating as hell. I never doubted I could play in the league — with every game I was getting more confident — but I did begin to doubt that anyone else would believe in me.

I mean, I was starting, but still Harter was complaining that he couldn't win with a five-three guard. As I mentioned, at the time he never said much directly to me. It was more to the media and to management. When I heard what he had been saying, it really pissed me off. Here I was busting my tail, and if he thought that way, he should have told me. Don't tell me I'm doing fine, then tell the media I'm too short. I deserve more respect than that. Maybe he felt he was telling me the things he thought I needed to hear to help me stay on top of my game, and at the same time, he was covering for himself. I don't really know. What bothers me is that he never told me to my face how he felt. He never said anything in my presence but that he believed in me. Then he'd slam me to everyone else. That shows you what kind of guy he is.

I just don't think he saw what was going on out on the court. I was making guys better. I could do things to make us win. My teammates believed in me, I am sure of that. If my shot wasn't working, I could still contribute. There aren't too many players who can walk off a basketball court with no points and still be the MVP of the game, or at least help the team win. He was looking just at the negatives.

To his credit, I think he got as much out of us our first year as anyone could. I mean, we won twenty games. That's a lot for a new team. But the second year, I think his negativity got to be too heavy. He was always downing us. Things weren't going well as it was, and here's your leader, your coach, telling you how he's trying to keep you in the league, or how your game doesn't matter, or that some other player is going to embarrass you out there. It just took the fight out of us. When we lost, it wasn't directly because of Coach Harter. It was because we didn't do the job. But the atmosphere off the court didn't help get the best out of us, that's for sure. We all just got a little tired of it.

It didn't take long before we heard that changes were in the works. George Shinn talked to me, Dell, Rex, and J. R. Reid. He asked us how we felt about the coach: Did we think he was motivating us? What was the problem with the team?

I told him, "Hey, he feels I'm not the person for his team, so how can I say he's the person for me?"

Everyone else had his own problems. I don't know if that led to his firing. People said the players got Dick Harter fired. I don't think that's so. I think it was between him and Mr. Shinn. Mr. Shinn made the decision himself.

Harter went to Shinn's office and said he wanted to trade me. He said I was too short, that I couldn't play in the NBA. Shinn tried to tell him I could play. He agreed that I was short, but I made up for it in all the other things I did, on and off the court. I fit our system well. I was a good guy in the community, a good family man. I never turned down a request to do a community project. Mr. Shinn knew that if he had to go somewhere to work for a worthy cause, he could always get me to come along.

But Harter wouldn't listen. He got down on his knees and held up his hands and said, "I'm Muggsy, trying to defend you. This is what it looks like. And you want to keep this guy?"

Mr. Shinn knew right then, there was no way he could keep this coach.

Harter was fired on January 31, 1990, and Gene Littles, our assistant coach, took over. We were happy to see the changes made. When Gene took over, everything changed. I knew he was totally behind me. I had security for the first time. He said, "Here's the ball, run with it." And I ran with it.

He put in more of an up-tempo offense. Harter ran a lot of plays, like the Bullets did, only a little less structured. With Gene, we ran and ran. That's where I really made my mark. Once Gene took over, we took off. We had a much better second half. And that's when I got to starting full time. I remember thinking, "This is when it all begins."

Gene and I became close friends. We talked about everything, family, friends, basketball, you name it. I was fortunate to have a coach like that. I was thinking back to Dunbar days. He was a young Bob Wade.

Gene knew the game. He knew the X's and O's. He got the most out of us. It did take a while, though — we went 2–20 over his first twenty-two games. But we could feel that we were improving. We finished the season with nine wins in our last twenty games — not championship material, I know, but a pretty good improvement for a team that hadn't changed all that much. Gene was so positive. He never left the room without saying something positive to the team. Even after a loss, he'd go over the mistakes, but he focused on the positives. That kind of thinking is so important. It takes you from "I hope I can" to "I think I can" to "I know I can."

That's when we started to make a little noise around the league. Teams took us a little more seriously. Although we won one less game than the year before, we still believed we were actually a better team. I know I really came into my own. My scoring was up to 9.4 per game, I was among the leaders in the league in assists with 867 and steals with 166, my shooting percentage was just under fifty percent, and I played more minutes than anyone on the Hornets except J. R. Reid.

I felt like I was becoming a team leader as well. Sometimes that meant challenging my teammates to play hard, sometimes it meant leading the way in off-court social activities. Occasionally it meant taking on problems within the team, or asserting myself as someone who wouldn't back down from anything.

For instance, that year we had acquired a player named Richard Anderson. When he arrived we expected big things from him — he was six-ten and we needed inside help. One day, several players were walking through an airport, all joking around and insulting each other as we always do. Anderson became involved somehow, and I called him "Whopper" because he was such a big guy. It was meant in fun, but he didn't think it was funny. Well, he challenged me physically — he grabbed my coat or something — and I just got furious. You don't challenge me that way. I won't back down from anybody. It didn't matter that he was six-ten and I am five-three. That never entered my mind. I had to do something, so I grabbed his necktie and pulled it so hard it snapped and tore away from his neck. Everyone was shocked, but they always forget that

I am a strong little fella. Of course, my teammates rushed in and made sure nothing else happened. But I had made my point.

I certainly didn't like doing things like that, but sometimes they happen over the course of a season. And these things are necessary. They help build a team spirit, a togetherness.

Gaining the players' respect is something I had to do both on and off the court. On the court, I really got the fans' respect, too, and at the end of that season they voted me the team's most valuable player. When I won the team MVP it really made me feel good. When I received the award before our last home game, I was thinking about the Bullets. It was vindication for me. No team had ever cut me before, and I was happy to show them they had made a mistake.

Those first two years in Charlotte were special to me. I finally felt like I belonged in the NBA, like I was really a part of it. I never felt that way in Washington. In Charlotte, it all came together. Surviving the Dick Harter era was tough, but it helped me. Being around guys like Rambis, Reid, Cureton, guys who had achieved a lot in the league, made me a better person, a smarter player. The competitiveness and desire was always there in me, but they helped me with the mental toughness I needed. I can say that all these guys helped in some way, even Wes Unseld and Dick Harter.

But now things were really changing. Entering our third year, we knew that a lot more would be expected of us. Not only did we have a new head coach who could really get a lot out of us, we also had a new front office. Carl Scheer had resigned as general manager to become president of the Denver Nuggets. Mr. Shinn replaced him with Allan Bristow, who was Denver's assistant coach, and Allan hired Dave Twardzik as head scout.

When Allan Bristow took over, I knew good things would happen. He had always believed in me. While he was in Denver, he had wanted to draft me out of college, and then he tried to trade for me when I was in Washington. He had played and coached under Doug Moe, so he loved the up-tempo, passing-game offense. He knew how I'd fare in a fast-paced offense like that, and he built a similar style in Charlotte. Gene Littles also liked the fast game, but Allan was going to speed it up even more. Muggsyball was back.

Finally, I had people who believed in me, and an offense I knew I could run. Everything was coming together. All we needed was a little more time.

Making a Buzz

Listen, did anyone lose their child?
— Michael Jordan, with Muggsy Bogues at the 1991
All-Star Stay-in-School JAM

B Y OUR THIRD SEASON I was pretty well known in Charlotte, but there are always people and things to keep you
grounded. I was a "small" star, especially compared to guys
like Michael Jordan, and he liked to kid me about that, as do
a lot of my friends.

Besides, fame is all relative. Things always happen that can put
you in your place. For instance, take what happened early that
third year.

Some of my teammates and I were in a barbershop in town. I
was waiting my turn, when in walked a wino, staggering and
drunk. The poor guy looked like hell. He stared at me a second and
said, "Hey, I know you."

I decided to kid with him. "Yeah? Who am I?"

"You play for the Hornets. You that little guy."

"Nah," I said. "I'm not him."

"Yes, you are," he said.

"Oh yeah?" I said. "What's my name, then?"

"Monk Bogues. That's it. You that *Monk* Bogues fella."

I don't have to tell you how that went over with my teammates.
For a long time afterward, I wasn't "Muggsy" anymore. I was
"Monk."

But that was all right. Even the drunks in Charlotte loved us.

The fact is, we were all becoming famous around the Carolinas. The whole area continued to support us so well, even after two losing seasons, that we were determined to start giving them their money's worth. Entering our third year, we wanted to be more than famous. We wanted to be good.

The Hornets management was doing everything they could to help us out. The third-year team was almost completely different from the first two, as they continued to look for a combination of players that could produce on the floor.

How fast do things change in the NBA? As we began our third season in Charlotte, only five original Hornets remained in the lineup: myself, Rex Chapman, Dell Curry, Dave Hoppen, and Kelly Tripucka. And Hoppen didn't last the season. That left just four of us to survive three years. That's a quick change. Plus, we had a new coach, a new general manager, and a new player personnel director. At least the mascot, Hugo the Hornet, stayed the same.

But then, when you win only twenty and then nineteen games, you have to change. And we were changing for the better. We had added guys like J. R. Reid, Armon Gilliam, and Kenny Gattison. And now, with our pick in that year's amateur draft, we added Kendall Gill.

Gill, who was the fifth pick overall, was out of the University of Illinois. He was another guard, which caused some concern. We were loaded with guys between six-four and six-seven — Gill is six-five — who could play guard or small forward, and there wasn't enough playing time for all of them.

And the situation got even more confused when the team signed Johnny Newman, a six-seven guy, as a free agent from the New York Knicks. Now we had Rex, Dell, Kendall, Kelly, and Johnny all fighting to play the shooting guard or small forward position. I was the only true point guard we had, so one of them was going to have to get minutes at the point as well.

Our big guys were J.R., Armon Gilliam, Kenny Gattison, and rookie Steve Scheffler. They weren't big enough, though — J.R.,

Armon, and Steve are six-nine, and Kenny is six-eight. So Armon was traded for a *bigger* big guy, veteran six-eleven center Mike Gminski, and later in the year we added another big guy, six-eleven Eric Leckner.

As you can see, this was still a team looking for an identity. The pieces hadn't come together yet. It was changing fast, but growing slowly. We had more talent, but we still struggled. We still couldn't get a good chemistry, couldn't get a rotation going that kept everyone happy. A lot of people were unhappy, especially at the two and three spot. The minutes weren't there for everybody. Kendall and Johnny took a lot of Rex's and Kelly's minutes, which didn't make them too happy.

At first, Kendall was going to take my spot — Kendall could play the one or two guard — and I'd be the odd man out. Once again, the coaches thought I'd be better coming off the bench, and they thought the team needed to find a bigger point guard. But once again I proved that I was the best point guard in camp, and it didn't work out the way they planned.

It actually was the best thing for both me and Kendall. He wasn't a natural point guard like me. He was better at the two. With the two of us as the starting backcourt, we both had a strong season. Kendall really blossomed in his rookie year.

Dell was still coming off the bench and was very successful at that, but now Kelly Tripucka and Rex Chapman were also on the bench. Both Rex and Kelly ran out of luck, and their games suffered. Rex couldn't handle coming off the bench. He couldn't really play the three. I felt bad for both of them — more so for Rex, since I liked him so much — because they had been with the team from the beginning. But something had to give. The management realized they had to make a change and avoid conflicts. Nothing happened until after the season, but we all knew someone — or maybe more than one — would have to go.

Even with those problems, things were looking up that third year. Gene Littles began to make his mark. We had a strong preseason, and with Kendall joining Rex, J.R., Armon, Kelly, Johnny, and Dell, we had a lot of scoring power. We were still a donut team, though — good around the edges, nothing in the center. But at this point in our history, management was concerned with acquiring as much talent as possible and putting them all on the floor. In the first years of a team, you just grab whatever is out there. Then, when a trade became available, they had the ability to make a deal. That's how we got Gminski, a veteran who was perfectly suited to be a backup to J.R. and allowed him to play his true position, the power forward. It's only later that you can begin to fine-tune a team and pick up the specific things you need.

Things began positively that season. We took the Knicks to over-time in our season opener at home. More than twenty-four thousand people attended that game, the biggest crowd ever at the Hive, and it got us so geeked up that, even though we lost the game, we won our next two. At 2–1, we had a winning record for the first time ever.

I know, 2–1 is not exactly going to get you to the playoffs, but it means a lot to an expansion franchise. I can't tell you how important it is when you make these small steps up. For a new franchise, each small achievement is very, very important. That year we won our first game ever against two of the league's best teams, the Boston Celtics and the Detroit Pistons. Beating a good team for the first time, or winning a game in another team's arena for the first time, or holding a superstar in check, all these little things begin to add up over time. It's like they say, you can't run until you walk. We were starting to walk a little steadier that year.

In fact, by the end of that year, the Charlotte Hornets had made a real buzz around the NBA. We all started to enjoy the game more than we had in a long time. For the first time, we felt like a *team*, not just a collection of guys. We were gathering an identity, other teams were taking us seriously now. They could no longer count us as an automatic win. I really feel that our third season was the year that made the Hornets.

We finished the month of November at 8–7, our first winning

month ever. But then we lost eleven straight in December. Our weakness in the middle, and our being overstocked with shooters, led the team to make the Gilliam-and-Hoppen-for-Gminski trade. That really helped us.

Things began to pick back up. We beat Sacramento by a club-record forty-two points one night, then shot 60 percent as a team to beat San Antonio on the road. We beat Boston and Detroit, and in late March we beat Golden State and Philadelphia for our twentieth and twenty-first wins, a new club record. We won five more games in April to finish with a record of 26–56. But more important, we finished with a lot of respect from around the league.

As I said, the team made a big move up that year. Kendall Gill was a tremendous addition. He had a lot of enthusiasm, and he wanted to make a name for himself. He ran the floor well, played competitive defense, and really wanted to win. Johnny Newman, who came from New York, also helped us a great deal. He was eager to play, because, like most of the older guys on the Hornets, he had left a situation where he just didn't fit in. He had that motivation to prove his old team wrong. He came in and performed well right away.

Under Gene Littles we were now playing a faster game. We had a lot of jump shooters, and Dick Harter's offensive style tried to free them up with a lot of screens. Gene speeded the game up, which helped me out. He let me create more, make more decisions, force the action, do the things I had always done. He let us play Muggsyball. That was the best thing he could have done. That's when your natural talent takes over — instead of worrying where you need to be and how to set up the play, you just run the floor and compete to the best of your natural ability. We all started relaxing and playing really well, especially during the second half of the season. We were making real progress.

There was a lot of progress off the court as well. Kim and I had gotten married, bought a beautiful home in the suburbs, and were settling into Charlotte. Brittney was happy and healthy. My first daughter, Tyisha, was having a difficult time living in the city of Baltimore, and her mother and I agreed that it would be best for her if she came to live with Kim and me. It was tough for her mom to give her up like that, of course, but she knew that the city was no place for a kid to grow up anymore. Tyisha was having problems in school and at home. Once she came to live with us, you could see the difference almost immediately. She has relaxed, and is doing much better in school and at home.

My two little girls are terrific. We thought we would be a foursome forever. Then we got more great news.

Kim had had two miscarriages trying to have one more child. She was having some medical problems, and the doctors told us that eventually we wouldn't be able to have more children. During the last month that we would be able to have a baby — in fact, on Kim's birthday — we found out that Kim was pregnant. It was a miracle. All I told my wife for months was "Kim, give me a son. That will make me the happiest person on earth." When we found out it was a boy, I was ecstatic. We had a sonogram every month to make sure it was still a boy. Kim says that I got on everybody's nerves — but the doctors were very happy to make more money off of me!

Kim went into labor on March 29, a game night. I was out of control: "Is it coming? What's happening? What's taking so long?" I was bothering everybody. Finally Kim said, "Muggs, why don't you go play tonight, and when you come back I'll be ready."

I asked, "Is that OK, doc? She won't have it while I'm playing?"

The doctor said, "No, she won't. Now go play."

I called Kim from my car on the way to the game. I called from the locker room. I called from the bench before the game. I called at halftime. I called after the game before I showered. And I talked to her on the car phone all the way from the arena to the hospital.

I brought Dell Curry and his wife, Sonya, and we all started making fun of Kim and her condition — she looked like hell, of course. But by 2 A.M. they say, "This is taking too long. We're leaving." Kim finally had Ty at 4:52 A.M. I was watching ESPN

"SportsCenter" while she was pushing the baby out. I looked at the baby and he looked at me, and that was all she wrote.

Everybody at the Hornets called and sent flowers. "I never got so much attention," Kim says. "Fifteen minutes after delivery I gave a radio interview. Muggs had been talking about having a son for so long, everybody in town knew. It was crazy."

Don't get me wrong, it's not that I love my son more than my daughters. It is just that, having two girls already, I wanted a boy. And Tyrone Jr. — we call him Ty, not Muggsy Jr. — is a handful of boy. He's just like me. He and I are best pals. He really made our family life complete.

There were still big changes to be made after the season, but the biggest happened when the team named Allan Bristow head coach and moved Gene up to the front office as a vice president. I am still not sure why Gene left coaching. I know Allan wanted to coach again, but I thought he was happy in the front office. And I thought Gene was happy, too. But these things happen in professional sports.

I had mixed feelings about this change. I admit I was a little upset, because I liked Gene and we had a good relationship. I was starting to play up to my capabilities, and I owed that to Gene letting me play my kind of game. I felt some loyalty to him. I still do. I was very close to Gene, and I was sorry to see him go upstairs.

But the NBA is a business, and you have to take what comes. I had no problems with Allan, and I came to like him a lot. I also respect Allan, and he has done a good job as coach. Knowing that he had tried hard to get me when he was an assistant under Coach Doug Moe in Denver, and that he wanted me for the system he played, helped ease my worries.

Allan had first become aware of me when I played in the World Championships in Europe. He had never heard of me, didn't know anything about me. He remembers, "I had the TV on with the sound off, and I watched, fascinated. I was falling in love with this guy. I have a fascination with small guards, and they don't get any smaller. I love guys who can press, who can make things happen. He was coming up from behind guys and just taking the ball away. It was amazing. Doug Moe had been watching, too, and the next day I asked him, 'Did you see that little guy? He'd be great with us.' I couldn't wait for the next night's game."

He told me the story behind his trying desperately to draft me out of college. Indiana was picking ahead of Washington, and the Pacers had agreed to the deal that if Reggie Miller had already been taken, Denver would get Indiana's pick and take me. But Miller was still available, so Indiana kept their pick and took him. Denver also tried to get me from Washington, but the Bullets felt like they couldn't trade a first round pick, so Washington traded them another small guard, Michael Adams, instead.

And when I came to Charlotte he *still* tried to get me. Denver offered Charlotte various things, players and draft picks, but George Shinn wouldn't part with me. Carl Scheer, the GM then, told Allan he'd get killed P.R.-wise if he traded me. "I figured, if I can't get him, I'll join him," Allan says now. "When I came to Charlotte, I knew he wasn't going anywhere."

Dave Twardzik, our player personnel director, knew what I could do, too. "When I was with the Clippers and the Pacers, coming in to play this franchise, Muggsy was the guy who gave us the most problems," he says. "Every game, he does something where you go, 'God, how did he see that?' I am a former point guard, and I don't even see the things he sees. He may have the best true point guard mentality of anyone in the league."

Allan and I spoke before the season, and he told me we were going to run a passing-game offense like he did at Denver. He thought I was perfect for that style, and I agreed. I was geeked up to get the ball and go.

That off-season was a positive one for everybody. The whole mood was brightening. Then came the college draft, and the mood got even brighter. We won the lottery and got the right to choose first overall, and everyone knew we were going to improve a great deal more.

The best college player out there was Larry Johnson of UNLV, a monstrous six-seven, 250-pounder, who could dominate the boards and provide some vicious slam dunks. He also happened to be exactly the kind of player we needed. He would give us the power presence we really lacked inside, and take some of the pressure off J. R. Reid, who was not playing up to the level we all expected. I couldn't wait to get L.J. into camp, get the big fella running with me, and see what we could do.

CHAPTER 16

Grandmama and the Little Fella

*You look at a highlight film of me, it's just a highlight film of
him passing me the ball. I'd kill for the little fella.*
— Larry Johnson

I WAS WATCHING THE 1991 DRAFT LOTTERY ON TV, like
every other basketball fan, and when we got the first pick, I
went completely crazy. I knew the front office people were de-
bating between Larry Johnson and Dikembe Mutombo, the big
center from Georgetown. We needed a true center, so they were
hyped on Dikembe. But Allan wanted Larry in a big way. They
liked his work ethic, and they felt he could be a force right away,
where Mutombo might be a year or two away.

They asked me my opinion. I hadn't seen much of Larry. I knew
Mutombo and thought he'd be a big help blocking shots and working in the paint, but I couldn't recommend one over the other.
They said Larry was the type of player who could take over a game,
and we needed that, too.

It was a tough decision, because you never know when a really
good center is going to be available. They are pretty rare. In the end
they decided to take their chances and wait on a center, and they
chose Larry. I am sure glad they did. Mutombo is a great player for
sure, but for my money Larry was the best choice they could have
made.

A day or two later I called him on the phone to welcome him to

Charlotte for the 1991–92 season. I told him, "Hey, big fella, I will take you to *the land.* If you work hard, I'll get you the rookie of the year award."

He laughed about that. We hit it off right away. He is a loud, fun guy like I am, and it took two minutes on the phone for him to realize, "Uh oh, I got a little version of me here."

And I kept my promise. After the all-star break, we turned it up a notch, and "L" stepped up and snatched the rookie award away from Dikembe.

Larry made a huge difference right away. He gave us inside power, rebounding, and the toughness we had lacked for three years. He worked so hard, and everyone fed off him. Including me. That's how we got our relationship together so quickly. I told him if he ran and worked hard, good things would happen. I told him not to concentrate on just getting points from his inside game. Don't just bang-bang-bang. Work on getting points in the transition game. Run the floor with me. Make it easier on yourself, become more versatile. Get the easy buckets, and then the tougher buckets will come, because your confidence will be growing. Don't wait for the game to come to you. You have got to be a part of the game from the get-go.

I knew he could make his teammates better by being more versatile, by passing off, taking the J, doing things besides just pounding inside. He has so much talent, he can do anything he wants to do.

We are both big talkers. We are so competitive. He has a lot of city in him. I like that guy because he doesn't hold anything back, nothing is hidden. He loves the game, and he loves people, loves conversing. We talk about everything. We give each other advice. He asked me about getting engaged before he proposed to his girlfriend. He asked my opinion, and that meant a lot to me, the fact that we can share those special things with each other. I love good friends, and I speak from the heart. Larry knows we can speak openly to each other. I love the big fella. He's grown and matured a lot in just a few years. I hope I have helped him.

We even talked and joked about his big new contract. After his second season, he negotiated a long-term deal worth a total of $84 million. As soon as he signed, he left a message on my answering machine:

"Hello, Muggsy Bogues, and Mrs. Bogues, and the kids. Muggsy Bogues, whenever you call me on my phone I don't want you to say 'Hey, Larry.' I don't want you to say, 'Hey, L-ster.' I don't want you to say, 'Hey, Mr. Johnson.' When you speak to me, you call me 'Mr. Eighty-four.' When you get that down, give me a shout. Peace."

Oh, man, I laughed so hard when I heard that. He's the kind of guy who is so down-to-earth, he hasn't got a dime in his pocket. A lot of guys get big heads from their success. Larry appreciates it, but he's still himself. His priorities are straight. He deserves what he gets. That's the kind of guy I like being around.

Heck, he's the only guy I know who can wear a dress and still get respect. When his commercials for Converse came out with him dressed up as "Grandmama," we kidded him to death. And he took it great. A lot of people couldn't do that, going on television and marketing himself nationally as an old lady. But he did.

I could kid him about it because I had been with Converse before I switched to Reebok. Whenever any Converse representative was around, I'd always say, "Hey, Larry, I know Converse doesn't like me anymore, but see if they can't come up with 'Grandmama and the Little Fella.' Can we promote something like that?" We would have a lot of fun with that.

In his second year, Larry was fined $8,000 for smashing Milwaukee's Eric Murdock with a forearm to his head because he thought Murdock had been banging me up a little. "When Muggs is getting bumped and bruised on the court, he goes absolutely crazy, and ain't nobody gonna get my little man," Larry says. "You gotta stand up for your little man. He can take care of himself, but I like to help him out." Hey, big fella, I appreciate the help.

Larry is great to joke with. After the fine came down, we decided to play a practical joke on him. The next time we played in Milwaukee, we told the ball boy to give Larry a note we had written that said Larry was going to get his ass kicked. It was signed "Eric Murdock." Larry paid it no mind, but we all had a good laugh.

Larry was quiet when he first came to camp, like most rookies are. He got a feel for everyone, and didn't disrespect the veterans. He took his time to feel comfortable, just like all rookies do. Larry had missed the entire training camp while he was negotiating a contract, but he made an immediate impact. In his first game he scored fourteen points, and in his second game he scored eighteen points and grabbed eighteen rebounds. He continued to develop, and the team responded. We didn't get off to a great start under Allan. We were only 12–33 through January. But then we went 9–4 in February, our best month ever, and Larry led us to a tremendous second half. We went on an 18–11 stretch, by far our best performances to that point.

Larry really dominated. We created a play called "Dallas," named for his hometown. It is an isolation play that has him go one-on-one with his man while we clear out of the way. He won a game against Indiana when he took "Dallas" to the hole in the final seconds.

Sometime during this 1991–92 season, a new feeling began to spread through the team. It had begun the year before, when we created that buzz around the league with our improved play. That buzz really grew with Larry in the lineup every night. People could see that the Hornets were putting something together. And we could see what was happening.

The front office was working hard, giving us some talent, searching for a winning combination. The first two years we had to hope a team didn't play well for us to win. During the third year, we could steal a game or two from a good team, but we also had games where we just had no chance to win. But by this fourth year, we felt we could win any night, against any team. Like I said before, it was building from "I hope we can" to "I think we can" to "I know we can."

Where do all these positive changes come from? They come from knowing what you want. They come from trying things and admitting mistakes and building to a goal. If there was a sad part to it all, it was admitting those mistakes. Because some things just didn't work out.

For every Larry Johnson, there was a guy like J. R. Reid. We just didn't get the maximum out of J.R. He came to us as the next Michael Jordan, according to some people. He was a fifth pick overall, and that carries a lot of pressure. They expected this Carolina boy to come in and do it all. But he had to make adjustments. Playing center at six-nine was a big adjustment. His first year he never got to play his true position, the four. His second year, he got to play more of the four, especially when we traded Armon Gilliam. But he still didn't produce the way everyone expected. I don't know why. He worked hard, but he wasn't consistent. Some players take four or five years to get where they want to be. It doesn't always happen in one year. No one knows that better than I do.

His third year, Larry came in and made a name for himself from day one. So J.R. didn't get the chance to prove himself that year, and he had the added pressure of being compared to Larry. He also got hurt and missed two months of action with a bad back. He came back in January, but by then the team knew he wasn't the "go-to" guy we all expected. Larry was. There were rumors that J.R. would be traded.

I tried to lift his spirits. I helped play a major practical joke on him. The idea came from Charles Barkley and Rick Mahorn in Philadelphia — they were playing jokes like this all over the league. What they did was, they got a local news crew to tape a phony news bulletin. They taped a regular TV show — I think it was "21 Jump Street" — and then cut in with a sportscaster saying, "We interrupt this show with a special report: J. R. Reid has been traded to the 76ers for Rick Mahorn." Then they had an interview with Charles about the trade, and Charles was saying all kinds of nasty things about it and about J.R. He was dissing J.R. like crazy, saying it was a terrible trade, there was no way J.R. could replace Mahorn. Charles really hammed it up — he's quite an actor.

They sent me this tape, and I put it in my VCR. At the same time, I had a video camera installed in my fireplace to tape J.R.'s reaction. When the time came, I invited him over to my house to watch "21 Jump Street," and turned on the tape instead of regular TV. It worked perfectly. It looked real, and sounded real, and J.R. believed it. He started running around the house, saying, "I've been traded! I can't believe it! I have to call my agent! I have to call my agent!"

But to make the gag last, I had already called the phone company, and they set things up so any call made from my phone got a busy signal. There was poor ol' J.R., trying to find out what was happening, unable to call anyone, getting more and more excited. He was so agitated that I couldn't hold out any longer and started laughing. The next day I brought the tape of him watching the show and running around my house into the locker room and showed it to everybody. J.R. took a lot of abuse, I'll tell you. And he was a pretty good sport about it.

I've pulled quite a few jokes in my time, but that one was probably the most elaborate. It took weeks to set up. I think it was the only one that ever turned out to be true, too. Early in the next season, he really was traded, to the San Antonio Spurs for Sidney Green and a first- and second-round draft choice.

Kelly Tripucka, one of the original Hornets, was another casualty that year. I think he had played his role well up to that point, but he wanted to be paid more money, and when Allan Bristow came in, he just didn't fit into their plans and was not re-signed before the season started. Kelly kind of wore out his welcome. There was a well-publicized incident that happened the previous year that told the story about Kelly. He was struggling on the court, and the fans were booing him. When the reporters asked him about it, he started crying — on TV! He said people shouldn't boo during the bad times if they cheer for the good times. The tape got picked up and played on ESPN. People around the league couldn't believe it. This guy is making a million dollars and he's crying about getting booed.

I know that his feeling came from his heart. Things were tough for him. He gave an all-out effort every night, and his game just wasn't together. But if you are struggling as a player, and the fans start booing, you can't get caught up in that. The fans can act however they want. You are getting paid to play, so go play. Don't worry about what the fans think. They have the right to boo. I didn't have any sympathy for Kelly.

I wasn't sad to see J.R. go — he became very bitter and unpleasant about his role on the team and really wanted out of Charlotte — and I didn't miss Kelly, either, since we were never close friends. But it was hard to see my boy Rex Chapman leave. He never got his game together in Charlotte, and in the middle of that fourth season, the team traded its first college draft choice ever, to Washington for Tom Hammonds.

I think Rex didn't understand the NBA game at that time. He didn't pick up the nuances as quickly as people thought he would, things like when to shoot, when to drive, how to be a factor. He came out of college eager and hungry, and wanted it to happen fast. But it didn't. Then he got hurt. Then the media started nagging him. He just never recovered from it. And he still is recovering a bit. The same things are happening to him in Washington. He's been hurt, and the media is even tougher there than in Charlotte. All he needs is some time to stay injury-free, and he'll be OK. He had a fine year last season, and one day Rex is going to put it all together and be a heck of a player. I know I am rooting for him.

In the middle of all these changes were Dell Curry and I. By the end of the fourth season, we were the last original Hornets left. It was stunning how fast all these changes were made. But it felt great, too.

All those players had come and gone because the team had a vision. And Dell and I were still in Charlotte. Each year, as we saw what was happening, we felt better and better. After all the talk over the years that we'd be the first to go, here we were the only two still here. Someone up in the front office knew that Dell and I were the heart and soul of the team.

I know that I hope to end my career in Charlotte. I can't see myself playing anywhere else. I certainly hope management feels the same way, because I will always love Charlotte. I know the fans are happy with me, because there was another practical joke, played on the team itself, and it really showed how the fans had taken to me.

On April Fools' Day a local radio disc jockey announced that the team had traded me. Immediately, the team started getting calls from everywhere. George Shinn says he got more calls that day than ever before or since. "I didn't take 99 percent of them," he says, "but some were from friends that I did take. They said, 'Have you lost your mind? I heard on the radio that you traded Muggsy. Are you crazy?' I told them it wasn't true. It really shook up a lot of folks."

I am very grateful that the fans like me so much. I think it is because I always give everything I have on the court, and because I am always available for good causes in the community. But the Hornets team president, Spencer Stolpen, thinks there is more to it. "To a certain extent Muggsy represents the Hornets to the rest of the world," he says. "The international popularity of the Hornets started before Larry and Alonzo were on board. Why is our merchandising number two in the league? It's partly because of the uniform and the colors, but also because we were the underdog in getting a franchise — the smallest of the eleven cities trying to get one. Here's poor little Charlotte, leading the league in attendance, and second in merchandising. Muggsy is the same thing. We shouldn't be in the NBA, we shouldn't be doing well. Muggsy Bogues shouldn't be in the NBA, he shouldn't be doing well. But we're doing it. He represents what Charlotte represents."

We went 8–6 in March of '92, putting us within striking distance of the playoffs. Under Allan, we became one of the feared teams in the league. He continued to play the passing-game, motion offense that Gene had installed, but he sped it up even more. That was fine with me. Our whole system is based on quickness and fast breaking, and when we are playing the way we are supposed to, I am my most effective. We are at our best in the transition game, and so am I. When you run, you cut down the impact of size. If you get big guys running, they get smaller, so to speak, because they spend more time and energy transporting themselves than being stationary and big. Only in the half-court game, when I have to slow down, do I become five-three. It's like in boxing. If Sugar Ray Leonard is moving, you can't hit him. If he is still for a few seconds — like in a half-court game — he'll get hit.

I started just about every game that year, and only Larry Johnson played more minutes than I did. I averaged 8.9 points per game, was among the league leaders in assists and steals, and led the league in assist-to-turnover ratio.

My game really came together because the coaching staff committed to me and my style of play. I felt like a leader on the team, in games and in practices. It was great that we were having success because of it.

We fell off in April, losing nine of our last eleven games, and we finished at 31–51. It was a solid five-game improvement over the previous year, which was good, but it didn't get us into the playoffs. That was both bad and good. The playoffs were a realistic goal that year, and we were truly disappointed to miss out. Everyone had us competing against Miami, the other expansion team that entered the league the same year we did, and they made the playoffs that year and we didn't. But we didn't feel too disappointed. We didn't want to be a team that went to the playoffs one year and then didn't go again the next. It was better that we didn't go. We gained more important things than the playoffs. We learned that we could win. We won in places we had never won before, like in San Antonio and in Utah, and that helped our self-confidence quite a bit. It made us even hungrier. Like I said earlier, each small step adds up to a pretty big stride.

Plus, by missing out on the playoffs, we returned to the draft lottery, which assured us of one of the top picks in the draft.

Once again, the lottery gods were smiling on us, because we drew the second pick overall. And once again I was thrilled. I knew we'd get the best center available, and maybe the best center in the last several years — Alonzo Mourning of Georgetown.

I had played a little against 'Zo in the summer leagues around Washington and Baltimore. We had some good runs at Georgetown. I knew his game. He had everything we needed: tenacity, intimidation, shot-blocking ability, meanness. Plus he could score from inside and outside; he had one of the sweetest J's for a big man I had ever seen. We couldn't have asked for a better fit or a better guy.

After the draft I began to look at our team in a different light. I saw 'Zo, Larry, Kendall, and myself starting, with Dell and Johnny Newman and Kenny Gattison all getting lots of minutes as well, and I thought to myself, "Man, all of a sudden, the Hornets are *something.*"

I knew we would make the playoffs the next year. I just knew it.

17

Triumph and Tragedy

I was so excited to come here, because I knew he'd get the best out of me. Muggsy Bogues is like a little Magic [Johnson]. He makes everyone else better.
— Alonzo Mourning

THE 1992 DRAFT HAD TWO of the best big men available in a long time: Shaquille O'Neal, from L.S.U., and Alonzo Mourning, from Georgetown. Shaq was probably better known than 'Zo. He was a loud, fun, boisterous guy in college, and had made a name for himself off the court as well as on. He was a great player, and a great guy to have for marketing purposes. 'Zo, on the other hand, had this reputation of being superserious, never smiling on the court, never having fun. People thought he was angry, or intimidating, or other negative things. He was a dominating center, everyone agreed, but he didn't have that fun-loving personality that Shaq had.

Everyone figured Shaquille would be drafted first. That's why I was so glad we got the second pick. Because 'Zo was the guy I wanted.

I knew him from summer league games in Washington. I saw him go against Patrick Ewing and Dikembe Mutombo every day during the summer. I knew what he could bring to the table. I saw the tools he had, tools other people didn't see in his college days because of the zone defenses he had to play against. I knew what he was capable of doing, especially his scoring talent.

In addition, he fit our plans and our team better than Shaquille did. 'Zo and Larry made a great center–power forward combination. They complemented each other perfectly. Shaq and Larry might have clashed. Their games are more similar, and they might have ended up competing against each other instead of helping each other.

After the draft, I talked to 'Zo on the phone, the same way I talked to Larry. I said, " 'Zo, I already got one rookie of the year for the L-ster, and I can carry you too, big fella. I got room on these small shoulders for both of you."

He didn't win it, though. Shaq had a great year and got a lot more publicity. But Alonzo could have won. I felt he deserved it. He stepped his game up and made the big difference in us making the playoffs. He was the exact piece we needed. We couldn't have ordered one from the factory any better.

Plus, people's perceptions of 'Zo as a person are all wrong. It is another example of how the media can distort a guy's image. On the court, he's got that hard face on all the time, and he keeps it on off the court sometimes, too, especially around people he doesn't know well. As a result, he's portrayed as this mean, hard guy, but he's actually one of the kindest people I have ever met. He just doesn't smile all the time. Me, I'm always smiling and laughing. 'Zo isn't that way. He needs to feel comfortable around people before he opens up. He shows himself slowly and carefully, to people he knows well. Once he knows you, he's a wonderful guy. You can't judge this book by its cover. People don't want to believe it, but 'Zo is a very happy fella.

'Zo is also a smart, well-spoken guy. He knows what he wants in life and goes at his own pace. He is well liked by everyone on the team. He and I are becoming close friends, and we talk a lot.

As I said earlier, it is crucial that guys on a team get along well. Only a rare team can be successful with guys fighting each other. More often, there has to be a sense of togetherness and respect among all the players, and I think our success in Charlotte comes from that. We have our occasional differences, of course, like any family, but all in all I don't think there are any deep problems like you hear about on a lot of other teams. We have players who know their positions, their roles, and are happy with them. No one has too big an ego, at least not bigger than anyone else's.

I am convinced that when everyone cares about one another, you perform better. You don't have people complaining, people loafing, not passing to certain guys. Here, everyone wants to win. We all cover each other's back. It makes us feel secure, like there is a shield around us.

Adding 'Zo made that shield so much stronger. He gave us a legitimate superstar in the middle. We had never had a true shot-blocking center before, and no defense is really complete without that. Just his presence in the paint makes teams think about what they are going to do. He alters all their plans, makes them think hard about every shot. He gets everything going in there. In the same way that I dictate the play on the outside, he dictates on the inside.

Now, for the 1992–93 season, we finally had all the ingredients. After five years, the Hornets had progressed from a collection of castoffs to a well-built, powerful team ready to contend for the playoffs for the first time. I don't have to tell you how excited everyone was to get to training camp. Especially Dell Curry and myself. After all the lows, we couldn't wait to experience the highs.

'Zo didn't come in until after the season started. They had to do some contract haggling to get him in under the salary cap. Several guys had their contracts restructured, including me — my third contract in five years. But that was OK. I deferred some money to be paid out later, meaning that my salary that year would be lower, but they extended my deal a few years and sweetened the pot overall a little, so I was happy. Heck, I might have given them some money back to help bring in 'Zo. (Don't tell my agent I said that!)

We got things rolling early that year. We won our season opener for the first time in our history, beating my old team, Washington. Larry had twenty-nine points and thirteen boards. Our third game was in Orlando against the team that had chosen Shaq first overall.

Shaq is a player, boy. He had thirty-five that night — partly because 'Zo wasn't with us yet. But we pulled out a 112–108 win. We lost our fourth game to go 2–2, and that's when 'Zo finally arrived. In one of his first games, he destroyed Golden State with thirty-four points and fourteen rebounds, and we came back from a twenty-one-point deficit to win in overtime, our biggest comeback win ever. 'Zo was such a presence, he even took out our own players. He knocked Dell in the head with an elbow and Dell needed eight stitches to close the wound.

That week, Johnny Newman broke a finger, and to replace him, we signed a free agent — my old Dunbar teammate David Wingate. The club asked me about 'Gate, and I gave him a great recommendation. I knew his defense off the bench would make a big difference for us down the stretch. And his offense came through, too. In his third game with us, the Sixers were so worried about 'Zo and Larry, they left David alone, and he scored twenty-three. We then beat Detroit in Detroit, for the first time, and won our fifth straight.

Next came some big games. We lost to Phoenix, when Dan Majerle hit a long three late in the game, and we lost to Utah when Larry went one-on-one with Karl Malone in the last seconds — the "Dallas" play — but his shot wouldn't fall. That was a wild game. Allan went crazy over a bad call and was thrown out of the game. He took his jacket off and threw it at the official, then kicked it onto the floor. We let him have it over that. We heard later that his wife was so mad at him for losing his cool, she made his daughters watch the replay of it on "SportsCenter," just so they could laugh at him and embarrass him. I thought that was really funny. Allan just thought the worst part of it all was that he had ruined a perfectly good sports coat.

Even though Allan's actions were comical, they said something about the Hornets. We were showing the league that we would not be intimidated by anyone, officials or players or opposing fans. We won a game against Detroit in which 'Zo and Bill Laimbeer, the Pistons' nastiest — or dirtiest, depending on who you ask — player, got into a big fight, and both got ejected. I loved seeing that. For years we had been pushed around, but with 'Zo in the middle, we now had that toughness you need to win. No one would push us around again.

We were 14–13 after the Christmas break, our best start in history, and we felt like we were ready to challenge the league's best. 'Zo was averaging eighteen points and ten rebounds a game, Larry was averaging twenty-seven and ten, and I was also averaging a double-double — twelve points and ten assists. I had a huge game in Washington against the Bullets, eighteen points, seventeen assists, and no turnovers, and I truly loved showing the Bullets management and fans what they had lost when I was let go. In fact, in the years since I had left, the Bullets had become aware that the one thing the team was missing most was a true point guard. To this day, they are still looking for someone to play the point.

We lost a game to the world champion Chicago Bulls — our seventeenth straight loss to them — but after the game their coach, Phil Jackson, had some good things to say: "They're really young. We're a much more experienced team. They have the speed, quickness, and resilience that comes with youth. Some ingredients must come with experience. They will get plenty this year and will be tough at playoff time."

Jackson was being prophetic. That experience came a few weeks later, when we finally beat his team, in Chicago, 105–97. Larry had nineteen rebounds, and 'Zo scored nineteen points and added fourteen boards and nine blocks. We then lost to the Lakers, to fall to 19–20. But we would never be under .500 again.

We won seven of the next ten games, and at the all-star break we were 26–23. Larry became the first Hornet to play in an all-star game, and we were all so happy for the big fella. He was the third-highest vote-getter on the East team. He played only sixteen minutes, the fewest of any starter, and there was some controversy about that. He said the next year he'd play more than sixteen minutes even if he had to check himself into the game. And who was gonna stop Big L.?

We came out of the break still hot, and won big games against New Jersey and San Antonio. It was important to beat playoff teams. It helped our confidence a lot knowing we could beat any team in the league.

We went on the road and won in the Boston Garden for the first time ever, as 'Zo had twenty-five and Larry got sixteen rebounds. Late in March we slumped, especially at home, and lost five in a row. We fell from fifth place to eighth overall in the conference, and were in danger of falling right out of the playoffs. When we lost a game to Atlanta that we had fought back hard to almost tie, we knew it was time to suck it up. Two nights later, Larry played a great game, to beat Philadelphia, with thirty-four points and fourteen rebounds. We lost to the Knicks in another close game — Patrick had seventeen points in the fourth quarter — but we knew we were capable of beating them. And then we beat Detroit, with 'Zo scoring thirty-six and a career high twenty-two rebounds.

'Zo and Larry really took charge in getting us into playoff mode. Larry became the first Hornet to record a triple-double, and he did it twice, in back-to-back games. 'Zo's numbers continued to improve, and he was averaging more than twenty-one points, eleven boards, and four blocks per game. He was going head to head with the best centers in the league — he and Shaq had a great night against each other. And I remember a game in New York, when he first went up against his friend Patrick Ewing. As Georgetown boys, they had been playing with and against each other every summer for a few years. We knew they were good friends and fierce competitors. We were all anxious to see what would happen.

They tore the house down. 'Zo had twenty-two points, seventeen rebounds, and six blocks. Patrick had twenty-eight points, nine boards, and three blocks. We beat them in OT as 'Zo held Patrick scoreless. That might have been the most important regular season game we played. People around the league really noticed our effort there, and started to see what we were capable of.

We could see what we were capable of, too. Inside the locker room, there was a real feeling that, hey, we can do this. We can not only make the playoffs, we can be a force. Winning really brought us closer together than ever. But we knew we couldn't count on other teams to get us in. We had to do it ourselves.

We went 6–3 in early April, and when we beat Milwaukee at the Hive, we clinched our first playoff spot.

When the last seconds of that game ticked off, I wanted to hold on to the game ball forever. I thought about Dell and myself as the two original Hornets, and everything we had been through. It was a feeling I can't really describe.

But there was still work to do. We won our last five games. The last home game was special, because we beat Chicago again, in a nationally televised game on TNT, at home in front of our 194th-straight sellout crowd. That really sent a message to the rest of the league. We were coming.

We finished at 44–38, our first winning season. And after both Atlanta and New Jersey lost their last games, we finished fifth in the conference, earning us a date with the Boston Celtics in the first round of the playoffs.

The playoffs are a whole different thing. It takes so much strength to handle the stress and strain. Every possession is important. You need total mental focus. I even felt nervous for the first time. I had been in the playoffs with Washington, but I wasn't playing at all. This felt like my first trip. It really was the first time for all of us, and we were all so pumped up. Our first goal was to make the playoffs. Now we wanted to make some noise.

We fought hard for the fifth seed so we could get to play Boston. We knew we could take them. We were only 1–3 against the Celtics that year, but we were in all the games, and we beat them in Boston at the end of the season. We felt we matched up with them better than with any team. They were older and slower than we were, and we thought we could harass them into making mistakes. We could outrun them, and with Larry and 'Zo we could outmuscle them. They were the best team for us to play.

Before the series began, the team moved into a training facility out of town, to be away from family, friends, and all outside distractions. Some people thought that was a bit excessive, but I thought it was a good thing to do. It's not that I wanted to get away from my three small children and leave them with my wife — I know that was hard on her — I just thought it would be good for us to focus totally on the task at hand.

We did a lot of film study. The team broke down into guard meetings and big-men meetings. All teams do that. You have to specialize like that because you are playing a team for three to five games. You have to know everything about your opponent. You go over each player step by step and play by play. I knew their guards inside out. I could tell you what Sherman Douglas ate for breakfast.

Stepping onto the parquet floor in Boston Garden for that first game was a tremendous feeling. I was totally into the game, so I tried not to get involved with the emotion, but you could feel it. And it was an extra-special feeling for me, because here on the floor were three Dunbar guys reuniting in the NBA playoffs. 'Gate and Reggie Lewis and I all had a special feeling about that. It was big. 'Gate and I always teased Larry Johnson about our high school team and how many people we got in the league. To see three people from the neighborhood we grew up in, just to make it in the NBA, and then make it to the playoffs together, to do something we had dreamed about together as kids, was a great feeling.

But it wasn't all sentimental. The competition among us was fierce. We all would be going back to Baltimore at some point, and somebody was going to have bragging rights. We all knew that something would be said, I promise you that. The loser would have to pay.

We knew each other's moves so well we didn't have to study

film. I knew all of Truck's moves, where he liked to score from, where he liked to receive the ball. I knew that to stop him we'd have to make him work constantly and tire him out.

Wingate was the same way. He saw Reggie every day, every summer, for a long, long time. But we both knew that Reggie had improved tremendously over the years. "Sometimes he's almost unstoppable," Wingate said.

Reggie knew me as well. "Muggsy's doing the same things he's always done," he told the media. "He pushes the ball as fast as he can. He goes to the hole, looks like he's driving, but I know he's going to pass. I always play him to pass."

We knew it would be a great competition for us all. Tragically, it never came to pass. Just five minutes into the first game, Reggie fell to the floor. I didn't even see it happen. Time was called, and his teammates helped him to the bench. No one knew what had happened, if he had tripped, or was bumped, or what. He looked a little dizzy to me, but it didn't seem that serious. I saw him on the bench later, and saw that he was with all his team's doctors, taking precautions, so I wasn't too concerned.

But seeing it on film later that night scared me. I was thinking, "It's Hank Gathers, all over again." Gathers was the college player who collapsed and died on the court from a heart problem. But Reggie had no history of that as far as I knew. He played a little more in the second half of that game, but still seemed wobbly, so they pulled him out. He didn't play in the next game, in Boston. When we came back to Charlotte he didn't make the trip, but I talked to his mother-in-law and she said he was going to be tested. I tried to check in with him to make sure that he was all right, but I never got through to him. At the time, I wasn't concerned about that. I figured he'd be tested and treated, and we'd be playing ball together again soon.

In the meantime, we had our hands full with the rest of his teammates. In the first game of the series, we were tied at the half, but Boston went on a 30–18 run and took the game from us. They won, 112–101.

We weren't worried, though. We had played poorly, and they were beating us with one particular play, a screen and roll for Sherman Douglas that they were very successful with. We knew that in the next game we would have to adjust our rotation to cut that down and make them try other options. That helped a lot.

So did the support we got back home. Even though we had lost our first-ever playoff game, no one got down. We could see the atmosphere around the organization, and the city. They almost didn't care if we advanced, they were happy just to be in the playoffs. We heard that the streets of Charlotte were almost empty while our game was on television. There was so much praise from everyone, we felt we owed it to them to play even harder.

Rumors about Reggie were already circulating around game two, that he had a heart problem and that he never should have played at all in the second half of game one. But it was still mostly a mystery to everyone. There was a lot of conflicting news. I couldn't let it bother me. We continued to focus on the game.

The second game was wild. There were seventeen lead changes and nineteen ties. Kevin McHale, the Celtics thirty-five-year-old veteran who was retiring after the season, had thirty points and ten boards in what would be his last game in Boston. But Larry Johnson came back from an off game and held Boston's Xavier McDaniel, who scored twenty-one in game one, in check; and he scored twenty-three for us. 'Zo had a monster game, with eighteen points, fourteen rebounds and six blocks before fouling out in overtime. And our defensive changes helped shut down Douglas. The game went to double overtime, and in the second OT we held them without a single bucket. L.J. scored early in the OT, and that was enough to win, 99–98.

Back at the Hive for game three, Dell Curry went wild, with nineteen points in the first half. We went on a 15–0 run, and he hit two big threes, to go from 35–34 to 50–34. L.J. took over in the second with twenty-nine more, and we really started to take advantage of our speed and youth. We had a ton of steals and basically drove them all nuts.

I had Sherman Douglas so tied up that he totally lost concentration on the clock. He was twisting and bobbing and going through his legs, and he got his mind totally off the clock. They got called for a ten-second violation. (Offensive teams have to get the ball past the mid-court line within ten seconds, or they turn the ball over.) Alonzo couldn't believe that: "I had *never* seen a ten-second call in the NBA before that. It *never* happens. It was like Muggsy just wouldn't let him get the ball up court. It was incredible." It was after this series that Sherman said I was so annoying, he wanted to slap me. That let me know I was playing my game to perfection. That was the best compliment he could have paid me.

We crushed them, 119–89, a huge margin for a playoff game, the third-worst in Boston's history.

The crowd was wild. The intensity in Boston was great, but the Hive was truly alive that night. We were up two games to one, with a chance to clinch the series at home. We knew we had to do it now. We sure didn't want to go back to Boston for a fifth and deciding game on their court. Allan warned us about getting overconfident, but he didn't have to worry.

In game four we played great for three quarters, and led 88–70. But we relaxed, the worst thing we could have done, and — creep, creep, creep — suddenly they were back in it. When Sherman Douglas made a steal and layup with less than a minute left in the game, they actually went ahead, 103–102. The nerves were on edge, boy. We just couldn't let this game get away. It would have been devastating. Going back to Boston for game five would have been a tremendous challenge — they would have had a huge advantage.

It came down to the final 3.3 seconds, and we had the ball under their basket. We had a play called to get the ball to our best shooter, Dell Curry, but the Celtics anticipated that and had Dell covered tight. Dell got the ball to 'Zo near the top of the key. He dribbled once, saw that he was open, and then let go a twenty-footer as the clock expired.

When it went in, the whole building exploded.

We all went absolutely crazy when 'Zo hit the shot. We piled on him in the center of the court, and the fans all rushed out. I thought I was going to be smothered under that pile. The feeling was unbelievable for everyone, for the city, the franchise, the players, the fans.

It was amazing — that one shot made the ESPN Espy Awards as the shot of the year. It was typical of 'Zo, though. The big fella had been everything we had wanted as a rookie, and he was leading us deeper into the playoffs.

It was on to New York. Madison Square Garden. All the stars were in the front row — John McEnroe, Spike Lee, Bill Cosby, all the actors and actresses. It really felt like a playoff atmosphere there. It felt like we were going for the title.

The Knicks were heavy favorites, but we still felt like we could win. Counting the end of the regular season, we had won eight of our last nine games. We knew we had to come at them aggressively from the opening tip.

We had them, too. We were up by ten in the second half, but in the fourth quarter they held us to only fifteen points while they scored thirty-one. They won the opener easily, 111–95. It ended up being the only game that wasn't decided in the final minutes.

Game two was close until we went on a 29–9 run and led by thirteen with less than seven minutes left. But again we couldn't hold the lead, and they came back. Patrick was huge, and Hubert Davis hit a key three to tie the game and send it to overtime. They beat us by four, 105–101.

It hurt going down 2–0, but we had played them so well, we felt we could just as easily have been up 2–0. Especially in the second game, which was a tough, hard-fought game, as exciting as a playoff game can be. "It was just an incredible, incredible game," said Pat Riley, the Knicks' coach. "I've been in a hundred and fifty, two hundred playoff games and I don't think I've ever been in a game like that."

Game three was my show. Back at the Hive, we won in double OT 110–106, our second double-overtime of the playoffs. We were down by six with four minutes left. I made three key steals, hit a basket with fifty-three seconds left to take the lead, then made two free throws at the end to ice it.

I finished that game with sixteen points, eight assists, and five steals. The steals were the key part. I had gotten under Doc Rivers's skin, and had him so worried, I felt I could take the apple from him almost anytime I wanted.

I was the hero of game three, but I was the goat of game four. We were down by fifteen but came back to tie it in the final minute. Rolando Blackman hit a J from twenty feet, and the score was 94–92.

Down by one with 5.4 seconds left, I had the ball and an open lane to the basket. I saw an opening and drove the lane, catching everyone by surprise. But as I flew toward the iron, the ball got away from me. No one touched it. No one hit me. I just lost control. I turned it over. New York ran out the clock, the game, and as it turned out, the series.

A lot of the guys were down after that loss, myself included. I had just won a game with the biggest shot of my life, and now I had lost one on the worst turnover of my life. I took full responsibility, and told the media I simply lost it. I believe that if you are going to accept being a hero, you also have to accept being a goat. A lot of players duck out of the locker room after a loss or a poor performance, so they won't have to talk to the media. I think that is wrong. Players who hide are not being true to themselves.

But even though we were down, we came back the next day convinced we could still win. We felt we had given two games away, and could have been up 3–1 instead of down 3–1. Three of the games had been incredibly close. We needed to stay close in game five as well.

And we did. Game five went down to the wire, until John Starks took over and scored seven points in the last 1:15 to win it for them, 105–101.

Of course we were pretty depressed, but we had a lot to be proud of. We had a great run, the best record in the franchise's history, and our first trip to the playoffs. We'd knocked off the famous Boston Celtics in the first round. And we'd played a tough New York Knicks team — a team many thought had a good chance to challenge Chicago and make it to the finals — and stayed close, giving them everything they could handle.

"They pushed us to the limit," Doc Rivers said after the series. "They just wouldn't go away. Muggsy is such a little pest, Mourning and Johnson are such forces. You have to take your hat off to that team. Boy, in another two or three years, forget it."

It was nice to get our "propers," but still, we all hate to lose. Me as much as anyone. They were a well-coached, veteran team, and they deserved to win. Maybe our inexperience had something to do with it. Hey, they got the job done and we didn't.

Even though we lost, we had to count the whole experience as positive. In fact, those two playoff series probably got the Hornets and me more notice than anything else during all my years in the league. I really learned how important the playoffs are in terms of attention being paid to your game. I had been doing the same kinds of things for years during the regular season, but people just weren't watching as closely, I guess. At least not in the big media centers like New York and Boston.

To this day I still watch tapes of those playoff games. The whole season was special. When we didn't make the playoffs the year before, we felt disappointed. I remember the last game in Minnesota that year, everyone feeling sad that we were finished, but determined to get going the next year. We had set the stage to make the playoffs that fifth year, and we did it. Things were running their course. All the changes and acquisitions over the years were paying off. A big load had been lifted from our shoulders. And the whole city was proud of us — Hornet fever stretched for hundreds of miles.

Win or lose, the fans of Charlotte still loved us. And when they threw us a parade a few days after losing to the Knicks, twenty-five thousand people lined the streets to see us drive past in open convertibles. And they went crazy. We got into it as well. Mike Gminski had on shades and a Hawaiian shirt, and slicked-back hair like Knicks coach Pat Riley. Sidney Green hollered, "What's up, fellas," every time someone yelled his name. People were throwing hats and shirts at them to sign.

When I drove by, people in the crowd rushed my car, patting me and shaking my hand and asking for my autograph. My car had to stop for all the people, and fell behind the rest of the parade.

That's when I heard this big woman screaming. She was the craziest. The whole crowd was crazy, but above it all, I could hear her the loudest.

"I got my Muggsy! I got my Muggsy!" she shouted, dancing in the street after I gave her an autograph. "You can have the rest of 'em, long as I got my Muggsy!"

We all went up on a stage, and I was selected to talk to the crowd. I basically told them we were disappointed because we weren't playing anymore. But we looked back and saw what we had accomplished, and accepted that we had a higher goal to reach the next year. We had a hell of a season, and felt good about that. "There are going to be some great times in the Hornets future," I said.

We were ready to go home and have a good summer, and come back better than ever in 1993–94.

But my summer was a nightmare.

On July 29, 1993, I learned that Reggie Lewis had died.

Reggie's passing was like a punch in my gut. I still can't believe he is gone. The day he died was one of the most emotional days of my life. I was scheduled to be speaking to some kids at a summer camp in Tennessee, and I had just flown into town and checked into the hotel around 10:30 at night. I had been traveling all day, but for some reason I was feeling really good, and I called Kim to see how everyone was doing. I was all chatty, but she cut me off.

"Have you heard?" she asked.

"Heard what?"

"Reggie has passed," she said.

I was totally destroyed. I cried into the phone with her for a long time. Here I was, stuck in this hotel a long way from home, all alone. I couldn't sleep. I didn't know what to do. I called a lot of people, just to talk. I called Coach Wade. Kim had phoned him before I had checked in with her. She was worried that I'd hear the news over the television or from some stranger, and she told Mr. Wade to have me call home if he heard from me first. She was really worried about me.

Coach Wade and I stayed on the phone a long time. I broke down a lot, but Coach Wade let me get it out. When I needed some help, he was there for me. I just cried and cried.

"It's not true, Coach. It's not true."

"Yes, it's true, little fella."

"I thought he was cleared by the doctors. I thought he was OK. What's going on?"

"They say he was in a gym just shooting around and he passed out."

"Shooting around? But the doctors said he was all right. How can this be?"

"I don't know. I don't know."

"Why, Coach? Why? He's so young. He's got a family. It's not fair."

We'd talk, and I'd lose it, then we'd just be quiet for a while. Then I'd lose it again. We talked for hours. I called Kim again, three or four times. Everything rushed at me; Reggie's wife, his child — and another one on the way — it was so heavy for me.

I went to the camp the next day, but it was so hard. I broke down all over again. I explained to the kids what had happened, and they were very understanding. But I couldn't wait to get on the plane and come home.

It was so frustrating because I never got the chance to tell him what he meant to me. From the time he had collapsed in the playoff game against us up until his passing, I hadn't had the opportunity to talk to Reggie. I tried a few times, but he was busy with his doctors. I had talked to his wife and family, and they had all been very positive. And then all the news seemed to be good, that his problem wasn't that serious and that he was getting great treatment. So I didn't press to talk to him, because I figured we'd have lots of time to get together. His death was such a surprise. Like everyone else, I just never expected it.

When we had our first preseason game in Boston after his passing, in the fall of '93, it was tough for me to play. I was doing fine during the warmups, getting loose and ready to play, not thinking about anything but the game. Then, just before we took the court for the tip, it hit me. I looked over at the Celtics bench and he wasn't there. It just wasn't right. We had come into the league together. To me, he *was* the Boston Celtics. He was always there. And now I didn't see him.

I broke down and cried all over. I couldn't believe Reg wasn't there. My Charlotte teammates knew what was happening to me and they were all great. They helped me a lot. I said a little prayer on the bench that night, and I do it now every time I play in Boston.

I took the court that night with red eyes and wet cheeks. But I also had a little smile on my face, because I knew Reg was looking down on me from a better place. I know I'll have those feelings every time I play in Boston. I'll feel a lot of sadness, but I'll feel a lot of joy as well. This is my commitment to him, to tell him how much I miss him and wish he was here, and also to let him know I love him and cherish the times we had together.

The summer went from bad to worse. Three days after Reggie's funeral, my father and Kim's uncle both passed away on the same day.

Kim and I were just numb. We had been through a lot of tough times, but nothing like this. Three people that we were so close to, all dead in the same week.

As tough as losing Reggie was, losing my father was even tougher. I had been trying to help him out over the years. After he got out of prison, he struggled to stay straight. I had given him some money and done whatever I could, but I guess he couldn't get himself off the street. His health had slipped — I am not sure, but he was probably using drugs — and he had spent some weeks with pneumonia in a hospital. The street life caught up with him, and it killed him.

I was so sad, because I had really tried to get close to Pops. I accepted him, even for the things he did that were wrong. We had our rough moments when I was younger, but I have no regrets about our relationship, or the things he did. He lived life the best way he could, and even though he made mistakes, he always kept his kids straight. In fact, in the hospital just before he died, he had told my brothers how proud he was of all of us, that all his kids had stayed straight and clean, that we had escaped the streets.

I will always remember the good things about Pops. He was my friend. He was a man with dignity and principles, and no one can tell me he wasn't.

At his funeral, people were called up to say a few things about my father. Most of the people were talking about the Lord, and salvation, and I got the sense that most of them didn't really know me or my dad. After five or six of these people, I walked up and tried to tell the truth about Pops. I talked about how he wasn't the perfect father, but we never went hungry growing up in the projects; that my mother, even when he was in prison, was always faithful to him; that even though he was a person of the streets he never let his family go without. I made a commitment to my father that I was stepping in and that I would take care of the family in his name. I was quite emotional, as you can imagine, and everyone had tears in their eyes, including me. But it was something I felt I had to say.

I miss my Pops tremendously. We kind of took our love for granted in my family. My Pops was there for me in his own way, but it wasn't a very open or affectionate love. I know better now. I try to tell my kids I love them all the time, to be more affectionate. I want to be there for them, too.

I am still stunned that a year that was so satisfying professionally became so devastating personally. When things like that happen, you really straighten up your priorities. I mean, basketball means the world to me. But that summer I learned that other things are much more important. I don't think I'll ever forget that again.

CHAPTER 18

Leading My Troops

Muggsy is the only player I clapped for when he came out of the game. I try not to be a fan when I come to a game, but Muggsy makes me a fan.
— John Thompson, Georgetown coach

IN 1993–94, EXPECTATIONS FOR US were really high. Our own were the highest of all. Coming from a successful first appearance in the playoffs, we believed in ourselves. We were not overconfident, but we knew we had a chance to win it all. Some writers even predicted that we'd win the Eastern Conference.

But things happened that just were beyond our control. We were devastated by injuries. Larry was hurt over the summer, and 'Zo went through training camp with a sore knee. Even though they played the preseason at less than 100 percent, they were still an asset to the team. We felt like we were on top of things, but then all hell broke loose.

'Zo went down with a torn muscle in his calf. Then Larry went down with a slipped disk. We still played above .500. Then three more guys, key role guys, also got forced out of the lineup. Scott Burrell hurt his Achilles tendon, and LeRon Ellis got mononucleosis. Then Kenny Gattison got the flu. That was five guys — almost half the team — out of the lineup. I had never been through anything like this. We couldn't play and we couldn't practice. It was frustrating as heck.

We got Marty Conlon from the CBA, and picked up free agent Tim Kempton. They did a good job, but we just didn't have enough to win. We tried to hold our own on the perimeter with our jump shooters, but our inside game was devastated. We lost eight in a row. We knew we were better than the teams we were losing to, but when you are outmanned there is nothing you can do.

We never got down. I tried to keep the guys loose, to help them to understand what was happening to us. I really tried to hold the team together, to maintain a good, positive attitude. I tried to stress that at least we had a light at the end of the tunnel, there were reasons we were struggling, we knew it was not our fault. As Allan Bristow told us, "The healthy don't have to suffer for the sick."

But we did suffer. The lowest point came when we lost to Dallas, at home. Not to put the Mavericks down, they played well that night, but they had the worst record in the league. They were just not at our level. We had only eight guys in uniform. I was pissed off mostly because teams could take us for granted, like they did during our first years in Charlotte. I think that was rock bottom. We had to turn things around.

I called a team meeting during the losing streak. I am the captain, so I have to know when things are getting out of control. After practice one day, I called everyone into the locker room. I said we needed to get our act together. We needed to rotate quicker, needed to rebound more aggressively, had to get back on defense faster. We couldn't be tentative, couldn't be afraid to make mistakes. We needed to play the game hard for forty-eight minutes. We needed to take care of ourselves, our game, and not worry about the other teams. We just had to do what we were capable of, and things would take care of themselves.

Everyone talked a little to get out frustrations. We had worked so hard to turn things around, and now it felt like the early days. I knew that shouldn't be true. I knew what expansion felt like, and this wasn't like that at all. Back then there was no solution to our problem. We were bad, and there was nothing else to do about it. But there was a solution now. We just had to look at our bench — we had more talent dressed in expensive suits than in uniforms. We had to remember that they would be back eventually. In the meantime, you can't lose your confidence, can't get down on yourself. If you do, it will just be tougher when the big guys do come back. Confidence is not like a light switch, you can't just turn it on and off. It's a routine you have to be in. When you feel good, good things will happen. If you feel bad, if you are in a zone where nothing good can happen, then you will fail.

The meeting definitely helped. Open communication always helps. I've learned that more and more the longer I've been in the league. I guess that is what being a veteran is all about. I think I am really learning what it takes to win in the NBA.

I tried to keep everyone motivated. Practices were especially tough, because we just didn't have enough healthy guys to get in the proper work. I really had to work to get everyone involved mentally. The guys look to me to lead practices. "When he's into it in our practices, he elevates everybody," Coach Bristow says. "He really can make a difference. Our practices are not nearly as good without him — and his energy. He pumps up guys, Larry more than anybody."

We kept loose, went out and performed well, played the game hard, and when the big fellas came back, we played like a contender again.

We also continued to have fun, which was important. It's tough to enjoy things when you are losing, but I manage — especially with the big fellas. Larry and I were wrestling in the hotel in Boston, and we were scaring everybody. Little old ladies wouldn't get in the elevator with us. They thought we were seriously fighting. Larry was trying to get up under me but I am so low to the ground he couldn't put me down. We went at it for an hour, and all the fellas came out to watch. I've wrestled everyone on the team, and no one can beat me. With Larry, it was called a draw.

Unfortunately, we had dug ourselves too big a hole and we couldn't recover. Before 'Zo returned in a game against Phoenix, we had lost sixteen of seventeen. When both Larry and 'Zo were out, we had a 5–16 record. With them both in the lineup, we were well over .500, and almost made the playoffs. That tells you all you need to know about how important the big fellas are. We made a great run after they came back.

And that brings me to a point I need to make. I need to talk about Larry.

At the beginning of the season, when he was struggling, a lot of fans got down on L.J. He was going through some stretches where he was only scoring four or six points per game. He wasn't playing well, because he was hurting. But because he had just signed his big contract, people jumped all over him.

It was not fair. A person is the same after he signs a contract as before. He is the same guy who went out and scored the only triple-doubles in Charlotte history, the same guy who scored twenty-five to thirty points a night and grabbed all those rebounds. He was still doing things to help the club, even when he shouldn't have been playing at all. His presence means so much to us, even if he's not in perfect health. Other teams play us differently when he's in the lineup. He makes things happen.

He could have sat out until he was at 100 percent, but he chose to come back and do whatever he could. He did it for the team's sake, he came to play when he could have been sitting comfortably in a nice suit on the bench. Still, people criticized him because he was making so much money.

Shoot, the Hornets got a *deal* by signing him to that contract. In the years to come, when he is healthy, the fans will see that I am right. They got a great deal. He is one of the greatest players I have ever seen in my life. His emotion, his love for the game, makes us so much better as a team. His stats may have been low, but he did so much for us — not in the box score but in our hearts. He helped us be successful early in the year.

The injury was something he'd never experienced before. Basketball is all about feeling good. If you feel good you can give your best performance. When your body isn't right, you can't perform. People forget how physical our job is. They didn't give him the benefit of the doubt. But he'll be back, he'll be the L.J. of old and everyone will jump back on the bandwagon.

He shouldn't have had to go through that kind of abuse. It was so sad. He didn't complain about it publicly — he was no Kelly Tripucka crying in front of the cameras — but we talked about it a lot. I told him not to worry about the fans, the organization, the media, the contract, or anything else. I said, "Just get healthy, feel good about yourself. Look for a long, happy life, not a two-year career. Look out for Larry. No one knows how you feel but you. Don't come back just because we are playing lousy. We all know you want to come back and help. But don't come back until you are ready. Especially mentally. Don't do it for the fans, for management, or for your teammates. Do it for you."

I tried to help him the way Moses Malone had helped me in Washington, by being a big brother of sorts. A lot of people were talking to Larry, trying to tell him what was wrong with his game, but he shut them all up. Larry said, "Look, I only listen to a few people, and one of them is Muggsy. Only these guys can tell me what to do, and what I am doing wrong."

I was sidelined a few games myself with a bad hamstring, and when I was on the bench I tried to act like a conductor, telling Larry where to go, what to do, as if I was the point guard in the game. Larry knows that I really understand his game, and he listens to what I say. And Larry had his best game to that point.

It was remarkable what Larry did last year in the face of such pressure. With the pain he was in he had to be careful. It was killing him to sit out and watch us lose. 'Zo was the same way. I love the big fellas to death. Their desire, their relentlessness, their competitiveness, their determination, their love of the game. They both deserve every penny they make.

'Zo is by far the best center I have ever seen. *By far.* Oh, man, his drive to win — he is a warrior. He has all the tools — left-handed hook, right-handed hook, outside jump shot, power moves inside, he runs the floor, he dribbles — he can do it all. And he still has room to grow. He is only twenty-four. Man, his talent is scary.

I would gladly go off to war with those guys. They love winning, and I love people who love winning.

We knew that even if we didn't make the playoffs, it wouldn't be the worst thing to happen to us. We knew why we were losing. Just to be in the hunt for the playoffs after what we had been through was saying a lot. To have L.J. out for thirty-one games, and 'Zo out for fifteen, and still be a decent team, is something. Not many teams could lose their two best players, their two big men, and stay competitive. At least we were competitive during that stretch.

We got back into our game by stressing defense. We have been known as a fast-break offensive team, but we always played tough D too. We also tried just about everything offensively to get us going, including gimmick plays. One time we had me post up Mark Price, and I got the ball down low. Their defense didn't know what to do — you could see them thinking, Should we help out? I moved across the lane and took the shot. I don't remember if it went in, but at halftime Bill Hanzlik, one of our assistant coaches, said, "Hey Muggs, I kind of like that play where we got it to you inside. They don't know what to do." I looked at him dead serious and said, "Did you see the big fella come down and double-team me?" I felt for a minute like I was Larry Johnson or something.

We even tried an isolation play for me. Larry has his "Dallas" play, and now the coaches drew up a "Wake Forest" play, where I get the ball up high, everyone else is down at the baseline, and I run time off the clock until I get a shot. We called it against the Knicks, and I scored. They called a time-out, and I came back to the bench totally geeked. I hadn't had a play like that called for me since college. I was yelling, "Good play, Coach! Let's go to it more often!"

I enjoyed being the "go-to guy" for a few games, but I know our real go-to guys are Larry and 'Zo. I'm the one who gets it to them, then they go to it. Things turned around immediately when 'Zo returned. We beat Phoenix his first game back. We won that game with defense. The confidence of all the other players rose with 'Zo back in the middle. You could see it in everyone's eyes. While he was sidelined, other teams had just been walking down the middle and laying the ball in. They had no fear of getting their shots blocked. Now it was a different story. 'Zo changes everyone's strategy, including ours. I can start to gamble a little more, go for steals, because I know 'Zo is there to cover my back. In one game late in the season, we were playing Boston, and we needed a steal at the end of the game to get a chance to win. Dee Brown was bringing the ball up for the Celtics, and I just told him, "I'm gonna take that." And I did. I could take the chance because of 'Zo.

We finished the season strong, and even though we fell short of making the playoffs, the good finish let us know we were still a playoff-caliber team. I think we are even better than the team that did go to the playoffs in 1992–93. Before the season started we made two key acquisitions in Hersey Hawkins and Eddie Johnson. And we made a key subtraction by trading Kendall Gill.

Kendall had surprised everyone when he said he was unhappy in Charlotte, and he demanded to be traded. We all thought Kendall was happy. He was a key part of our success, and I liked playing with him in the backcourt. When he started complaining that I was passing to other players more than to him, I was shocked.

Back in the chapter on how I play the game, I told you that the point guard's job is to distribute the ball. Kendall thought I wasn't giving him the ball as much as I was Larry Johnson or Alonzo Mourning. That's ridiculous. If you looked at the stats, Kendall was getting plenty of shots. He had over one thousand that year, which is quite a lot. Larry and 'Zo got a few more, but it wasn't because I was disrespecting Kendall. If I have a choice between a Cadillac and a Volkswagen on the break, I'm going to give it to my Cadillac. That's just how the game is played. Not everyone understands that. Kendall didn't. It was not because I don't like Kendall; I always liked him, and still do. It just makes basketball sense to give the ball to the strongest finisher. It's an easy bucket for him, an easy assist for me, and two points for the team. That's just smart thinking.

The controversy about Kendall was a surprise, but it was resolved when Hersey and Eddie came in, and he was shipped to Seattle. Both Hersey and Eddie really helped carry the team while Larry and 'Zo were hurt, and both became fan favorites for working so hard during the tough times.

As I look at our lineup now, I think we have the best personnel we've ever had. Because of all the injuries, it still remains to be seen how good we really are. We haven't all been able to play together enough. A lot of teams have been together for many years, and they know each other's games well, what everyone is capable of. That is where team chemistry comes from. Our run at the end of the 1993–94 season sure makes me optimistic, though. We have the talent, and when we get the time together, the chemistry, we could be very special.

I'll say it right now: the Charlotte Hornets will be back, and better than ever. And I'll be at the point, leading my troops.

Role Model

*He's one of the most accessible guys on the team. You don't
hesitate in picking up the phone and calling him for a favor. He
cares. He understands the responsibility of being who he is.*
— Spencer Stolpen, president of the Charlotte Hornets

I AM A ROLE MODEL.

A lot of celebrities speak on the role model issue. A few years
ago, Charles Barkley said his thing — he told kids to let their
parents be role models, instead of athletes or musicians or other
celebrities. That's a good point. I don't disagree with that. Besides,
Charles does a lot for kids, he respects kids, he only wants kids to
get what's best for them. He was just being honest. Maybe what he
said just came out wrong, or was misunderstood. But when he said
he was not a role model, I think he was wrong. The fact is, we are
all looked upon as role models. He is a role model, so am I. With all
due respect to Charles Barkley, professional athletes are role models
whether we want to be or not.

And there's nothing wrong with it. I think of it as an honor. I
always go back to my hometown of Baltimore, to my roots, to try
to give the kids something to hope for. If you're doing good, positive
things, living a good life, and if someone can pick up on that and
get something out of it, that's great. Kids need a model. If they see
how one person has done it, it gives them hope.

If children can see the way I live my life and get something positive, get some self-confidence so that they can go out into the world and try to do something they might otherwise be afraid of trying, that can only help them. If they see someone who beat the odds, who took a challenge head-on without worrying what other people thought, and just did it because he believed in himself, it might give them the idea that they can do the same thing. It gives them a chance, and they can say, At least I tried to accomplish my dreams, and I did not give up.

I am all for that. I sure know that my role models helped me in that way. Friends like Dwayne Wood and Reggie Williams and Moses Malone and Dell Curry, coaches like Mr. Howard and Mr. Wade, and my parents and brothers and sister all showed me a model to follow. Without them I wouldn't be where I am today. If I can motivate people to try to make their life better, I am proud to be a role model for that. I'll wish you well. Don't shortchange your life. Don't shortchange what you want to become.

I especially want kids to be happy, and to have an opportunity to try to make their dreams come true like I did. We all have dreams, big dreams and small dreams, even dreams that we don't think are realistic. But you never know until you try. If you don't try, you'll never find out. I say, Take a chance. If you fail, that's all right. Success comes with failure. Everyone who became successful, at some time or another has failed. I have certainly had my failures, my disappointments. That's when you really appreciate success. You know what it takes to get there and to sustain it.

Sometimes my own success hits me. I can be doing anything, it might be the most irrelevant thing, and it hits me. A lot of people look up to me, respect me. I'm doing something no one expected me to do.

It really struck me recently, when the Charlotte public bus company did a promotion and painted the pictures of Larry Johnson, Alonzo Mourning, Hugo the Hornet, and me on city buses. When I saw my face on the bus, I was shocked. That was something. That was a first — a huge bus with Muggsy on it rolling down the street. That really touched me, that people would be riding "my" bus. I mean, I used to ride the bus all the time back in Baltimore. I rode the MTA to school, to friends' houses, to my grandmother's house. You put your money in the box, you got your transfer ticket, off you went. To see people, especially kids, climbing onto the Muggsy bus really affected me. That was wild.

When things like that hit me, I try to let it go quickly. I try not to dwell on it. I don't want to sit down and think, Muggsy, look at what you've done. I know it is there in the back of my mind, but I don't let it come out, because that's when I let my guard down. When I am away from the game, maybe I can sit down and say, Gosh, I really did some things. But I can't afford to do that now. I'll become comfortable, and that's dangerous. That's when you become your own worst enemy. When you become comfortable and relaxed, bad habits creep into your performance. You can't be thinking too much about the past, the history. You have to concentrate on the present. Focus is important, no matter what you are trying to accomplish, whether it is in sports or education or work. The past is past. You can reminisce later. If you can't perform now, then you are history yourself.

I think I have a good grasp on difficult situations, and how to make the right decisions and to stand by those decisions. I have always tried not to let anyone else dictate what I should be or do. I don't think anyone should dictate your life, because if you do, I don't think you'll find the gratification, the satisfaction, you're looking for. Plus, you won't feel responsible for the things that have taken place in your life. You will feel that someone else has led you to things you might not have been too sure about. By making your own decisions, you get the life *you* want.

I constantly teach that to my own kids. I make sure they understand that I am going to be with them no matter what, to encourage them and help them and guide them to the things they want. But I am also going to make sure they understand that they have their own identity and that they shouldn't be afraid to make their own decisions. After all, it could be the right decision. And if not, you live by that and learn from it, and make better decisions in the future.

My three kids have been the best thing to happen to me in my life. The whole family experience has worked out better than I ever thought. We have a pretty big household now — we went from one child to three almost overnight, with the birth of little Ty and with Tyisha coming to live with Kim, Brittney, and me — but I truly love being able to spend time at home. I don't have as much time as I'd like for that. The travel in the NBA is constant, and my off-seasons have gotten busier, with exhibition games overseas, summer camps I run in North Carolina, and endorsement opportunities that have kept me running around the past few years. So I get home whenever I can.

Of course, man does not live by family life alone. Fame has its advantages, too. I have gotten to do some great things because I play basketball. I've met some fun people and traveled to some fun places.

I played in an all-star game that Magic Johnson had set up during my rookie year. My coach was Arsenio Hall. Everybody got playing time but me. We did it again the next year, and he still didn't play me. When I was called to be a guest on his talk show I wanted to get back at him. I told the producer about it, but we never got it in. So I am saying it now: Arsenio, you are one lousy basketball coach if you don't know enough to play the little fella!

Seriously, I really respect Arsenio. I had always wanted to be on his talk show. I had seen Spud Webb there, and Larry was on it once. I had been in the studio audience, and Arsenio had acknowledged me. But I had never been out there sitting on the couch with him until recently.

I also always wanted to do a "Webster." I saw Patrick Ewing on it once. I want to do a spot where I come in and mess around as myself. I see myself making a guest appearance on a show like "Fresh Prince of Bel Air." I can see it in my mind — the Fresh Prince playing ball, he thinks he's got a game, and the little fella shows up and takes him out. I think it would be great. All you TV producers out there, just give me a call.

I am still waiting for that, but in the meantime I have done a spot on "Saturday Night Live," and on David Letterman's show. Those were both great fun. I was on "Saturday Night Live" with Charles Barkley, and they wanted me for a skit where he is running a clothing store for big and tall guys. When I got to New York, I found out that they had another skit that was supposed to have in it Chris Mullin, the former St. John's star now with the Golden State Warriors, but Chris had to cancel. So they asked me to sit in. It was a funny skit where Charles is talking to the Stuart Smalley character, and I have to tell Charles that I love him. All through rehearsals Charles kept cracking up — we couldn't get through it without laughing. We did it fine when we were live, though I could see Charles really working to keep from laughing.

The Letterman show was fun too. I was on with Siskel and Ebert, the movie reviewers, and before the show they were fighting like cats and dogs. Those guys really don't like each other! I thought it was an act, but now I know it's real.

I've also had the chance to make some TV commercials, which is a tremendous opportunity. I have shot commercials and print ads for Sprite, AT&T, Reebok, X-AM jeans, and other companies. It is a lot of work, but it really is fun — and I won't lie, the money isn't bad, either.

The Sprite commercial, called "Muggsy vs. Goliath," took two days to shoot. The guy playing Goliath really was a Goliath — he was seven-six and weighed 389 pounds. I had to run around him and through his legs (I actually could fit through them) and do a somersault to the basket. I admit, that wasn't me flipping through the air. They hired a nationally ranked gymnast to pull that stunt off. I can do many amazing things on the basketball court, but that isn't one of them.

The AT&T commercial also played on my size, naturally. I represented a "small" business, going up against the big boys. This time the giants were played by my old college teammate Anthony Teachey and another former ACC star, Cozell McQueen of N.C. State. That was a fun one to do, because I had speaking lines, and I have come to enjoy public speaking. There is a bit of the ham inside the little fella. I like to put on a show on the court, and I am learning how to put on a show off the court, too.

The endorsements and TV shows are nice. I admit, my ego likes the recognition that comes with fame. But like I said earlier, there is always something happening that keeps you from getting too big a head. For instance, as we were taking a cab to the "Saturday Night Live" studio, my marketing agent, Rob Urbach, noticed that the cab driver — a woman — was wearing a Hornets baseball cap. Rob asked her about it, and she said Charlotte was her favorite team. I just kept quiet, knowing that Rob was enjoying playing this little game with her. He asked her what she liked about the Hornets and she replied, "Oh, I love that little guard!"

She didn't recognize me. Rob kept prying about why she liked the little guard, what she'd do if she met him, and so on, until she finally got suspicious and looked closely into her rearview mirror. I flashed her a smile, and she turned all the way around to check me out. We almost hit a car in front of us!

But the thing I like best about being famous is that it allows me to work with and for kids. One endorsement I do is for a regional bank in the south called First Union. In one ad I dressed up like Albert Einstein, with the frizzy hair and big mustache, for a program the bank sponsors that gets kids to work to improve their grades in school. That was hilarious — I admit, I'm no Einstein. But I have learned how important education is, and I want to get that message across to my young fans. (It's working, too — more than ten thousand kids participated in the program's first year.)

I also get to speak directly to kids at schools. Typically, Gil McGregor or someone else at the Hornets sets things up with a local school. Last season, for instance, Gil picked me up after practice one day, and we took a limo to a rural school down in South Carolina, about forty minutes from Charlotte.